INSPIRED

ALSO BY MATT RICHTEL

NONFICTION

An Elegant Defense
A Deadly Wandering

FICTION

Dead on Arrival
The Doomsday Equation
The Cloud
Floodgate
Devil's Plaything
Hooked

INSPIRED

UNDERSTANDING CREATIVITY

A JOURNEY THROUGH ART, SCIENCE, AND THE SOUL

MATT RICHTEL

MARINER BOOKS

Boston   New York

HarperCollins books may be purchased for educational, business, or sales promotional use. For information, please email the Special Markets Department at SPsales@harpercollins.com.

FIRST EDITION

Designed by Michelle Crowe

Library of Congress Cataloging-in-Publication Data has been applied for.

ISBN 978-0-06-302553-0

22 23 24 25 26 FRI 10 9 8 7 6 5 4 3 2 1

To my family

Contents

INSPIRED

Author's Note

This book posed a particular challenge for me. It has to do with pronouns. Authors typically make a choice about whether to write in the third person (they) or the first person (I) or the second person (you). I don't feel I have the luxury of the conventional options. That's because I'm writing about great creators and the scientists who research them (they), my own experience (I), and also about what this all means to the reader (you). I thought about pretending that I wasn't going to use all pronouns, just sort of try to slip one by you. But that just seemed like a good way to get fairly called out, or lambasted on Twitter. So, I'll just own it: pronounwise, I bounce around a bit. I could try to justify this on the grounds that it is an example of creativity. Gross. Ultimately, my decision to use different pronouns reflects the fact that this book is journalistic, conversational, and personal. I'm telling you a story about a journey I took to discover how creativity works, visiting with some of the world's leading creators and thinkers about creativity, and much of what I found applies to all of us. So, humbly, I ask that you forgive the fact that I'm talking to you, and about them, and, occasionally, myself. When this journey comes to the end, I hope the inconsistent pronouns will be the last thing about this book you, they, or I remember.

Prologue

In the beginning, as the biblical story goes, darkness was upon the face of the deep. Pitch black, everyplace. Quiet, natural, desolate, but roiling with emerging life. Organisms competed to survive, innovative by their very nature, mutating new forms of cells, giving rise to more advanced combinations of traits, developing hearts and lungs, protective fur, powerful sight, claws, arms and legs that eventually let them stand upright, one baby step after the next until there was an actual baby step. By a human being. Still, there was darkness, at least at night, until . . . Aha!, a person discovered how to create fire. And it was good.

Then, others found inspirations drawing pictures on the cave wall, made visible in the firelight; the paintings stirred emotions, as did the songs people wrote and sang around the flame. The creations came naturally, spurred by deep primal urges as visceral as hunger. And they became more refined with craftsmanship. They were beautiful, ingenious, sometimes dangerous.

Fire could rage out of control and a village or forest burn down. So other people eventually came up with buckets for water and then fire hoses, and salves for burns, and antibiotics for healing. One creation built on the next, little inspirations mixed with skill becoming like magnets drawing other ideas, a virtuous cycle. Often with a curious twist.

Many of the new creations posed new problems later known by a phrase that someone coined: "unintended consequences." Think of the combustion engine, which allowed us to travel farther and faster in cars but had the unintended consequence of causing many people to die in road collisions and—aha! a new idea—seat belts, and they were good. Then the exhaust from the cars led to climate change and a person came up with the battery-powered Tesla. And it was really good, especially when it self-parked. And the scientists begat solar technology, abundant energy extracted from rays of sunlight. But what about all those displaced coal workers? What discoveries would help them, the legions feeding their families from mining fossil fuels?

This book is the story of human creation—a rolling series of inspirations, little, medium, and immense, virtually all their creators lost to history. This is nature's call-and-response: rising challenges and new solutions, creation and disruption and creation again. It is the story of how we create, and how any of us can. How you might.

There are many troubling things in the world today. This book is the good news. It's about hope. The marvelous accident of persistent creativity. The promise that new ideas will come again and again, as inevitable as the ocean waves and the up and down path of the sun.

This isn't philosophy, or esoteric science. This is personal. This is about the inspirations stirring in each of us—for a business, screenplay, recipe, community program, political movement, painting, phone app, technological advance, new medicine, or song; heck, for that matter, perhaps an entire musical? Why not?

Because it's just a germ. Because would-be creators are afraid, feel they lack expertise or that the idea doesn't exist for a reason, that it sounds nuts when said aloud. Because people are taught to color inside the lines. Because, in a way, the act of creativity is terrifying.

Just about every creator has been there. They feel a spark, an urge, a calling, the muse. Or they realize they'd felt it all along and they give in to it, embrace it, and they create—often with an abandon of self-fulfillment and joy unknown in virtually any other pursuit. Sometimes they change the world.

Where do these ideas come from—the creative force behind art, science, music, business, technology? How do they become something new? Not from any miracle and not merely from luck or hard work. Inspiration, innovation, and experiment—creation and the creative process go by many names—can all be explained by biology, neurology, and other basic sciences. Creativity was inside of us all along—inside *each* of us—in the beginning. From darkness, creativity lights the way forward, as it has done over and again in the past. It is in us now, especially now, in crisis, even chaos. This book is about how it works.

Our story starts in Jerusalem.

BOOK I

FROM CRADLE TO MUSE

Wherein a visit to Jerusalem and a chance meeting
with the Kangaroo Man provides a profile of a creator
but reveals creativity's mortal foe, doubt.

Heresies

"King Herod was the Steve Jobs of his time."

The day after Thanksgiving 2019, I stood in the Jewish quarter of the Old City of Jerusalem. One week earlier, in Wuhan, China—4,500 miles away—the first known human being became infected with the virus caused by COVID-19. But that morning for me had a blessed feel, sun-bathed, unusually temperate. The "city of peace" felt calm, subverting an underlying turmoil of the world poised to surface and explode.

The square hummed with a throng of tourists, city dwellers, the pious. Devout Jews and Christians coursed across the cobbled stones to holy places. Around only a few narrow corners hustled too the Arabs and Armenians who also consider this place a portal to the heavens.

Where better to consider the source of human creativity than in a city many believe central to all of creation itself?

My guide, Amy, pointed to stones beneath our feet that the king laid more than 2,000 years ago. They were part of an empire-building mania led by this Roman-appointed ruler, streets that led to ports, fortresses, new ideas for gates and military defenses. Amy tells me he was "a man who thought larger than life": Herod the Great.

He could also have fairly been called Herod the Vicious Paranoid Killer. He was a terrible person, a madman who ordered the murder of children and his own allies. It was all part of his conniving effort to hold on to power, his inspirations yielding the great and the evil.

His prolific creation was doubtless inspired by his surroundings and his peers. Judea around the year zero thrived with restless en-

ergy, competing ideas, cultures clashing. It drew half a million people, a significant population by even today's standards. This is key, it
turns out. Throughout history, there have been outposts of explosive
innovation, hot spots of creativity, cooperation, and fierce competition: Florence, Harlem, Athens, Morocco, Paris, extraordinary
periods in Russia, Mali, Japan, China, India, Mexico, and Egypt, in
Silicon Valley, Hollywood, and, certainly, Jerusalem. It was the ultimate company town, and the industry was religion.

A mythology has developed surrounding the image of the anti-
social, isolated creative genius. It is among many misconceptions I
began to see, little heresies, shorthand fables and narrative conveniences baked into the story of creativity. This book seeks to clarify
the record, and this opening chapter is an overview into, and a down
payment on, the science and story I will use to support a different
view.

Population-level research, for instance, tells us that what gets created
appears to come through a collective energy. Picture the teeming hub
of ancient Jerusalem—Jews, early Christians, Romans—gathering,
sharing, arguing; the ideas and energy gaining steam, then being
poured out through an individual. Some person became a portal,
a wellspring, a channeler, a veritable winged sage transcending the
monotony of learned behavior and accepted technology.

Created here, the greatest stories ever told, if readership numbers
are any guide.

A mere stone's throw from where I stood with the tour guide are
rooted the origin stories of Judaism, Christianity, Islam. Here, we
learn from the New Testament, Christ carried a cross to his death,
and burial at the site of the Church of the Holy Sepulchre. The
golden mosque that looms over the city houses the Dome of the
Rock, among the holiest sites for Muslims, where Mohammed in a

dream flew on a white steed named Burāq to a spot that Muslims—and Jews and Christians—consider the "foundation rock" of the Earth. It was on this jagged opening, the beloved narratives have it, that our human story began.

And just below the Dome of the Rock stands the Wailing Wall, as holy a remembrance as there is in all of Judeo-Christian storytelling. The wall, reaching skyward as men and women bow before it, was the western edge of a temple which, the stories tell us, held the Ark of the Covenant. The Ark has been lost, last seen thousands of years ago.

As I looked around the square, I could see one extraordinary creation after the next. Like the Bible, the city has stood a rugged test of time—and seemingly every image testifies to the underlying force of creativity to, in fact, define the human experience.

Clothing, cameras, Gucci bags, North Face backpacks, and knock-offs galore, Israeli soldiers in green fatigues shouldering M4 semi-automatic machine guns, sewage grates, vehicles of various shapes and sizes designed to manage the narrow streets and alleyways carrying trinkets, bags of refined cumin and turmeric bound for the Arab Quarter.

I pulled out my iPhone, itself a wonder I held in my hand: a camera nearly as powerful as any that has ever existed, attached to a computer processor to rival those that took up entire rooms only several decades ago (the "supercomputers" that we marveled at because they could play a solid game of tic-tac-toe against a human foe). This phone would become an enabler of my own invention, helping me to remember, many months later, what I would write here. Material creations like these serve us as tools, emboldening creation and helping us create the building blocks and stones of the next innovation. In some ways, the even more powerful creations are the spiritual ideas that emerged in places like Jerusalem—and at sites in India, China, France, Germany, and on and on. They have a virtually cosmic role: They shape our reality.

Such is the power of creativity that it forms and re-forms our very understanding of the world. Creativity is, in this way, the true first wonder of the world. From it springs everything else.

This makes creativity seem so grand, elusive, the stuff of legendary thinkers in historic places. But King Herod didn't build Jerusalem any more than Steve Jobs built the iPhone. Their creative contributions and ideas resulted from centuries of innovation, made in increments by the inspired. This shouldn't seem particularly revelatory. More compelling, though, is why this is so: Creativity lives inside each of us and, collectively, we create our world.

It is not, as many have come to believe, the province of the few, another well-traveled misconception. Creativity is, in fact, part of our more primitive physiology. It comes from the cellular level, part of our most essential survival machinery. We are creativity machines.

When a fish first crawled onto the land, it did not do so in a single aha! moment, a sudden burst of inspiration, adaptation, or evolution. When a bird-like creature first took flight, it did not magically sprout wings. Rather, the ability to crawl onto land, or to first fly, built on one prior creation after the next, changes to anatomy over millennia, incremental transformations laying groundwork. These happened by the accident of evolution.

Random changes in genetics altered in tiny ways the programming of an organism. Some changes had no particular impact. Many actually led to the organism's death because the change left the new creation unfit for the environment. Some changes gave the organism a slight survival advantage, changing, for instance, how well it metabolized energy or protected itself against threat.

Bit by bit, small changes could add up. Eventually, they might lead to the anatomy that became the basis for a wing, or webbed feet. In rare cases, a profound mutation led to a clear survival advantage, and that genetic change—or creation—took over and made the prior genetic version of that organism obsolete. It was creativity, but mindless, unconscious, random.

Then, as animals became more advanced and complex, some were creative in ways that might feel more familiar to the way human beings create. For instance, animals like birds and monkeys, even some insects, display versions of creativity recognizable to our eye, like the singing of songs, or the building of tools or nests. New mutations come about, confer survival advantage, take hold. Nature endures through the powerful, relentless machinery of regular and consistent creation, but it does so without conscious direction.

Human beings bring to this process an almost Godlike twist. We can create at will. We were born to create.

In fertile brains, we make random connections among ideas. These are highly similar to the emergence of mutations in the genetic coding of more primitive organisms. Ideas materialize, draw one another, connect, rearrange, like new genetic material made of imagination. Then, in other parts of the brain, we scrutinize these ideas, vetting them almost instantaneously for their viability. Can they survive in the world? Should they?

In short, ideas bubble and rise, accidents of connection, mutations, some bold and relevant, most destined to die in the ruthless terrain of reality. Even for the most creative.

Once, a creativity scholar told me, Albert Einstein felt overcome by a creative spark. He felt certain he'd discovered a unified field theory to explain the whole of existence. He confided in a colleague.

"Interesting," the colleague answered, "but under that theory the universe can't exist."

A tight parallel exists linking the fact that a fish crawls onto land, or a reptile takes flight, and the trial-and-error way in which the Theory of Relativity ultimately came to Einstein, or how modern astronomy sprang from Galileo's brain, or sounds of glory and ennui emanate from the trumpeting lips of Miles Dewey Davis III. The machinery of change, the factories of creativity that live inside each of us, are directly analogous to the machinery that exists inside cells to replicate and mutate genes.

This means that creativity is not mere habit. It is as natural as reproduction itself, the mating, combination, and recombination of ideas. As with mating, though, we can choose to create. This is where the analogy with nature departs. Our discoveries are not completely accidental or random.

Creations can be pursued. How creators do it has become the source of a growing body of scholarship. We are learning, through creative research—powered by innovative technology—how to wield our creative power with greater precision.

These are among the subjects I hope to illuminate:

- **NEUROSCIENTISTS HAVE** begun to use imaging to map the brains of creators and understand the regions where ideas get generated and where they are assessed. Spoiler alert: there is yet a long way to go.
- **PSYCHOLOGISTS HAVE** increasingly refined personality models to discover prevailing traits in creators, including the critical insight that creativity doesn't require one to be of particularly high intellect. It's good news for many of us: Average intelligence will do! Raw talent counts, to a point. Of equal importance, if not greater, are qualities that can be developed, like openness and curiosity.

When it comes to intellect and creativity, I'd boil the relationship down to this:

An intelligent person answers a question.

A creative person comes up with the question in the first place, and then answers it.

- I HAVE learned too from astrophysicists who liken creativity to the birth of a new universe—and the *aha!* moment as happening at the "edge of chaos" where stability collides with disorder. In this case, instead of an idea falling into an infinite abyss of failure, it becomes a new foundation for the human experience.
- THEOLOGIANS DESCRIBED to me human creation as an outgrowth of the divine. These religious ideas, remarkably enough, tie closely with the way creativity takes place in Constitutional Law—and the decision-making of high courts across the world, including the United States Supreme Court. New research also shows that deeply religious people can struggle to be creative because they subvert their ideas to the wisdom of an all-knowing God.
- POWERFUL INSIGHT into creativity also comes from the field of visual sciences. What people create depends in large part on what they see. Literally. A creator's toolbox grows through travel, new experience, emotion, and veering outside everyday comfort. It is often said that creators connect dots among ideas, and so it is worth noting that creators can connect only dots that they have seen, felt, experienced.
- CREATIVE PEOPLE, science tells us, not only see more material but tend to be willing to consider a greater pool of information as relevant than do less creative people. In other words, creators aren't so quick to dismiss information as irrelevant or unworthy just because it doesn't conform to existing beliefs. By considering more information, creators have more raw material to process, more dots to connect.

It is almost impossible to overstate the significance of the idea that a person's creativity depends on obtaining these inputs of information—seen, felt, heard, experienced. I think of this as the Spice Rack Theory of Creativity (a cheap name of my own invention). A mind rich with raw cooking spices—joy, agony, empathy, intellect, and openness—can more ably mix and match. A handful of scientists, as you'll read, have developed simple tactics to help people be aware of their internal spice racks, side-tracked as they can be by distraction, fear, lack of training.

- SCIENCE HELPS illuminate the obstacles that inhibit creativity. Some obstacles are taught to us at an early age, but the most basic reason we resist creative impulses is more primal: New ideas scare the heck out of us. This research explains our subconscious bias against creativity, and that might clarify why people resist it in themselves and discourage it in their children. Creativity and creators can make people deeply uncomfortable. Creativity requires confronting this fear. A small but growing body of neuroscience offers hope through concrete steps people can take to manufacture the environment and mental state in which to conjure creativity.
- RESEARCHERS WHO study creativity have developed a vocabulary for innovation. They speak of "The Big C" and "The Little C." The Big C is creativity that transforms the world: the wheel, antibiotics and vaccinations, democracy, the atomic bomb, the Beatles catalog, and on and on. Little C creations register less seismic tremors of iteration upon which Big C's get built. Little C's are experimentation. They are crucial. These might be smaller technological, scientific, or artistic developments that become the grains of sand that become the pillars on which Big C's are built.

All this science arrives at a pivotal period in history.

Never before have so many technological tools existed to connect us and allow creativity on such a grand and widespread scale. Jerusalem or Silicon Valley, Hollywood or Florence, at your fingertips. No prior epoch, by any stretch, has fostered the reach across time and space to communicate, learn, share, write, illustrate, make music, build a business, publish, manufacture, market, sell: each a version of creativity. The power to execute inspiration enabled, now, for the masses.

In this era, people interact through vast networks, uninhibited by borders, vacuuming up ideas and connecting them with their own. Creating. One indicator of creativity is the number of patents granted, and it has soared: In 2019, the US Patent and Trademark Office granted 391,103 patents, a steady rise from 71,230 in 1969—fifty years earlier. (The first US patent, granted in 1790 and signed by George Washington, went to Samuel Hopkins for making an ingredient called potash, used in fertilizer.)

Recent years have shown us the rise of creators from nooks and crannies. I'm not talking just about YouTube and TikTok sensations who gather eyeballs by doing pet tricks but about communications more substantive. These outpourings illustrate that the personal cost of putting out an idea is virtually nothing, but with potentially massive impact. In December 2018, a fifteen-year-old named Greta Thunberg in Stockholm won a newspaper contest with her essay on climate change; she posted her ideas to social media and soon had a million people joining her in speaking out to confront climate change. People like Thunberg provide a powerful testimony to the way a medium can spur creativity in a surprising way: by making it easier to fail and therefore easier to try. Of no small note: This reference to Thunberg is not a political statement, and this book is not ideological or partisan. Creativity belongs to no party or ideology.

Creators can certainly be ideological or even create new ideologies. But creativity itself? That defies partisanship.

Tesla innovator Musk, a die-hard political conservative, counts among the great creators of his generation. And late in this book, I'll share an idea about one of the most powerful, innovative ideas I've ever heard for forging ties between police officers and African American youth in the United States by taking small groups to tour the beaches of Normandy together. It was the brilliant brainchild of a retired rock star, with conservative leanings and deep gratitude for the work of military and police, who found his true calling in healing the broken parts of his community.

Speaking of rock stars, in the early 1960s, Bob Dylan was invited to speak to the National Emergency Civil Liberties Committee, which presumed he shared its progressive views. Onstage, he rebuked them.

"There's no left and right to me anymore," Dylan said. "There's only up and down and down is very close to the ground and I'm trying to go up without thinking of anything trivial, such as politics."

And creativity is not the same as fame or fortune, not even remotely. Creativity is essential to our nature while fame and fortune are so fleeting that even legends have only their brief day.

Early in the reporting for this book, I was playing basketball in the driveway with my eleven-year-old son. I told him I was hoping to interview Bono for this book.

"Who?"

"The singer for a very famous band called U2."

"Oh," my son said. "Is Bono a him or a her?"

Later in this book, you'll hear from Bono himself on creativity and legacy as he ventures a theory on how U2 became one of the most commercially successful bands of all time. The answer is not through talent or creativity alone, Bono posits, but in great timing.

So, no, creativity is not ideological, nor the same as success. In fact, if this book argues for anything, it is the democratic nature of creativity as a singular form of freedom and personal expression. In a related breath, I'll argue that elitism, superficial ideology, and the blinding light of material success can grossly undercut the ability to create by discouraging authenticity.

Another myth: Creativity is good. It is not, in fact, inherently positive. The process is not in and of itself bad either "neither moral nor amoral," a big thinker in the field of creativity has written. The moral underpinnings of creativity don't come from a creation but from the values of its creator and, even more so, from the way the creation is used.

As I walked to the gates of Jerusalem, I was about to be shown this lesson firsthand. I soon came to see how our greatest creations can turn deadly.

I hailed a taxi and climbed inside.

The cab lurched forward. The driver punched the accelerator with such great enthusiasm I felt like I had been transported to New York City, home to the world's most impatient cabbies. We flew out the entrance to the gates. The driver made a sharp right turn and wove around the edges of the walled fortress. He slipped across lanes, honking, cursing beneath his breath.

Then he suddenly began poking at the iPhone attached to his dashboard. Maybe, I thought, he's checking a map. He was not. He was scrolling through pictures of shirts and jackets, described in small-type Arabic on his screen.

The driver was internet shopping.

I'd have asked him to stop driving-and-shopping if the moment weren't so journalistically rich. What the heck was he doing?

"I'm curious. What are you checking out?" I asked.

"My friend sells clothes. He got in a new shipment. What do you think?"

Um, that we might die.

The taxi flowed with the haphazard traffic—bursts of speed, quick changes in direction, sudden stops in moments of congestion. And my taxi driver stopped. He explained that his friend sells clothes outside the Arab Quarter, and he didn't want to miss the latest deals. I suppose he wasn't taking into account the possibility that he wouldn't be able to shop if he killed us in a collision.

Creations are not inherently good or bad. It really depends on how they are used. From virtually the moment that the automobile became available to the masses, people began to die in car crashes. Today, riding in a car is among the most dangerous activities we will ever undertake, as measured by the level of risk of serious injury or death. Now add in the mobile phone, originally marketed as the "car phone." It was a powerful creation in the sense that people couldn't previously speak on the phone while driving. It was a terrible proposition from the standpoint of safety, at least when the use of a phone while one is driving leaves a driver inattentive. Add to the mix internet shopping. Pretty amazing creation, right? Not at thirty miles an hour, weaving around commute-hour traffic in the old city.

The way that creations get used and the niches that they inhabit typically cannot be predicted by their creators. This becomes all the more unpredictable as the systems of the world become more complex, with one creation combining with and careening off the next. Information, weapons, ideas, technology.

As we drove around the edges of the city, I noticed the incongruent image of a Hasidic Jew, dressed in ancient garb, inhaling deeply from a nicotine vape pipe. The discovery of these nicotine pens was aimed by their creators at taking the place of cigarettes. This creation, beloved by many, has, in the last year, itself become deadly to users because of innovator-added chemicals that seemed to make the product cheaper but wound up killing some people who inhaled the poisonous fumes.

In the broadest sense, this is the creativity paradox. It is the idea that our greatest creations can have troubling side effects that, in turn, require and inspire even more potent creations.

Creativity, like cellular mutation, is a messy, clunky affair in which most new forms do not take root and some are noxious. Nazism, slavery, poison gas. We see their evil now, but someone at some point thought they were good ideas.

Some innovations prove so powerful that it is not possible to say yet whether they ultimately will be of more help or harm, like the nuclear weapon, a petroleum-powered economy, the antibiotic— tools of such immensity the full measure of their influence cannot be understood but by the passing of epochs.

These remarkable, lasting creations suggest that creativity is chiefly aimed at improving or saving the world. Certainly, some innovations may do that. Or perhaps they'll change your family, your community, a region.

In this way, creativity defines our world and claims the most extraordinary of niches: It is the place where individual expression and satisfaction meet societal meaning and advancement. It holds keys to both personal and collective salvation. Many pursuits in this world ask a person to choose between the selfish end and societal advancement. Creativity, though, allows us to nurture our individual spark while also potentially changing the world.

"The best way to predict the future is to invent it," Alan Kay, who helped invent the personal computer, is credited with saying.

It's a nice way to think of creativity, as a societal salve. This is one more significant misconception.

As individuals, we don't create to save the world. Not at first.

Creativity is personal. It stems first from the thrill of inspiration.

The cliché, of course, is that necessity is the mother of invention. This isn't totally false, but it is only partly accurate.

The reality is that necessity is a subset of a more sweeping concept: authenticity.

Individual spark is the true forebear of human creativity. Creators often start not with a desire to solve a problem, but with much more personal inspiration akin to a cellular mutation. An idea pops into the brain. Aha! And it inspires the individual in the way of a muse, a delightful, exciting, new proposition. A creator might well solve a problem because he or she has directed much mental energy to that problem and the idea that surfaces could well be related. But some of the most creative people in the world, interviewed for this book, can testify that the open mind delivers exhilarating ideas that may or may not be precisely on topic.

The experience of discovery and creation can be deeply thrilling and satisfying experiences. The reasons are primal.

One reason: The process of creativity allows people to unburden themselves. Research shows that creators get an opportunity to share themselves with the world. They can do this without necessarily sharing parts of themselves they consider shameful or deeply personal. The research suggests that when people think and create "out of the box" they can free themselves of feelings of shame without necessarily revealing the full or direct nature of a secret. This research argues too that creativity can improve physical health by helping a creator be unburdened of psychological weight that dampens effort and performance.

Relatedly, sometimes creative thinking serves the restless soul by giving the brain an activity—simply, something to do. A friend of mine who is an author, and one of the best editors ever to work at the *New York Times*, once described his brain to me as a "wood chipper." It had to be fed. He gave it regular creative projects so it would not "chip itself." Creativity can be the opposite of destruction of your own world.

When the inspirations are authentic, honest, they allow the creator to connect to others and thereby provide them a source of relief. This can be true of art, business, policy. In fact, there are times when a creator's honesty can touch other people in deep ways even if never intended to do so.

Right around the time of the Cuban Missile Crisis, Dylan released a powerful song called "Hard Rain." The chorus asserts a "hard rain gonna fall," and many listeners assumed Dylan referred to the terror of imminent nuclear destruction. Legendary journalist Studs Terkel asked Dylan about that on television.

Not "atomic rain," Dylan said, "just a hard rain."

Years later, on the cusp of the pandemic, Dylan would write and release a powerful new song titled "I Contain Multitudes."

"I fuss with my hair, and I fight blood feuds," he sang. A conceit and a brawler, as in each of us, conflicting perspectives, complementary and clashing styles. "I'm just like Anne Frank, like Indiana Jones, And them British bad boys, the Rolling Stones."

This leads me to an essential, encompassing, and often-overlooked core truth about creativity.

It doesn't come from one particular kind of place, environment, or circumstance. *Creators are not one thing.* Inside of us, multitudes, the seed corn of variety, novelty, creation—songs, stories, murals, speeches and policies, medicines, technologies, recipes, turns of phrase. They are distinct moments made by individuals, as vast as life, as natural as the instinct to survive.

This idea that we have so much material inside us to draw from should be freeing to would-be creators. It ought to give permission for each of us to draw from our eclectic mix of humanity to create art, business, and flourishing new ideas. But people get locked into identities, narrowed by fears that interfere with natural creative impulses and limit our access to our own natural capacities. In some ways this is quite understandable; the impulse to constrain and narrow is undeniable, and simple answers can help dull the feeling of the chaos of life around us. It might feel as if safety and rigidity provide sanctuary amid the ecstatic swirl of the twenty-first century. I know this firsthand, having resisted creative impulses for years, scared of the multitudes within, resistant to them—a defiance that caused me to implode emotionally, before finding my voice.

I also know the truth of the value of multitudes within from listening to the various creators I'll introduce in this book. One of these remarkable individuals is woven throughout.

Rhiannon Giddens is an emerging pop star, with a voice to rival Whitney Houston's and a folk sensibility. Her searing album *Freedom Highway* draws from hope and despair baked like hardtack from a slave lineage. But she also wrote a hit song for a spaghetti-western video game called *Red Dead Redemption*. She's among the best-known banjo players in the world.

She's working on a musical with renowned rocker Elvis Costello, while preparing the debut of an opera called *Omar* she wrote about a Muslim-African slave brought to Charleston in 1807. Her partner is an Italian jazz pianist, educated in the Hague. The middle ground has proven to be Ireland, where they currently live.

When Giddens accepted a GRAMMY in 2016, she paused on the red carpet for an interview. She explained that her work was aimed in part at paying tribute to all the women who had come before her. Nina Simone, Dolly Parton, Sister Rosetta Tharpe. Spirituals, soul, country. "I didn't want to be locked into a genre," Giddens told the TV crew. "I said: American music is about more than genre. I made the record to show what I think about American music."

Giddens was born to a Black mother and white father; the pair married in North Carolina shortly after the law allowed interracial couplings. Later, they divorced when her mother came out as a lesbian. Until Giddens was eight, she and her sister lived with grandparents whose worldview was shaped by the legacy of slavery, leaving the grandma and grandpa fiercely protective and loving, sometimes furious and violent. But for all of that, Giddens believes that the most influential of all her childhood experiences were the endless hours she and her sister spent playing outside, alternately bored and imaginative, in their grandparents' yard, 'round that giant old oak tree.

Giddens's reality was shaped by one contradiction after another— love and anger, permission and discipline, sobriety and addiction, the city and the country, crime-riddled streets and elite schools, Black and white. Straight and gay.

All of it led to inspiration in 2020 during the COVID-19 pandemic and the overlapping trauma of the deaths of Black men and women at the hands of police officers. She began to fear deeply for the life of her nephew, an artist in North Carolina on the front lines of protests. Giddens would become inspired, as I'll show you, and bring her multitudes to bear in profound creative ways. Hers is the story of the emergence of a true creator but also how that emergence can take a person beyond creativity, and its trappings of notoriety and money, to self-acceptance and happiness.

When I spoke about creativity with another remarkable talent, Carlos Santana, the legendary guitarist, he implored me to understand the keys to happiness, satisfaction, and success that come from his tapping into this power. "The main cancer on this planet is that people don't believe in their own light," he said. That's what he calls your individual creative spark: your light. "We're at the age of enlightenment, where we can put that nonsense aside," Santana added. "The keys to the kingdom come from your imagination."

The language of creators can sound mystical, the language of academia clinical. I hope to act ably as a translator for both, having worked as a *New York Times* journalist who has spent a career interviewing scientists, but also as an author and musician. I understand what it's like to feel overwhelmed with inspiration, to flop and succeed, to experience the call and betrayal of notoriety and public acceptance, and to know, again and again, a simple truth: The act of creation is an end unto itself—one that provides more joy than do the resulting creations themselves.

Life span has increased, our material needs met as never before. But happiness has not risen in lockstep. Perhaps the secret isn't in the products of our creativity, but in the process itself.

"Too many people adhere to the idea they are not creative," said Dr. Lynne Vincent, an assistant professor of management at Syracuse University, and one of a growing number of scholars who are, as she puts it, "demystifying and discovering what it means to be creative."

A big first step is "coming to terms with the fact you are a creative person, and understanding what creativity means."

Despite the Jerusalem taxi driver's best efforts at distracting himself, he dropped me safely at an Airbnb that my family and I had booked using the wonder of the creation of the very internet that let the cabbie shop-n-drive. My family and I soon packed our bags for a visit north, where we'd spend Thanksgiving.

There I stumbled upon a fascinating creator, the Kangaroo Man.

His is the first story among dozens I weave together here, from the scholars and Giddens and Bono; Einstein; Golden State Warriors coach Steve Kerr; comic movie–director Judd Apatow; social media stars you haven't heard of but whom your children swear by; technology entrepreneurs who made hundreds of millions of dollars on their inspirations; a Nobel Prize winner who came up with new cancer treatments—these and a cast of dozens of others will appear and reappear to testify to the way it all works. They add up to a comprehensive view of this most essential of human traits, set against the backdrop of a particular time and place. Now.

You see, a terrible virus had begun to spread in Wuhan, China, in late 2019. It would kill millions of people, and, secondarily, create a black hole–like vortex that inhaled jobs and livelihoods. It was a time of great social unrest too with a surge in the momentum to confront racial inequities.

Noxious biology, economy, and sociology swirled—a virus that was the creation of random mutation, and systemic racism with roots in the creation of slavery. Both poised to explode.

And did I mention the wildfires? In the fall of 2020, the American west went up in flames, then Australia had firestorms—millions of acres consumed by flame, the natural world reacting to the heat of our creations. The sky turned dark with ash and pollutants that made it deadly dangerous to go outside, rendering the air in the most advanced technological regions the world has ever seen the most toxic.

This was hardly the first time extraordinary challenges confronted our species. In fact, time and again humans have created their way out of threats, from the tiny to the existential. So much progress had been made already, born of human creation—from medicines to ideas of fairness and equality to laws that seek to enforce them. History teaches the good news: We would create our way out again.

In the lull before this extraordinary moment in history, the Kangaroo Man stood in the dust amid his creation, a fulfilled man with a powerful, telling story about innovation.

Leap of Faith

Creativity finds a way, like life itself, even in places where it seems starved of the conditions and culture needed to thrive.

The morning after Thanksgiving, my family and I visited a kibbutz called Nir David, about a two hours' drive north of Jerusalem. I'd had cousins who had helped found the kibbutz as the state of Israel began to take shape. This nation was a creation of the world, partly in response to anti-Semitism. It was not welcomed by the Palestinians who lived on this land. One man's creation is another's disruption, even destruction.

The Palestinians attacked here on April 20, 1936. Palestinian Arabs, furious with the growing population of Jews in land then controlled by the British, streamed into the fields of Nir David, which was still under construction at the time, and scorched the crops. Women and children hid in a shelter. Men fought, seemingly destined to succumb, until British forces arrived. The kibbutz endured, narrowly, and time and again over the decades that followed, the agricultural collective would be defined by its ability to scrape by. This didn't leave much room for creativity beyond that which was needed to survive.

In fact, a typical kibbutz, at the time, had all the flare and individuality of the Soviet State. The basis for the collective was socialism. Every person received roughly an equal salary. Residents ate the same food in drab dining commons, tomatoes and cucumbers for breakfast, with other meals heavy on the hummus and pita. The collective's Spartan housing took the form of cottages, with beds and modest sitting areas, a bathroom. So shared was the burden that it was unusual even for grandparents to sneak sweet treats into the home to give their grandchildren. When it came to workload, jobs were assigned, in the field, kitchen, factory, the accounting office. The children were raised with similar uniformity. They would spend the night with their parents but then were raised collectively in day-care and schools, like dozens of siblings by a cadre of babysitters, returning to their parents to sleep at night. The parents had no time to play ball or child-rear; they worked the fields for the common revenue and common defense.

It is overly simplistic to think of this as an ideological extreme, the way we'd think of failed communism. This was somewhat different, born of necessity for several dozens of families fending off hunger to the left, armed attack to the right. These realities intensified after the Holocaust, when pioneering members of the kibbutz traveled to Poland to retrieve survivors and integrate them, all while facing increasingly hostile attacks from Arab nations and Palestinians aggrieved by the way the world created the State of Israel in the aftermath of World War II.

This was a hardscrabble place. Not fertile ground for a pianist or painter, an eccentric entrepreneur, a policy maker outside the boundaries of the survival edict. Not the sort of place, it seems, for such a creator to spring up. Not ideal conditions for the rise of the Kangaroo Man.

His name is Yehuda Gat.

"People didn't believe I could do it," he said, shortly after I met him outside the cages filled with kangaroos that we'd come to let our children pet. Gat's eyes twinkled and I pulled out my iPhone to record his story. "They laughed at me."

He is in his eighties now, having grown up on the kibbutz. For many years, he lived within the confines of the culture, as a young man fulfilling his duty of going to school to learn agriculture. He helped raise turkeys on the kibbutz. In the army, part of mandatory service for Israelis, he joined a paratrooper unit. He spent time in Chicago, doing outreach for the government for Americans aspiring to move to Israel. There, he developed a deep love for the Chicago Bears. Around 1990, Gat was back at the kibbutz, which was trying to figure out the next job for him. It was suggested he be given two goats and two sheep to tend to and for children to visit.

He was fifty at the time, his bushy beard starting to gray. The goat idea didn't appeal to him, but it led to a spark. Gat somehow got it into his head that he'd create a Winnie-the-Pooh theme park and a petting zoo potentially drawing tens of thousands of people— "something different from what I've done and different from what other people do, and build a zoo to connect people with animals but not with cages but via education," he described it.

Maybe that doesn't sound so crazy at all, or entirely novel, but it was certainly unusual for the time and place.

And the more Gat thought about it, the more he couldn't banish the idea from his head.

"I didn't care about *nothing* else. I had just zoo. I went crazy, not crazy, but you couldn't talk to me about anything," he said.

Community members thought maybe the idea would fade. "He had a crazy idea. Everyone said it would wear off," said Yael Ziv, a cousin of mine who grew up on a nearby kibbutz and whose husband grew up on Nir David.

Nir David, uncertain what to do with this community member who was suddenly obsessed, arranged for him to take a class for people interested in starting projects. Maybe Gat's inspiration would indeed wear off. After six months in the seminar, Gat told me: "My tutor said to me there is no way—NO WAY—you are going to start a Winnie-the-Pooh park."

A friend mentioned to him that maybe he could limit his park to Australian animals, like kangaroos. Kangaroos? Kangaroos!

Yes, yes, yes, yes. Gat sat down and faxed letters to more than eighty zoos in Europe, asking if he could buy a kangaroo. One answered, telling him that they could provide a single kangaroo, a big one, but warned it would be unfriendly. The zoo sent two kangaroos. "They were very, very aggressive."

He wasn't a laughingstock, but there were chuckles. At one point, he planted eucalyptus trees to feed koalas. "Right in the middle of the field," said Oron Ziv, Yael's husband, who was the head of farming at the time and a former tank commander in the Israeli army. "This guy must be really crazy," Ziv said, verbalizing the conventional thinking.

Gat insisted he would find a way and would create a tourist industry, with twenty thousand visitors annually to Nir David. The reaction his vision inspired first took place when he walked into the dining commons where all the members of the kibbutz eat their meals.

"People were jumping up and down on two feet," he said.

What is creativity?

The possibilities are vast.

"Creativity is an umbrella term that subsumes various definitions and theoretical perspectives," as one recent paper in the *Journal of Neuroimage* describes the breadth of the possibilities. "It can be defined as a product, a process, an identity, or a personality type."

The most widely used association I've seen with creativity is that it is characterized by newness, originality, novelty. A second widely used association is that a creative development has "meaning." To put that another way, the creation makes a difference.

This is why many definitions of creativity settle on an explication that includes a convergence of novelty and value. Value is important, "because it allows us to differentiate creative thought and behavior from thought and behavior that is merely eccentric or odd," notes the *Cambridge Handbook of Creativity and Personality Research*.

To be creative, a concept can't be one that is only new. It should mean something, even in the abstract.

Some researchers add a third component: surprise!

Novelty, value, surprise!

Others say that surprise is just novelty with an exclamation point affixed at the end. Or, as one highly regarded creativity researcher told me with vigor: "The idea is bullshit. It's just an extension of novelty."

Welcome to the broader world of creativity research, which has blossomed in recent years, become more refined, and still, as you'll see, has nooks of uncertainty and even incoherence. Or, if you prefer a more pointed version of that sentence, this is how the lack of coherence is described by Arne Dietrich: "Given the time-tested ability of pop-psychologists and self-help gurus to expand in a vacuum, creativity has become a hotbed for useless piffle, nebulous fluff, and—to adopt an expression of art from the philosopher Harry Frankfurt— bullshit," Dietrich wrote in his book *How Creativity Happens in the Brain*. (We'll hear more from Dietrich in a later chapter about creativity and the brain.)

So I start with the most accepted, basic proposition that creativity involves novelty and value or influence. To be clear, this is not at all the same attribute as having "positive" influence. For instance: Hitler. Or Pol Pot. What they did might, in some way, check the boxes of newness and value, in the sense that these cretins brought temporary structure or value to a community, had novelty of scale, and certainly surprised humanity with the depth and commitment to genocide and novel combinations of tools and tactics to carry it out.

What this tells us is only that creativity should not be seen, on its face, as good or evil. It is a process. The results are subjective.

Harold Cohen developed a computer program called AARON that painted pictures. Pretty darn good stuff that hangs in galleries. His daughter, a painter, has less notoriety and draws images "for which most people would not be inclined to pay." For his part, Cohen "rates his daughter's creativity as much greater than that of his program," according to a sweeping article on the evolutionary roots of creativity published by the Royal Society of London.

The article notes how varied are the definitions of true creativity. Some think the idea should only be "applied to the great creators of great historical import."

As you'll read later on, though, there would have been no light-bulb, no smallpox vaccine, Martin Luther King, Jr., or cancer immunotherapy, and on and on without the Little C's that came before.

In short, a creator just might change the world, but that's not at all required, in the eyes of many scholars in the field, for a person to be creative.

Creativity has another key association that has less to do with the outcome and more to do with the personal experience of the creator. That association involves the concept of authenticity. Some scholars in the field of creativity embrace the idea that creativity often blossoms from a development of ideas that come from authentic experience and emotion. This makes sense. A creation of authentic origin might have a better chance than an inauthentic or fake one at resonating with others—and therefore having value.

When experiences are authentic, they can be pleasurable, honest, true. This means that, very often, creativity can be associated with immense pleasure.

Albert Einstein called creativity "intelligence having fun." He had more than three hundred publications to his name, many of which tackled the greatest mysteries of how the universe works, so Einstein knew whereof he spoke.

He also said that "Logic will get you from A to B. Imagination will take you everywhere," which seems to suggest that the intelligence element isn't as important as the fun part.

"Imagination is more important than knowledge," he said, and: "You can never solve a problem on the level on which it was created." It's clear Einstein believed creativity was among the most essential of human traits.

Many scholars I've spoken to agree. This line of thinking considers creativity the sine qua non of existence. Meaning: Creativity is absolutely essential to everyday life, to language, to moving ahead, and no profound creative leaps could be made without the universal, quotidian advances.

So I'll add to the definition: Creativity is absolutely, vitally, insanely important.

Novelty, value, surprise, authenticity, fun. But not necessarily good or evil.

All these notions and nuances about creativity have validity.

I tell the story of the Kangaroo Man for several reasons. It shows how people can become creative later in life and in settings that might not seem hospitable for originality. The story highlights one of the most important aspects of creativity: To have usefulness, an idea or innovation obviously doesn't need to shake the whole of the world, reform a religion, cure a disease, and so on. You'll hear in this book from people who have done those things. The Nobel Prize winner who helped pioneer powerful new cancer therapies blows the mind, for instance, but even for him the act was a by-product of a process. It wasn't itself an aim. Results of creativity may vary. Sometimes, as the kangaroo story shows, in surprising ways.

The last and main reason to tell his story is to illuminate an aspect of creativity most people don't discuss, one that is rarely included in the definitions.

Indeed it is the first aspect to understand, because no creative pursuit can go forward without appreciating this facet of creativity.

It can be *terrifying*.

Gat's story provides a powerful example of how one person found himself through creativity and changed his corner of the world, and why the ultimate impact of that can be hard to measure.

His story illustrates and introduces the arc of a creator's process, which involves overcoming doubt, embracing authenticity, allowing inspiration to bully obstacles, internal and external. It also shows us through example and science that creativity inspires unconscious fear that starts early in life, which can be overcome only by a resolute faith in oneself, one step after the next; but there is a dastardly punchline: The fear is reasonable because the outcomes of creative journeys are unknown.

The Kangaroo Man grappled with all these challenges, and it paid off.

Gat, mocked but not chagrined or deterred, wrote to Australia. He convinced the kibbutz to fly him there. He traveled to Australia six times, visiting more than two dozen zoos, where he learned how to care for kangaroos, koalas, emus, wombats. In 1996, he sat down across a table from Australian authorities on the sixth floor of a government building in Canberra. For two hours he described his vision. By the time he left, he was told he could have them all—the pantheon of exotic animals for his kibbutz petting zoo, a first outside Australia. On the elevator ride down, he recalled, a mentor of his in Australia told Gat that he must have been heaven-touched.

"Gabriel the angel touched your head when you came out of your mother," Gat quoted, remembering his old friend as being a devout Christian. Gat added, "I don't believe in Gabriel, but I cannot explain what happened that made Australia believe in me. I have NO idea, honestly."

He added: "If I'm a religious person, which I'm not, I think maybe the rabbi helped me, or God helped me."

Not long afterward the first kangaroo petting zoo outside of Australia opened at kibbutz Nir David. It became a hit, a smash hit, with a wide range of animals and birds. Prior to the pandemic, the park annually welcomed 140,000 visitors from all over the world, orders of magnitude more than Gat promised. When fully operational, the zoo brings in $6 million shekels a year, nearly US$2 million, of which about 25 percent is profit.

Australian authorities have come to cherish Gat to the point that they are discussing sending him three endangered kangaroos, a rare breed that spends its lives in trees. More than that, the zoo became itself a source of kangaroos for other zoos around the world, in Latvia, Warsaw, Jordan, Belgium, Canada, China. It's become all the more important now, with Australian forests burning, millions of animals killed. There's a home away from home these days, on a kibbutz, where the Kangaroo Man once seemed like a nutjob.

Now Gat is a beloved fixture, still a step apart in his world. When I spoke to him, outside the wooden fence of the kangaroo petting park, he held in his right hand a pail containing a dead bird that a snake wouldn't eat, and, in his left hand, parts of a dead mouse that the snake also did not find palatable that day. Behind Gat, in the kangaroo park, echoed the joyful squeals from a busload of Arab children spending a field trip petting and feeding dozens of the transplanted Australian creatures.

Ziv, the former head of the farms on the kibbutz, now is a believer. "He's got a vision. He was fighting against other people and he made it. Sometimes you need people like this to get things done."

I asked Gat his secret. He paused but then seemed resolute about what makes him tick. "I think I am very confident of what I'm doing. I am a beekeeper, a hobbyist beekeeper. The moment I decide I'm doing beekeeping, I do beekeeping. I decided four years ago to play jazz on the saxophone and I play saxophone."

Yet he came to his inspiration late in life. Can just anyone do this? No, he insisted.

"You have to be a dreamer but not forget to keep your feet on the ground. Not everybody could be that," Gat said. "They must have the flash in their eyes. They have to feel they will hit their target," he said.

Gat described his experience like this: "I was living on the edge."

Is he right? Is creativity an exclusive club?

The short answer is no. But to understand why requires breaking down the way a creator emerges by confronting deep, unspoken challenges.

Doubt

So you want to be a creator?

You have ideas. You think of them before you go to sleep. You've mentioned them at cocktail parties, to your spouse, to friends who have started businesses, to fellow engineers, to people who play guitar or do comedy at open mic nights. You have a family member who is a screenwriter. You've heard yourself say sheepishly, "I've had this idea . . ." or "Can I tell you my idea . . ." and then your voice peters out.

Or maybe you're not sure you have ideas. You sense that there could be one or two innovations in your pocket.

But what do you know from creativity? What business do you have pursuing the Big and little C-words? Does it have anything to do with you?

Before I tell you that you know more than you think you do and that the steps are much more accessible then you imagine, I must first explain the hidden barrier. I refer here to the D-words, The Big D-word, Doubt. Then there's the Little D-word—disgust.

Yes, creativity might disgust you, if you're honest. It's terrifying. Vomit-inducing, like a toxin.

Check out the science.

Powerful research comes from Jack Goncalo, a highly innovative thinker about creativity who, along with two collaborators, asked themselves a question: Do people really like creativity and creators?

This seems like a brainless question. Really? Do people really like creativity? Do we really like ice cream, puppies, rainbows?

In reality, the question they were asking is a fantastic one. In journalism circles, we sometimes call this kind of inquiry "the smart-dumb question." The idea behind such a question is that it takes an idea we think we are absolutely certain we know the answer to and asks if we really are, in fact, absolutely certain. Have we taken a basic assumption for granted?

Goncalo, to me, is one of the more interesting researchers in the field of creativity who, time and again, asks such questions. He's uncovered multiple insights, hidden gems about the process and psyche of creators. He teaches in the College of Business at the University of Illinois at Urbana-Champaign, but at the time of the study about creativity and fear, he was posted at Cornell University, collaborating with researchers at the Wharton School at the University of Pennsylvania and at the University of North Carolina. Sometimes it takes very smart people to ask smart-dumb questions.

The question he and his fellow scientists posted in 2010 led to a paper published in 2012. In the paper's first paragraph, they state their premise: "Do people desire creative ideas? Most scholars would answer this question with an obvious 'yes,' asserting that creativity is the engine of scientific discovery and the fundamental driving force of positive change. Furthermore, creativity is seen as being associated with intelligence, wisdom, and moral goodness."

However, the premise continues, research also shows that companies, research centers, leaders, and others "routinely reject creative ideas," and teachers "dislike students who exhibit curiosity and creative thinking."

You might too.

"We offer a new perspective," the research says, "to explain this puzzle."

My first exchange with Goncalo took place on January 13, 2020. By now, an infection being called simply "a coronavirus" had begun to spread, resulting in some alarm, but hardly hysteria. On January 15, the *New York Times* reported, two had died in China and forty others were sick. A handful of cases of the "mysterious pneumonialike coronavirus" had shown up in Thailand and Japan. The article speculated that the disease had spread from "a seafood market in Wuhan that sells other birds and animals."

An organism that likely had evolved some time ago—nature's creation of unknown age—had begun to find a niche in the human world. Curiously, it would have much to teach us about how creativity works and thrives. But at that moment, the disease still seemed remote. Even knowing it was out there, somewhere, our family had flown back from Israel in a packed flight; the gravest threat to our safety I felt was from our eleven-year-old son's staying up twenty hours straight to take advantage of the free movies (yes, he did). We also had flown back and forth over the winter holidays to Denver and then skied at Steamboat Springs, where I distinctly recall chatting with visitors from Italy, which would soon become a hotspot of infections with the incredibly contagious virus.

All the while, a biological creation lurked that would wind up underscoring precisely what Goncalo, now a professor of business at the University of Illinois, was poised to share with me: Creativity is terrifying, in ways we lie to ourselves about.

Goncalo and his fellow scientists ran two experiments. The first split research participants into two groups. One group was told they could receive extra money that would be distributed by a random lottery. They could get cash but couldn't control the outcome. The other group did not get any offer of a bonus.

This condition had the impact of making the lottery group feel uncertain.

The researchers then used an established research tool to measure how each group felt about creativity—not just how they said they felt on a conscious level, but also how they felt subconsciously. This is a kind of research that gets at what is known as "implicit bias." It's the same kind of research, broadly, that can be used to study how people feel about others of different races. People say one thing about creativity but, on a deep level, feel conflicted.

The researchers established through a questionnaire that study subjects expressed generally positive feelings about creativity. This was their "explicit" or stated belief system.

Then the researchers sought to unearth feelings that lurk below the surface. Using a clever computer program, they asked study participants to react so quickly to information that they don't really have time to "think." They just react.

This particular study involved having participants react to ideas like "novel" and "original," along with ideas that are less associated with creativity like "practical" or "functional."

In this research, these words and related ideas were paired side by side on a computer screen with two different categories of images. Some of the images had positive associations, like rainbow, heaven, and cake. Others had decisively negative associations, like vomit, hell, and poison. When these study subjects responded in a rapid-fire manner, without thinking, their subconscious, hidden views of creativity emerged.

On a visceral level, creativity felt toxic, the study revealed. "People actually had a strong association between the concept of creativity and other negative associations like vomit, poison, and agony," Goncalo told me.

The subset of study subjects in the "uncertain" category—who didn't know if they'd get money—were even more likely than the control group to have negative associations with creativity.

What this suggested to researchers is that people say they like creativity, but they also like stability. So when things feel unstable, or uncertain, they are more likely to reject creativity because it suggests even greater chaos.

"People want creativity and stability," Goncalo said.

It can be difficult to have both.

Creativity is disruptive. Creativity means changing how we relate to the world, go through our day-to-day lives, what we eat, listen to, watch, how we interact with one another. Creativity changes long-accepted behaviors, technology, and basic social contracts. It can be wrenching.

While this seems obvious upon reflection, it's not what we tell ourselves. "Saying you don't want creativity is like saying you don't like hope," Goncalo observed.

It would be hard to understate the significance of this finding in a modern world filled with change and chaos. Fairly, it is possible even to explain some of the rise of more authoritarian governments or leaders in some countries as a reaction to immense and fast-moving change. The advancements and innovations people say they crave, and many people authentically do, can run headlong into competing cravings they and others have for stability.

From a biological perspective, the origin of this tension derives from a deeper association: Creativity is death.

New ideas pose the threat of extinction in two different ways. This is not metaphorical but rather is drawn from the biological. I'll elaborate later when I introduce eminent biologists into this book. For now, in brief, the idea is that new forms of life and new ideas are almost always destined to fail. When viruses or bacteria mutate by accident, and when new combinations of cells emerge inside our bodies, these cells almost always die because they don't fit as well into the environment as the forms of life that came before. This is true of many ideas. Most don't work. They die off.

There's another way, though, in which change equals death. When the new forms of life, or ideas, do succeed, they displace what came before—and kill the past. New ideas kill habits, businesses, power structures, jobs.

In my early twenties, I took a job at a small newspaper, earning $16,000 a year. To pad the paycheck, I worked the 6 a.m. shift at a local Chevron station on what was known then as "the full-service island." I filled gas tanks and washed windows. Then along came credit card readers and other technology that did away with the jobs on the full-service island. And along came the internet that did away with many newspaper jobs, including closing down that first newspaper where I worked.

In the biological world, new life-forms can take over the landscape from the older forms of life less suited to a changing environment.

You are darn right creativity is scary.

So is the call of inspiration.

In fact, one of my favorite stories about how inspiration can be terrifying comes from the Bible. It's a story that took place not far from the land of the Kangaroo Man when, as the Bible tells it, a burning bush appeared to Moses.

"And Moses said: 'I will now turn aside,'" the King James Bible reads.

If you like a metaphor as much as I do, the bush can appear as the mighty flame of the wonder of inspiration. The bush was like the modern idea of a lightbulb. Idea! Free the slaves. Moses turned away.

That's not the end of the story. God told Moses he must help to free slaves. "And Moses said unto God: 'Who am I, that I should go unto Pharaoh, and that I should bring forth the children of Israel out of bondage?'"

A biblical scholar told me at one point that this was almost funny because Moses was, in a very modest way, talking back to God.

Really? I'm going to be the vessel that frees slaves? I'm a dang sheepherder! Find someone else.

God proved persuasive, and Moses relented and slaves were freed.

It's worth noting that the very name "Israel" means "wrestles with God."

While this idea yields plenty of possible interpretations, one of them is the idea that people are grappling with a creator, creation, the ultimate power.

One generation after the next had to feel the inspiration, hear it, succumb to it, and fight enslavement, of self and by others; the issue would rise again with terrible ferocity in 2020 with a fight against systemic racism in the United States dating back to its own not-so-distant sins of slavery.

Meantime, there's more that Goncalo has discovered that helps explain why people might keep creativity at arm's length.

Given the finding that people harbor subconscious bias against creativity, Goncalo and his peer researchers then asked a second question: Does that mean people might have trouble actually recognizing creativity when they see it? In other words, if people associate the process of creativity with vomit, might they conflate actual creativity with disgust?

This is precisely what the researchers found when they showed a new running shoe to two different groups: people who identified as having considerable tolerance of uncertainty, and those with less tolerance.

This new running shoe, the researchers told the study subjects, uses nanotechnology to "adjust fabric thickness to cool the foot and reduce blisters."

The people in the higher-tolerance group were more likely to see it as creative, the others less so. This finding, while not startling, particularly given the results of the implicit bias study, reinforces the kinds of conditions and people that are more conducive to creativity. Uncertainty and instability yield infertile ground for new ideas.

Examples abound from history where a new idea that would ultimately become accepted as highly relevant, even brilliant, was initially received as noxious.

In 1872, Claude Monet debuted a painting called *Impression, Sunrise*. It's a moody swirl of morning on the water as fishermen row to sea, a tinged-red sun rising in the distance.

Critics ripped it to shreds.

"A preliminary drawing for a wallpaper pattern is more finished than this seascape," wrote a critic in 1874 in an essay published in Paris. The scathing review borrowed from the painting's title to name the style of painting "Impressionism." It was meant sarcastically, as if to say: Monet, could you draw a real freaking sunrise already?

The painting now hangs in Paris's Musée Marmottan Monet, one of the world's greatest art museums, one that bears his name, and he is heralded as among the greatest of the grand artistic innovators. You could buy this wallpaper drawing for about a trillion dollars if it was ever for sale.

Centuries earlier, Galileo made people so desperately want to throw up that he was convicted of heresy for declaring that the Earth revolves around the very sun Monet had so creatively drawn. 'Nuff said.

In other cases, creativity and inspiration are quite understandably scary in that creations can yield mixed and unexpected results.

To illustrate, I return briefly to the story of the Kangaroo Man.

———

In 2010, after the kangaroo park was long since up and running, and Gat had more than fifty kangaroos, the animals began to suffer from a condition called "lumpy jaw." So inflamed and infected became the jaws of the kangaroos that they did not eat. They died or had to be killed to end their suffering. This doesn't happen in the wild, only in captivity, and it had long vexed Australians too. There was no cure.

Gat and the veterinarian at Nir David reached out to scientists at Hebrew University. One of the scientists was Doron Steinberg, a microbiologist and pharmacologist who a few years earlier had co-invented a new technology to prevent gum disease in human beings. It is called the PerioChip. It tucks into the gums and delivers antiseptic to prevent the growth of bacteria. Steinberg recalled that when he came up with the idea with his co-inventor and fellow Hebrew University professor, Michael Feldman, he felt overwhelmed.

"The feeling was like we were doing a worldwide breakthrough," Steinberg told me. He thought of all the physical pain to be relieved and money to be saved by substituting this technology for surgery. They were not mistaken. The technology is now sold widely in the world and has approval from the US Food & Drug Administration.

When kangaroos started showing up sick, the pair borrowed from their ideas, worked with two veterinarians, and developed an enamel that can be applied to kangaroos and that has, for all intents and purposes, eradicated the deadly effects of lumpy jaw.

When I heard this coda, I was struck by three lessons illustrated by the story of the Kangaroo Man.

The first has to do with how ideas build on each other, driven by cooperation, communication, mind melds, and brainstorming. Steinberg and his co-creator came up with the idea for the PerioChip in a lightning-struck conversation—in an elevator. "From one floor to another. It was so quick!" Doron told me. This kind of "aha" moment has become the subject of increasing study that I'll explore further later in the book.

The second lesson is really a question: Was this zoo such a good idea after all? It provided revenue for a struggling collective, brought joy to families who visited, and helped lead to a cure for other animals in captivity but at the expense of keeping animals in captivity in the first place. This is not the venue for a debate on the subject so much as the occasion to point out that there is a debate to be engaged in—about whether this creation and others are objectively good or bad.

The final lesson has to do with a subject I've already introduced: that many people, including some creators, believe that creativity isn't accessible to most people.

This point was reinforced for me again when I asked Steinberg the same question I'd asked Gat: Can just anybody be creative?

"No, no, no, no! I do not want to sound arrogant but you need God's gift for that."

"What do you mean?" I asked.

"You need it in your genes—a way of thinking, not to fear something that's unknown. When people say 'What are you doing? You're crazy!'—you need to be very courageous and not afraid."

"But," he continued, "I have colleagues, they hear that, and they go right back to their cave."

When I returned from Israel, I tested this idea by talking to several fantastic creators I've had the privilege to get to know. What struck me was the vehemence of their responses.

One such reaction came from one of the world's top-selling authors, who happens to be one of the nicest people and most supportive human beings I've ever had the privilege to know. When I asked this person if just anyone can be creative, the judgment came swift and harsh, with a preface: "Don't quote me by name," the person said.

Then the author let loose.

"Ninety-nine percent of people don't think out of the box. They can't. They receive opinions from others. They go about their lives in an efficient, wonderful fashion without having a creative thought in their lives," the person told me. "I guess I do not believe that creativity is accessible to most people."

In my conversations, I also discovered that even people I consider highly creative do not think of themselves as such and dismiss the idea that they could undertake pursuits they deem to be creative.

Several memorable exchanges I had on this subject took place with a terrific journalist and writer, a veteran *New York Times* business feature reporter named David Streitfeld. We started talking about writing books and I asked him if he ever thought about doing it. He seemed nearly aghast.

"Why would I write something when everything great has already been written?" Streitfeld said. He's tall and curly-headed, self-effacing, and funny and wise. We had that initial conversation several years ago. I never forgot it. And I went back to him during the reporting for this book and told him I wanted to ask him about his earlier comments.

"I'm already getting a dark feeling about you interviewing me for this book, unless it's an example of me being one of the least creative people you know and, even so, I'm not sure why anybody would care."

I burst out laughing at his visceral shock at the very idea. This is a guy who had been part of a team that won a Pulitzer Prize.

Streitfeld also said to me: "In essence, this is a subject I'm interested in because I do not have, for whatever reason, that ability—that trait—that you have and have cultivated in yourself and without which nothing writing-wise is possible, and with it, everything is possible."

I think it's fair to look at Streitfeld's thoughtful perspective in two ways. The first can be summed up with a question: Why bother? If a person doesn't feel inspired, why bother to create? I see this as very reasonable. An uninspired person shouldn't be forced to feel otherwise.

The second way, though, to look at Streitfeld's perspective is slightly more scientific. It suggests that the resistance a person feels comes from a state of mind that isn't set in stone. Inspiration can be learned.

Streitfeld had used a key word: He said he hadn't "cultivated" the trait that encourages free-flowing creativity. It's a good word. Creativity can be cultivated, and the first step—the more important step, arguably—involves addressing the doubt, self-doubt and outside expectations, that often hamper the creative impulse.

Because to put a fine point on it: doubt is essentially inherent to the creative journey. It must be grappled with. That means understanding when it starts.

In childhood, of course.

Seeds of Doubt

Researchers can pinpoint when the doubt sets in.

Fourth grade.

In 1959, a pioneering scientist named E. Paul Torrance sought to measure the creativity of 350 elementary school students. He did so by giving them a handful of cognitive tests aimed at gauging abilities seen as crucial to creativity, such as how flexibly they could think, how much they could elaborate on concepts, and their ability to come up with lots of different ideas. In creativity scholarship, this last category is known as "fluency."

Torrance gave the students rankings for their creativity based on these measurements. When they were in the earlier grades, they tended to be idea machines. They'd throw out one crazy idea after another, generating random thoughts, concepts logical and mad.

Torrance then sat back and watched what happened as the students aged. Once a year, each year from September of 1959 through May of 1964, he gave the students the same set of tests.

Over that period, he saw a sharp drop in creativity measures, especially in their fluency, or ability to generate lots of ideas. The drop happened in fourth grade.

"Many children end up with lower scores in the fifth grade than they attained in the third grade," reads Torrance's seminal scientific paper, published in *Gifted Child Quarterly* in 1968. The students' scores dropped 52 percent in their fluency with ideas, though they rose 21 percent in their ability to elaborate on the ideas that they did generate. "In general," Torrance wrote, "there is the strongest tendency for growth in elaboration and the weakest in fluency."

The children, while they appeared to be able to elaborate on some ideas, could generate fewer of them. They'd become less creatively agile.

One of the most lasting aspects of Torrance's study was the label that he gave to his discovery. He called it "Fourth Grade Slump." It had the Madison Avenue ring of great marketing. Plus, Torrance himself was widely regarded as one of the most original and pioneering thinkers in the field of creativity, and so his name added weight to the findings.

"It caught on. People refer to the fourth-grade slump as if it were universal and unambiguous," said Mark Runco, a contemporary leading thinker in creativity. He edits the *Creativity Research Journal*, teaches creativity at Southern Oregon University, and has himself developed tests to help measure creative potential.

Torrance had strongly held views on why students appeared to grow less creative.

"Torrance said the problem here is education," Runco explained. "A bunch of rules get instilled: raise your hand, sit in the right seat. His view was that by the fourth grade, children have internalized conventional thinking and the need to follow rules, which in turn inhibits the tendency toward original thinking."

The pressure to conform to thinking didn't appear just from their teachers but also from their peers. Ideas that in second grade seemed playful, funny, harmless, or loosely connected could now prompt teachers to say "Really? C'mon!" or classmates to laugh. Bit by bit, the theory went, children internalized the voices of outsiders condemning or mocking them and so developed a preemptive filter. An idea might emerge but be quickly dissolved inside the brain before it hit the mouth or before pen got to paper. What if the teacher thinks I'm an idiot? What if my friends think I sound stupid?

And more conventional thinking takes root.

Runco cites a simple example to show how children's thinking changes over time. In the earlier grades a student asked to draw a tree might think nothing of giving the leaves polka dots. "In the upper grades, no way: the trees have brown bark and green leaves," Runco said.

A biblical metaphor proves powerful here too. It has to do with the tree of knowledge of good and evil. The man and woman in the garden were forbidden to eat from it. When they did eat, they lost their innocence, realized they were naked, grew ashamed. It's a bit like children who learn, at some point, to become ashamed of themselves. (It's easy to let this metaphor get away from me, so I humbly beg readers to enjoy the surface interpretation.)

The idea that the change in thinking actually takes place in fourth grade has been tested since Torrance's seminal work. Some papers have replicated his findings. Others have refuted them. So the point isn't that the change happens precisely in fourth grade. But it happens during a child's formative years.

Other recent scholarship has reinforced that notion.

Kyung Hee "Kay" Kim, a professor of educational psychology at the William & Mary Graduate School of Education, won the 2018 E. Paul Torrance Award. It is bestowed by the National Association for Gifted Students for work deemed to spread and contribute to creativity, particularly among children.

A year earlier, in 2017, Kim had criticized the world's education system for becoming increasingly hostile to creative thinking. Kim blamed the problem on the rise of testing. She called the problem "Exam Hell" and said it had intensified greatly in the United States, which adopted testing regimens from other countries, since the early 1990s. Such testing, Kim argues, amplified and made much more

explicit the kinds of rule-based thinking that Torrance had identified as implicit in education decades earlier.

Kim, who taught English in Korea for a decade before becoming a
researcher and professor in the United States, argues that despite the
implicit rule-making of prior generations, much of instruction in the
United States in particular revolved around curiosity and independent thinking as tools used to come up with interesting solutions.
Broadly, she writes, the climate "nurtured their emotional, compas-
sionate, self-reflective, daydreaming, autonomous, nonconforming,
gender-bias-free, and defiant attitudes."

I suspect that the extent to which this is true could inspire a fairly
strong debate among scholars, though Kim certainly is well regarded. Certainly, the extent to which students learn to think freely
depends on what sort of school they attended.

Broadly, Kim's most persuasive point is that the education climate
has changed radically because of testing. In her 2017 work (an up-
date of research she published in 2011 titled "The Creativity Crisis"),
she argued that testing appeared to serve various constituencies:
politicians who wanted objective measures of success; colleges that
wanted to easily differentiate among students; parents who wanted
a clear, unambiguous way to see how their own children ranked; and
those with a broader societal desire to see the country's youth keep
up with the test scores of other countries.

In the process, Kim argued, tests with concrete answers caused
children to lose curiosity and imagination, discourage passion and
risk-taking, and ultimately to succumb to "conforming to others'
control."

The system "increasingly fostered conformity, stifling individuality, uniqueness, and originality in both educators and students," she
wrote. And she told me in an interview: "If, early on, you start thinking about the right answer instead of thinking about possibilities,
your brain loses flexibility."

Some fledgling neuroscience backs up the point. The neuroimaging research shows that when people answer questions using the same methodology over and over, there is atrophy in parts of their brain associated with more flexible thinking. I will delve more deeply into this idea in the neuroscience section of the book.

Meanwhile, one of the most powerful studies ever published about the relationship between intellect and creativity shows that children who perform well on intelligence tests are not necessarily destined for creative achievement.

In 1921, a Stanford psychologist named Lewis Terman embarked on this spectacular research. He gathered roughly 1,500 young people with very high IQ scores. For the moment, I will set aside the question of whether these scores are an accurate measure of intelligence and accept the idea that they do represent a particular type of established intelligence aimed at being able to solve problems and engage in abstract thinking. Terman's students, on average, had an IQ of 147, which put them above the 99th percentile in IQ scores.

The Terman Study followed these students over the course of their lifetimes, all the way until 1986. The finding was plain: These scores did not reflect future creative achievement. "The Terman group in general was surprisingly uncreative over the course of their careers," reads a powerful analysis of the relationship between intellect and creativity published in 2003 in the *Journal of Research in Personality*. "No major writers, artists, or scientists emerged from this 'genius' level IQ group." There's a coda. Two bright children who didn't meet the 140 IQ cutoff for the study did each go on to win a Nobel Prize. One was William Shockley, who invented the first transistor.

This is not to say intellect doesn't play a role in success. It just doesn't equate with creativity . . . And yet testing became increasingly an arbiter in measuring student performance.

One key reason for the rise of testing is the advent and spread of the personal computer. These devices have permitted the widespread ability to uniformly test people.

Yes, they allow the ability to create and in ways never before possible. But the way they've driven testing culture simply shows, once again, that our greatest creations can have side effects we neither anticipate nor, in the end, actually desire.

Then human beings fire back, with new ideas.

To that end, a recent backlash against testing appears to be reversing the three-decade push to have children check the right box. No wonder many big thinkers acknowledge now that the fast-changing nature of a complicated economy requires more flexible thinking.

Meanwhile, there are so many tools a school can use to foster creativity, but they aren't tools which allow the outcomes to be so easily measured.

One simple technique is called "What-if?" storytelling. It's only one modest example but the "what-if" game illustrates a larger point.

A few years ago, I wrote a children's book called *The Runaway Booger*. It's about a family in which nose-picking gets out of control and a giant booger gets created. Yes, it's super gross.

After I wrote it, schools and local groups began inviting me to talk to children about the book, and creativity. I did a little research and, drawing on the wisdom of experts, cobbled together the "what-if" game.

It usually starts after I've read the book to the kids and one of them asks:

"Why did you write about a huge booger?"

"Well," I say, "I just got to wondering: what if you picked your nose too much and wound up with a huge booger?"

At this point, I'm like the king of kindergarten (very possibly where I still belong).

"Why don't you try," I'd suggest. "All you have to do is say: what if . . ." And then they're off and running, building sentences and even full stories. "What if," a kindergartner once spewed, "you flushed the toilet and wound up in outer space?!"

"And what if," another student said, "you flushed the toilet again and went somewhere else!?"

The students caromed off into space and their imaginations. I didn't tell them that toilets are potty talk and potty talk is bad. I didn't tell them that you can't flush a toilet and break the time/space continuum. I did tell them I *might* steal their brilliant ideas.

Then something remarkable happened.

One student suggested that when you flush the toilet, it returned you back home. She was, in effect, giving the story a kind of conclusion, or a return to earth that, in some ways, was consistent with how someone might tell a traditional story. What I found so compelling about all of this is that, even though the students had let their imaginations flow, they also had some sense of conventional or rule-based storytelling that infused the story.

This is worth noting because it underscores a very important point about how much the rules that govern the world and various genres—art, science, technology—become integrated into thinking merely by existing in the world. People absorb structures. As creators learn more about their fields, they become familiar by feel with basic tenets of structure. This should give some permission to parents, children of all ages, and educators to allow more imagination, knowing it will not lead people off the rails altogether.

I mention this what-if exercise not in the spirit of providing any kind of catch-all counsel on how to raise a creative child. This is not that type of self-help book. I mean it to show that there are many simple steps that allow for creative processing and encouragement to be built in to communication with young people as a way to promoting creativity along with other skill sets.

These types of exercises are aimed at creating a safe space around completely open-ended thinking. The delight is in the imagination, shared by teachers, or parents. Such exercises need not replace tests or other measures but can complement them.

All this said, it would be overly simplistic, even grossly unfair, to blame schools alone for the fourth-grade slump. The schools reflect the political climate and the will of the people who create it. In other words: we, the parents.

The Seeds of Doubt grow at home too.

"Do not pick your nose."

"Do not run into the road, eat food off the floor, talk in a loud voice, slump your shoulders, draw on the wall with crayons, use that kind of language!"

A remarkable percentage of child rearing involves setting boundaries. This is good for survival. It is essential. Know the rules or die. A child who doesn't receive clear direction not to dash into traffic is a child who might be run over. This message cannot be delivered clearly enough. Do. Not. Run. Into. The. Street.

The trouble arises when parents expand the number and nature of such rules and make them overbearing. When rules abound, children begin to develop a habit of looking for the rule, and adhering to it. The children develop a kind of automatic filter—not just to dangerous ideas, but to more general ones that could overstep some boundary. The children develop a knee-jerk "no."

In the late 1990s, John Dacey, a professor of education at Boston College (now a professor emeritus) decided to study the homes of children who had exhibited creativity. These were children who had been identified to the researchers by schools as having produced creatively—not merely shown creative potential. The students, for instance, wrote a column for the school newspaper, or created a radio show.

Dacey decided to compare the parenting and atmosphere in their homes to those of children who had not exhibited any particular creativity.

The researchers visited multiple homes, armed with two hundred questions about various facets of life. One particular area of inquiry yielded powerful implications. The parents with creative children gave those children far fewer rules on a daily basis than did the families with children who did not exhibit creativity.

In the families with creative children, Dacey told me, "There might be one rule, like: Be a mensch."

Translation from Yiddish: Be kind.

By contrast, the researchers found that in families with children who exhibited less creativity, there were, on average, ten rules. When to go to bed, when to be home, how to behave in various situations. "They never wanted their kids to get into trouble, or to make mistakes," Dacey said. The families with creative kids "were forever taking risks, letting kids practice making mistakes."

The differences in rules and cultures came across sometimes in how the homes looked—more conformity with the less creative families, less so for the ones that raised creative children. One home that struck Dacey looked antiqued from the outside and on the inside had a dining room with antiques that appeared to be centuries old and bedrooms filled with modern furniture. Another family with a particularly creative child had a collection of forty-seven birds (curiously, Dacey said, the researchers found that many of the families with creative children had collections of some kind or another. He thought that, perhaps, it showed that children learned to fit ideas into different kinds of categories, which could be seen as a form of dot-connecting).

What Dacey took away from the study was that many parents, in an effort to protect children, "stifle them" by having them internalize the idea of limits, rules, boundaries.

This is not an argument for doing away with all rules. Rather, the idea is to recognize the power of rules to cement a kind of mindset. As parents shape the neural networks of their children, it is possible to have rules while also mixing in explanation and questions, indulging curiosity, allowing children to question and to seek their own reasons for why there are rules, when they apply, and what circumstances allow flexibility.

One way that parents may not realize they subdue creativity is through subtle language that may not seem so bad. But it can discourage open-ended thinking. Think for instance of the questions "That's not how we do things, is it?" or "We don't say things like that, do we?" These sentences have the impact not only of discouraging a certain behavior but also of discouraging independent thought. The emphasis is on what "we" do and don't do and therefore what is "right."

Speaking of the word "right," it is another potent but low-level rhetorical technique that can put children into a box. The word gets used to confirm a particular premise in such a way that it suggests there is no basis for other thinking. For instance: "Those two colors don't go together, right? And so the house should be painted yellow."

The psychology that underlies this parental guidance can be more complex than a parent's merely fearing that a child will face physical harm if not complying. Sometimes, the rules reflect the parents' own fear of being perceived as poor stewards of their kids, or as failures. This fear can be amplified, Dacey said, in the internet age, when a child's mistake can "go viral." The mass media culture also implies greater risk of some threats, like being kidnapped (LOCAL TEEN KIDNAPPED! NEWS AT 11!). It just doesn't happen all that much, but

it can feel near, elevating a parent's assessment of risk. Urging conformity and rigid rulemaking and rule-following.

Mark Runco, the scholar I mentioned earlier in the chapter,
pointed out to me that as children age, parents become less toler-
ant of ideas that sound unconventional, fearing that they might even
sound dangerous or malevolent or evil.

Okay, not evil, exactly, though that is the word that Runco used.
He meant "evil" to refer broadly to ideas that make it sound like the
child might be amoral and thus reflect poorly on parents.

"I often talk to parents and teachers and one of my simpler messages is the best thing they can do for creativity is tolerate," Runco
said. "It's not as easy as you think."

Runco elaborated: "You better be open to the idea they're going
to come up with a good idea but also in the opposite direction—a
horrible, evil, vile—some of the ideas might be vile. As a parent, you
say: That's not my kid. That can't be my kid."

Children might well not pick up such explicit messages. But what
might indeed come across is that there is some terrible, unspoken
risk of failing to live up to expectations. This thinking, in turn, can
limit a person's desire to take risks.

This leads to one of the most important points I will make in this
book: The number one enemy of creativity is perfectionism.

There isn't even a close second-place enemy.

If you can't make a mistake, you can't take a creative risk. And so
the opposite of perfectionism is permission. It is one of the most important concepts in creativity, and the mortal foe of perfectionism.

The core idea isn't to engender nonconformity for its own sake,
but to stoke a measure of permission around the idea of deviating
from a one-size-fits-all world. This includes the terrifying prospect
that a child whose ideas don't gain worldly advantage (or straight
A's) is a child who has failed.

"If you want to be creative, you have to generate lots of ideas—

and pick out the good ones," said Dean Simonton, a scholar who has made a life's work of studying creative genius. "The main point is that you're able to generate ideas without knowing whether they're going to pan out."

Over and again, Simonton sees the same patterns with major creators: Quantity of ideas outpaces quality, not fearing how they will be perceived or whether they will work. His research shows that Thomas Edison had 1,093 patents and Picasso "executed more than 20,000 paintings, drawings, and pieces of sculpture, while Johann Sebastian Bach composed over 1,000 works." That doesn't mean that high productivity and influence are the same thing, but it does suggest that your odds of creating something others find meaningful increase if you feel the impulse to create and take the risk to go with it.

"If you want to be creative you can't guarantee a solution in advance," Simonton told me. "It's true if you look at any creative genius. Do you know how many dead ends Albert Einstein went through? It was astronomical—Sometimes you make really, really horrible mistakes."

Simonton makes a related point that is vital. The point is that creators persevere without knowing whether their pursuit will succeed. For many deeply creative people, the act of creativity itself is the end game because the nature of the process is to venture into the unknown.

By contrast, the child who only learns to check boxes—and fears failing to do so correctly—can become befuddled later when life gets more complex.

What can happen when a child internalizes this kind of thinking is that the child becomes a more hardened person who, later in life, has trouble dealing with open-ended situations that require flexible or creative thinking. Dacey, before he retired and became a professor emeritus, taught a class of undergraduates about creativity. For the final project he told them, "You have to do a project that shows me you learned a lot."

The assignment drove some students nuts. "They would say: 'We know there are no rules, but please . . . *Give us some direction, Dr. Dacey!*' I had more students crying in my office, saying: Please give me/us some parameters."

That's a very hard position to be in as the economy becomes more variable and open—less manufacturing line work, more work with ideas and cooperation, and more demand for conjuring solutions than putting preordained pieces together.

This analysis might make it sound like parents should let their children roam a little more freely.

I'm not going to be so simply prescriptive. Permission is important. So are rules. After doing all this research, as a parent, I think about this balance in terms of (wait for it) eating utensils. Take the fork, for example. I want my kids to know how to use a fork when they eat. I also would love if they felt free to think of fifteen other ways a fork might be used. As a shovel. A back scratcher. A lockpick.

It doesn't mean that I'd actually have them use their dinner fork to dig for worms (maybe at a picnic or not during actual dinner). But if my daughter started playing with her fork in some creative way, I also wouldn't say: "Now, c'mon, Mirabel, that's not how we use a fork, is it?"

If she ate steak with a spoon, I might wonder if she was on to something.

One more thing: I try now not to feel like the ideas, observations, wondrous curiosities that my children utter are a reflection on me. I see some parents who seem humiliated when their kids say "the wrong thing." Sure, they shouldn't call Aunt Jane an old bat. They can, though, attempt lots of associations, wrong as they might sound to me. Those random connections don't mean I've failed to teach them properly. I've allowed them to connect dots.

I do think the best way to see how complicated these issues are in the real world is to witness a real-world example. What follows are stories of how creators take shape. Their emergence can be messy.

Creator Takes Shape

In the first chapter of this book, I introduced Rhiannon Giddens, a singer-songwriter who grew up in North Carolina. She offers a searing insight into how creators emerge and how the conflicting messages that adults send contribute to the complexity.

Giddens and her older sister, Lalenja Harrington, grew up in a world filled with a varied mix of perspectives and influences: white dad and African American mom, who later came out as lesbian, and a deep influence from the family's maternal-side legacy of slavery. This influence led to some very powerful rulemaking and, it would seem, with good reason. The girls' maternal grandparents, given the legacy of slavery and racism, were terrified that if the girls didn't conform—if they stepped out of line—they could face dangerous, even deadly, discrimination. They were funny, gentle, and fiercely loving, intense.

The grandparents lived in rural North Carolina in a shotgun house; in this case, "shotgun" takes on a literal meaning.

One day, when Harrington was seven, she witnessed a terrible argument. Grandpa was needling Grandma.

"They had one of those seventies houses with wood paneling for the walls," Harrington recalled. "I could see down the hall my grandmom had gone back to her bedroom. There were shotguns in every closet and I remember seeing the barrel of that shotgun come through the door." The girl shouted a warning and that "brought grandmamma around"; granddad got out of harm's way. "From what I understand, my screaming saved my granddaddy that day."

Each grandparent dealt with alcoholism. Each had a temper. Each suffered dearly from slavery's deep and lasting wounds and the systemic racism that followed. What the wounds taught the grandparents was that Black men and women who stood out got the lash, or worse, the noose.

For instance, when the girls' grandmother was herself a young woman, and she didn't follow the family's rules, her own father would hang her by the arms from the barn rafter and beat her. He was just one generation from slavery and sometimes he would sit on his front porch with a shotgun on his lap to deter the darker-skinned Blacks from courting his daughter.

When Giddens and Harrington were girls, their grandmother worked in schools. She was the only Black teacher. She would tell her granddaughters how the boys would carve "KKK" into their arms and let it scab over. "They'd hold it out and stare at her," Giddens told me.

"You said something to the wrong person, you could get killed," she said. "There was harsh discipline in African American households, and it was a straight line of trauma."

She would come to understand it better later; of course, what child can make sense of all that? At the time, it felt both normal and scary. The message was clear: You girls will stay well within the lines. Nothing pleased Grandmother as much as when her friends came over for bridge and, after hours of preparation, the two girls had been dolled up for display.

By contrast, one time Harrington got her hair cut short. Her grandmother didn't like it. "She didn't speak to me for a month." Harrington was eleven at the time.

When Giddens was even younger, she made the grave error of sticking her tongue out at her grandmother. As things went, her grandmother told Giddens's sister to go out and get a switch. That was better than when Granddad brought out the belt.

It's not that their grandparents weren't loving. But they were rigid about many behaviors, and they came by these rules honestly.

Were these the only influences in the girls' lives, it's not clear the creativity they each exhibit now would have emerged. (Harrington is a highly creative scholar who has developed teaching techniques to educate a group of children with intellectual disabilities.)

What may well have provoked the girls to evolve past the fourth-grade slump were a handful of influences in their lives that encouraged freer thinking.

Even at their grandparents' shotgun house, there was freedom—but it came from the imagination, and from outside the walls of the actual home. Out back, a giant oak grew to the sky, with massive roots popping from the ground like veins or tiny islands. The sisters spent hours inventing games, like pretending that the earth surrounding the massive tree was water filled with sharks. Their grandmother would shout, "'Get out, get out of the house. You cannot come back into the house until dinner time.' We were bored and made landing pads of dead leaves. That was it. We had that kind of boredom—complete and utter boredom," Giddens said.

She and her sister credit the boredom with forcing them to develop vibrant powers of imagination.

They got encouragement too to think independently from their parents—a Black woman and a white man—rebels in their own right, courageous lovers in a dangerous time.

When their father, David, married their mother, his own father disowned him, leaving him without land that others in the family inherited. And David's voice teacher, a German man, dropped him as a student.

"My mom called him The Old Nazi," Giddens said. "My dad had a beautiful baritone voice, a serious voice." Losing his voice teacher "broke his heart."

The girls' parents believed in the ethos of the era that personal truth and world advancement could be in concert, *needed* to be.

"Both of my parents have always approached things that way—permission and celebration, and that is valued," Harrington said. "A part of what I've gotten from both of my folks is this encouragement to try and to take risks and even if uncomfortable, to do it anyway."

Their mother, unlike her own mother, didn't dream of her daughters becoming debutantes or sorority sisters.

The girls also took encouragement from their father's mother. She was a white woman from a white world who appeared not to see color—"Grandma Giddens. She was like the sweetest woman you could ever imagine," Giddens recalled. This grandmother didn't reject her son or grandchildren, loving them unconditionally. As such, Giddens reflected, "She single-handedly changed a family."

In sum, the two girls got this mix of influences, rigidity and discipline, tolerance and celebration, the fear of being other and the feeling of belonging. The girls also lived at times on poverty's edge, while excelling in academics and winding up in high-quality schools. They moved in and out of different environments.

"It was like code-switching," Giddens said.

There was a lot of that for her. One year in elementary school, she recalled, she spent half the year eating lunch with the white girls and the other half eating with the Black girls. She preferred the company of boys to girls. But she also kept to herself a lot, reading science fiction books while she walked down the hallway. She spent hours drawing pictures, lots of horses. She fantasized about being an animator for Disney. "I can draw a decent horse to this day," she told me.

Our conversation turned to middle school and suddenly Giddens started to cry.

"I was really depressed; it was such a hard time. So I just don't like to be back there, that's all," she said. "Nothing of import happened, I mean, my house didn't burn down. It just wasn't an easy time," Giddens said. She was seven years younger than her sister, who was Giddens's guardian angel, the person who did her hair for her and gave her hugs, and she'd gone off to college. "She was a buffer for me in a lot of ways and my mom was just really angry and mad and depressed herself."

Her mom had come out as lesbian and worked as a drug counselor. She was a frustrated artist; she went to Alcoholics Anonymous meetings. She could be angry. Rhiannon remembers her throwing a glass against the tree out back. The neighborhood didn't always feel safe. Sometimes winos passed out in the yard. But then, thanks to her academic skills, Rhiannon was admitted into an elite math-and-science-centric boarding school. She met nerds, like herself. She saw another segment of society.

So many inputs. Did she have any clue these different experiences were building the muscles of creativity by stretching her to see the rich textures of the world?

Not so much.

She kept to her books and illustrations and pined for her sister.

But life finds a way. It began to do so for Giddens through several different experiences. One involved music. Prior to her senior year in high school, she attended a choral camp. For the first time, she was around people who loved music. She performed her first solo and, yeah, she could sing. It felt good. It was just a tool then, not for creativity, more for sound that could make herself and others feel good.

Somewhat later, she began to read her history. The experiences of her mother, and her grandparents, began to make sense. What they exhibited, far from being outlandish, could be explained. It might even be common. That wasn't material in her life to throw out. It was material to understand, to draw from.

"The more I started studying history, the easier I could understand where some of this stuff was coming from—and the courage it took to try to break out of it," she said. "I stopped being mad at my mom and stopped expecting to have a different mom from the one that I had. On the other hand, it means accepting all the beautiful things she's given me and the wisdom to see her as she is."

What had begun to form for Giddens was an acceptance of her inner multitudes. The less she fought these parts of herself, the more they took the form of a cohesive whole, and a creator.

In the years after Giddens graduated from high school, she got by on innate musical talent, both instrumental and vocal. She was accepted into Oberlin College and Conservatory, an elite music school. She was overwhelmed, in part because she didn't know how to read music. She had no formal training, unlike others there, but she also wasn't really sure what she wanted. She'd been carried along by a kind of mindless momentum. She pushed herself because that's what she thought she should do—working every job she could find related to music, while the uncertainty betrayed itself in various ways. Once, she showed up at an audition and had forgotten one of her shoes. After school, she burned out and faced an uncertain path.

"I never felt like a truly creative person," she said.

Years later, she would become friends with Yo-Yo Ma, one of the world's truly great musicians, and he told her a story about having been in the same place himself.

"He told me he'd been playing cello since he was itty-bitty, and he told me about reaching a certain age in his twenties and thirties and realizing he had to *choose* to be a cellist," she said. "That's what he did—he'd been playing just because that's what he did. Since then he'd been much happier with his life."

Initially, though, the world chose Giddens and not the other way around. She formed a band called the Carolina Chocolate Drops and their debut album, produced by a small music label, included sixteen cover songs—folk and hoedown, banjo and fiddle. It got a bit of attention. Their third album, *Genuine Negro Jig*, released in 2010, won a GRAMMY that year for best traditional folk album. In 2012, the band released *Leaving Eden*, with Giddens as lead singer and playing on fiddle, banjo, and cello banjo.

They were working musicians. That's nothing to take for granted. It's very hard to make a living as a musician—"living the dream," Giddens said.

She was unhappy—very.

"I was very frequently miserable. It would be time to go back on tour and I just wanted to cry," she said. She thought to herself, "I'm good at this and I'm supposed to do it," adding, people get "wrapped up in people petting them and it brings in money and you get caught up in this system."

She started getting sick, literally, physically ill. She developed irritable bowel syndrome. She grew depressed.

"The body tells you everything," she said.

What it told her was that despite the fact that on the outside she looked like an artist, like an authentic creator, she was not at all creating in a way true to herself. For the sake of the band's collective and commercial vision, she felt like she buried how she really wanted to tell stories. She felt the band was doing something "important" but that felt more and more like a duty inconsistent with where her artistic impulses were heading.

She thinks of herself at that time as symbolic of a larger trend.

"Our culture does not put a premium on self-knowledge. A lot of us are walking through life kind of like zombies and looking outward for what we need to find inward. That's why entertainment is so big. People aren't making their own stuff being pacified but being pacified by others' stuff."

She was one of those people pacifying others, by making material that looked and sounded good, and appeared to be drawn from an authentic place.

"I realized I was doing this because it was bringing in money."

This is a crucial moment in her story, and a key point in the illustration of how creators emerge. Time and again I heard stories from creators, and the scholars who study them, of a distinction between a person with creative tools and an authentic creator. Each can create material. The material can be creative. It is not authentic, though. The difference may seem scant from the outside. It is not. Especially for the creator. That's because the creator dancing to another's tune oftentimes is unhappy, even miserable. The creator can feel merely like a mimic, a grade-grubber, someone seeking approval. Then a more personal voice fights to emerge and the creator makes a choice. External validation. Or freedom. In the end, Giddens story—and the story of many creators—is about happiness.

For Giddens, deeply personal motivation had begun to form. During the long drives between Carolina Chocolate Drop gigs, Giddens tuned into a fuller version of her voice. It was a voice that came from the singular circumstances that had created Giddens herself.

On those drives, she had been reading and learning about narratives of slave women. They spoke to her with such power, particularly one story. It was about an enslaved woman and the mistress who owned her talking as the northern armies approached the plantation.

"At some point, the mistress says: 'When soldiers come, would you hide this plate in your cabin and would you say it's yours?' And the slave says: 'You sold four of my children to buy this plate, so it wouldn't be a lie.'"

Giddens read the story "and it would not go away, and it would not go away. And I thought about all the nameless Black people in history we would never know."

The song "Julie," about the slave's agonizing decision to leave the plantation, and all she had known, looks on video and sounds to me like the moment that Giddens arrived at herself, at least a version close to the one she looks like today (she is still very much in flux). Her voice and eyes carry a powerful mix of empathy and defiance, traits that I see as deeply authentic to her.

It was a coming-out party of sorts for Giddens. She'd begun to hear her true voice. "It was my first awareness," she said. "I didn't consider myself a songwriter at all."

She wasn't fully ready to embrace herself as one either. She continued to enjoy such external success that it fueled her.

She had put out a solo album in 2015 called *Tomorrow Is My Turn* that included mostly cover songs, including one by Dolly Parton. *Rolling Stone* named it a Top 50 album of the year. She opened for Faith Hill and Tim McGraw. She got a regular role on the TV show *Nashville*.

At the 2016 Country Music Awards, she performed with Eric Church in a made-for-TV country-rock moment. Giddens was on the cusp of stardom, and it wouldn't be but a few more small steps before she was a household name.

That validation, though, was conflicting with an inner voice guiding a different set of choices. "I was living the dream and was very frequently miserable."

It can be wrenching to learn to hear one's own voice amid the external noise.

For the moment, I offer next another look at a different creator emerging from a childhood cocoon. It's a story I know well, because it's mine.

Author Takes Shape

This book is not a memoir, and I do not intend to dwell on my own experience. I'll mention it briefly in places, starting here, because I can speak firsthand to a creator's journey. I didn't start out as creator. I went through significant transformation from ignoring my voice, to hearing and then expressing it. This book, in part, is aimed at my own raw curiosity about creativity.

I want to hunt down an answer to the same question a multi-GRAMMY-winning Hollywood director asked me: "What is the purpose of creativity?"

Where do these bursts of inspiration come from?

How do we wield them?

I began to ask these basic questions after I felt myself open to these bursts. What is this transformation?

As I say, I speak from experience. It wasn't always fun.

I grew up in Boulder, Colorado, a relatively small university town that, at the time, was solidly middle-class and not much more. My dad, Murray, was a law school professor who became a judge. He was a big, exuberant man, intellectual, a believer in Big Ideas and a reader of nonfiction tomes about historical turning points, and great wars and thinkers, like Churchill and Kennedy and Gandhi. He told me and my sister we could and should be anything we wanted to be, but I missed that message and mostly heard that there was one way to be—some sort of wunderkind mix of John Fitzgerald Kennedy and Mickey Mantle. Big doers, exuberant in making progress like my father.

He also planted in me tremendous seeds of curiosity. He has a professor's enthusiasm for drawing people out as they learn and is not prone to lecture. At the dinner table, he would ask me and my sister our thoughts about his legal cases, creating an at-home version of the Socratic Method, a tool used for deep analytical thinking in law school and the legal profession. When a challenge came up at school, he pressed me to think about my ideas, not to mimic his.

My mother, by personality and circumstance, took up much less space. This was partly because she ceded airtime to my father but also due to her own upbringing with her emotionally abusive father. He was deeply controlling, rigid in the extreme. Maybe to keep from enduring his harsh judgment, she kept a low profile. She also, through nature and nurture, sought strict control over her own physical circumstances and emotions. She felt that vulnerability could be attacked as weakness, or that was my take. So as a kid, I experienced a mother who was passively affectionate, not affirmatively affectionate. My mother never said to me or my sister the words "I love you." Later, she would tell me, she thought those words could sound inauthentic.

At the same time, she wanted to give us something she had craved: the freedom to make our own decisions. In this way, she is as open a person as I know; she wants people to be who they are and express themselves as they might. This allowed us a certain kind of freedom but also let her not feel too connected to us in a way that might harm her. The upshot is that I'm not sure I could tell how much she cared for me. The one time I most knew I had her full attention was when she laughed. She has a beautiful laugh, and when I make her laugh I know I have my mom's full attention.

What this all added up to was that I listened hard for two things: my mother's affections and my father's aspirations. Maybe I should be like him. Or maybe I should emulate the apparent confidence of the jocks who were my friends and teammates in school. I wore a facade, part jock and part jokester, fake-tough-guy mute much of the time, particularly when it came to acknowledging or expressing much in the way of authentic thoughts, feelings, observations.

This was nothing like what Giddens and her sister experienced in the way of the legacy of slavery, or the overt trauma of racism as a daily affair and the downstream impact that would have on self-expression and creativity.

On the other hand, she did have a legacy of creativity in her family. I couldn't see any in mine. What I did inherit, like Giddens, were seeds of doubt and the seeds of creativity—through curiosity and permission to be myself—and yet those seeds fought each other to a standstill for a long time.

On the whole, what I experienced was the kind of vanilla challenge to achieving self-acceptance that I share in this book because it is just so commonplace. A person need not have been expressly traumatized to struggle to hear his or her or their own voice. I couldn't hear mine.

Hence my collapse.

In 1991, working at a small newspaper, I was jogging on a tree-lined street when I felt dizzy. It was the first of many bouts I began having with some mystery ailment. I was given multiple courses of antibiotics. But this was no infection. Unable to pinpoint a single physical problem, I went to sit on a shrink's couch, suspecting subconsciously this was in my head. And then some.

Two years later, I'd wrung myself out of tears and tried every which way to find the key to my unhappiness. In the course of this, I turned my life into scorched earth. I pleaded with a shrink to tell me what was wrong. I was an enigma to myself, wrapped in the fetal position. Who was I? Why was I sobbing?

Finally, I quit asking. It dawned on me that this guy had no more answers for me than I had for myself. My voice was not only as valid as anyone else's, it was the one that should and would be my ultimate guide.

Maybe I risk aggrandizing this experience. Maybe I was just going through my twenties. It mercifully ended and I was left, overwhelmingly, with a handful of basic, elemental emotions. I've since seen that these are part of the makeup of many people who create.

One is gratitude. Foremost, I felt so grateful that I no longer suffered. In turn, this made me feel thankful—for everything. For the big things like a roof over my head and a job, but for tiny things too, like a great street taco and a decent night of sleep. My friends and family. Everything felt like up. By turns, I became almost grotesquely optimistic in the sense that I was alive, not feeling rotten, and mostly everything else was gravy.

This connects very squarely to creativity because it made me look differently at failure. If I wrote something and no one liked it, I still had street tacos, and they were so good.

I also emerged from my nadir with a deep sense of humility. I'd seen terrible demons, begged other people to explain me and approve of me, prostrated myself and pleaded for mercy. I now know that I can never judge another person. The recognition of my own frailty made me less ideological; I began to see that I cannot know another person or idea without really listening, just as it would have been impossible for another person to have known me when I appeared outwardly "successful" despite being an inward mess.

This connects directly to creativity too. The less I judged, the more I could explore, without threat, information, and inputs from various sources. Relevant clues and insights could come from all over the place, and I ceased to see those pieces of information as threatening.

But the most significant way in which this experience connects to creativity is that I no longer was judging myself as harshly, and I was far less subject to the judgment of others. What I said, and thought, the ideas that poured out, had the simple value of being a regular old human being's thoughts. The decisions I made became more about what felt right to me than about what might be considered the correct thing to do by external standards.

A quick example follows.

In 2000, after a decade of working at smaller newspapers, the *New York Times* offered me a job. I would be allowed to remain in San Francisco. The next year, the newspaper changed its mind and said I had to move to New York by October 1, 2001. By then, I'd met the woman who would become my wife, and I'd begun to sense seeds of inspiration—in what I wrote for the paper and in other creations that would follow: a comic strip, novels, songs.

I flew back to New York the summer before my return deadline. I sat down with a high-level editor and made my case that I should be allowed to stay in San Francisco.

"I'm happy," I told him. "And I think you're happy with my work."

"Very," the editor told me. "But this isn't about happiness. It's about what everybody does."

I told him I'd think about it. But that was all I needed to hear. I wasn't going to New York. This wasn't about mere happiness. It was about being myself. It was about trusting my voice.

On October 1, when I was supposed to be in New York, I sat in my home office in San Francisco and waited for my boss to call and fire me. The call didn't come. Here I remain.

There was no heroism in this. I'd emerged from an abyss and knew what it felt like to be free. For much of my life, I'd been on the run. My adrenaline had pumped nonstop, my fight-or-flight response churning as if I'd been running from a lion. But the lion was of my own creation, conjured from my perception of judgment by others and an understanding that all I had to fear was fear itself.

I'd also begun to feel touches of inspiration that I'd liken to a feeling of no less than euphoria. Ideas would come and they would feel so right that they would begin to take me over. I believed in them with a faith that would come to strike people in my life as a little on the light-headed side. Not long prior to being hired full-time by the *New York Times*, I told my father that I wanted to create a comic strip. To this day, he reminds me of how nuts it sounded, but I was sure. Even though I couldn't draw. I found an illustrator. He believed too. On September 1, 2001, a month before I was supposed to move to New York, according to the *Times*, our comic strip, called *Rudy Park*, was syndicated on a daily basis in newspapers around the country. The syndicate, United Media, was among the biggest media companies in the world and being syndicated by them was like having HBO pick up your TV show.

I wrote the strip every day, letting characters spin from my head with abandon, often feeling that grip of certainty that I was creating something beautiful that mattered, whether or not that was true.

It was at around this time that I heard a story that began to form my fascination with creativity and the creative process that ultimately yielded this book.

The story is about Charles Schulz, the creator of *Peanuts*. The editor of the comic strip I wrote was also Schulz's editor. One day, I asked Amy to tell me a story about Schulz, known to his friends as Sparky. She told me what he had told her.

Each morning, Sparky would wake up and start working on his strip and be struck by an idea. Thunderstruck. He'd think to himself: "I've got it. I've got the idea for the perfect strip!"

And he'd spend all day on that strip, bringing life to Charlie Brown, Lucy, Snoopy, seeing his morning's vision through. The next morning, he'd wake up and he'd look at what he'd done. He'd think: "Not quite." Then he'd pause and he'd think, "But, wait, wait! I've got it! Today, I've got the idea for the perfect comic strip!"

His belief was such that it overpowered any energy cost of undertaking a new creation.

I heard a version of this feeling from multiple creators. "It's a euphoria, definitely a euphoria," I was told by Mark Romanek. He's one of the most celebrated music-video directors in the world. He's worked with Taylor Swift, Jay-Z, Michael and Janet Jackson, Nine Inch Nails, Johnny Cash. He's won more than a dozen MTV Video Music Awards and multiple GRAMMY Awards. Coincidentally, he's also such a fan of Charles Schulz and *Peanuts* that he has a tattoo of Linus on his forearm.

When the euphoria hits him, an idea overtakes. That happened with his movie *One Hour Photo*.

"Three whole acts came flooding into my head. I remember it as a physical sensation."

Dear reader, this feeling, this certainty, an almost euphoria-like drive that overtakes, is the kind of sensation that began to open up for me. What was that thing? Where had it come from? Why was I hearing it more often?

In refusing to go to New York I was trying to hold tight to my own voice and the circumstances that let it thrive. I wasn't totally confident that I could go to a place like the headquarters of the *New York Times* and withstand the volume and influence of the external voices I felt sure would beckon there. I wasn't sure I could hear myself any longer.

That would take more work.

I was also increasingly developing the craft of writing. This must come too, but expertise or even basic craftsmanship is not at all the same as creativity.

I now understand that many creators wrestle mightily with this challenge around voice, including the most successful in our midst.

One of the most powerful examples I heard is that of Taylor Swift. A raw documentary about her, *Miss Americana*—itself a terrific creation—describes Swift's enslavement to the judgment of others.

"It was the complete and total belief system I subscribed to as a kid," she says in the documentary. "Do the right thing, do the good thing. The main thing I always tried to be was, like, just, a good girl."

She continues. "I was trained to be happy when you get lots of praise," she says. "Those pats on the head were all I lived for."

It's not that she wasn't creating. By the age of sixteen, she'd written 150 songs, including every one of the songs on her debut album that hit #1. She created, and it came from inside. But she wasn't yet trusting it, and it led to a crushing period of her life.

"When you're living for the approval of strangers, and that is where you derive all of your joy and fulfillment, one bad thing can cause everything to crumble."

The film explores how and when that crumble happened for her—an eating disorder, and a full withdrawal from career and the public—and Swift had a reckoning. "I had to deconstruct an entire belief system for my own sanity."

The documentary ultimately shows that ambition and audience can coexist with creativity—we are multitudes—but that there is a peace and purity of creativity driven by an individual embracing his or her or their own voice. It can nag until honored. Ignoring it can create doubt that undercuts any value of external success, to the point of raising a question for some creators whether their work matters at all if it doesn't feel right to them.

Swift is the rarest combination—innate ability to write a story, put it to music, deliver it with great nuance and a heaven-sent voice. What stands out most to me, watching her testify to her process, is the way she seems overcome. She gets ideas, sitting at the piano, willing ideas, channeling them, instantly accessing them, throwing them away, and being seized, struck, gripped with a kind of necessity that screamed: Yes, this, this, this, this!

It was just as the madness of the COVID-19 pandemic was starting in the early part of 2020 that Swift quietly, without fanfare, and essentially in secret, recorded her eighth studio album. It is called *Folklore.* The probing intimacy and tone vary from her prior work. It's the kind of creation that prompts people to say an artist "reinvented herself again." That's a horrible phrase I'd encourage wiping from the vocabulary of creativity because it suggests that Swift set out, first, to repackage herself. Hardly. She allowed herself to hear and express parts of herself in ways that inspired her, at that moment, in that way.

I heard firsthand another great story about a creator learning to hear his own voice. David Milch created the television shows *Hill Street Blues* and *Deadwood*, a western set in South Dakota in which the rhythmic, staccato-burst, profane, and rough human dialogue sets the television screen ablaze. I would infuriate my wife by pausing and rewinding and listening again to one exchange after another, like my son watching a YouTube video of a skateboarder or Steph Curry, wondering: How did that human being just do that? What a creation!

Milch was paid handsomely, upward of $100 million, according to a profile in *The New Yorker* magazine. The piece also noted that he lost a fortune too—perhaps $25 million on gambling, which beckoned to him at times, as did Milch's heroin addiction. He had lots of ideas, and not all of them worked commercially. Some shows he wrote, like *John from Cincinnati*—a story that takes place in a surfer town and is built around a naive, Messiah-like figure—essentially flopped.

Then Milch was stricken with Alzheimer's. In the summer of 2019, as the disease progressed, I had a handful of phone conversations with him, talking about creativity. He remained lucid, even as dementia took an increasing hold, and I had to be mindful that he had limited energy and that I should not take advantage of his waning state—with, say, leading questions. I felt like I got a stripped-down, raw version of a world-class storyteller, and it was in our second conversation that he gave me one for the ages about his early days and how he learned to hear and trust his voice.

"I had a very good friend, whose name was Judgy—because his grandfather had been a state supreme court judge," Milch began. "Judgy was a drunk, and it pleased him to drink with me in ridiculous amounts."

Milch spoke somewhat haltingly, while his wife, Rita Stern, sat in on the phone call with us, supporting him as he found his story— "lost in thickets of recollection," he said.

"As we speak," Milch said, "I'm remembering what my friend looked like. Judgy was as pure a drunk as in the ensuring fifty-five years I've ever met—and he communicated without impediment. We were both fourteen. We were in the basement of Judgy's house.

"What I drank was Scotch. What he drank was the first thing that came to hand."

Milch then began to gather steam, his ideas began to bloom—at least that's how it felt—but they also took a shape I couldn't yet recognize. Where was he going with this?

"I realized the virtuosity of lying, of tale-telling," he said, "that was inadvertently associated with booze."

The pair began to tell tall tales, the way boys do. And as they went along, David felt his inhibitions drop, the way they do when one is drunk.

"It gratifies in a way that gives you a sense of order and meaning and presence," he said. "The word I want to use is relief. You feel relief in that discipline of connection with your listeners. It's a paradox of being a drunk in that you enter a connection with your listeners— which may, in fact, be absolutely contradictory to the truth of the connection between you and them."

They told each other stories, and talked, uninhibited, sometimes with great lies, and Milch felt relief. "If you're with someone whom you consider your friend and the communication between the two of you is a source of solace and order and joy, that's pretty much as good as it gets," he said.

As he spoke, I could hear the narrator in him building to a conclusion, which he soon delivered. Over time, he told me, he learned that creativity feels something like the uninhibited expression he learned while drinking with Judgy.

"When you don't know what you're going to say next but you trust yourself to say it anyway. That's one of the constituent elements of friendship and also of inspiration. When you combine those, you've got the game."

It's worth repeating this core element of inspiration: when you don't know what you're going to say next but you trust yourself to say it anyway.

This is, in its most basic form, the voice. Your voice.

Crucially, the voice I'm referring to isn't some pure form of scientist, storyteller, musician, entrepreneur, politician, teacher. This deeply personal voice is merely one that can listen without judgment to ideas that get spit out by the brain. These are rarely full-formed ideas, but bursts of information, emotion, words, and phrases rather than whole sentences, let alone paragraphs or complete thoughts. They are seed corn. But they are your seed corn. They are you.

No one I've heard captures the revelation of embrace of self and freedom as does Bruce Springsteen—a poet laureate of authenticity and raw emotional power.

In a live Broadway show that ran in New York over several years, Springsteen talks of a particular moment, on a "regular Sunday night," that helped set him on his way to hearing his voice. He begins his story of creative emergence with biblical language, and with his humility and sense of humor.

"In the beginning, there was a great darkness on the waters," he tells the audience in the small theater. "There was a lifeless sucking black hole—homework, church, school, homework, church, school, green beans, green beans, fucking green beans." Then, he says, came "a blinding flash of sanctified light," and a "new kind of man split the world in two." Springsteen, just a little kid in New Jersey, had seen Elvis Presley on *The Ed Sullivan Show*. "Suddenly, a new world existed," Springsteen says with a pause, "the one below your belt," another pause, "and the one above your heart."

He continued: "A freer existence had exploded into unsuspecting homes all across America on a regular Sunday night. The world had fucking changed in an instant and all you needed to do to get a taste of it, was to risk being your true self."

This is your spice rack, the part that is uniquely you—that is not so inaccessible as it might seem. It is easier to utilize if a person feels encouraged from the start of life. And please don't mistake the lesson of Springsteen's story. He had to fight to hear his voice too, as he eloquently captures in an autobiography, describing how he wrestled with the condemning voice of his father. In an interview with *Vanity Fair*, Springsteen was asked if his father ever told Springsteen he loved him. "No," Springsteen answered. But if Springsteen said: "Love you, Pops," he might get, "Eh, you too."

Springsteen learned to embrace his own voice, and also to recognize the multitudes he embodies. "Whoever you've been and wherever you've been, it never leaves you," he said in the interview for *Vanity Fair*. "I always picture it as a car. All yourselves are in it. And a new self can get in, but the old selves can't ever get out. The important thing is, who's got their hands on the wheel at any given moment?"

His rich body of works speaks to someone who learned to hear these different parts of himself and to allow each, at different times, to drive.

The testimony of these greats, my own modest experience, and much lore suggests that struggle is a central stop on the way to tuning into yourself, and, ultimately creativity. Fairly, in a world that urges conformity, it can take work to hear your own voice.

I'd also caution that lots of people struggle, creator or not, and creators might be more prone to describing their journey aloud. So as long as you're going to suffer, might as well get something good from it—an honest reckoning with your personal spice rack.

There is a more basic question, though. Does it actually require such a struggle to hear the internal voice? Is the assumption accurate that destination creativity goes through the town of pain?

The short answer is: no.

It doesn't require nearly the suffering some creators experience to find their voice. It doesn't involve a mortal fight. It doesn't mean staring down your fears in a showdown with your soul, or developing an eating disorder, nor does it mean coming apart.

That's because there often is no lion.

Rise of the Voice

Threats abound. I'm coming to them—death, and lost love, and lost opportunity, and excruciating material hardship. Pandemic and systemic racism. But there is a big difference between real, definitive threats to our survival and lesser threats, ones we imagine, conjure, blow out of proportion. These are our proverbial lions, the terrors that we imagine chasing us and that cause us to tighten up, live in fear. These can interfere with creativity.

What many creators discover as they emerge—and learn to hear their voices—is to listen to their voices and impulses without judgment or fear of a threat that is more imagined than real. This chapter helps to explain one way to understand how to listen without fear.

To understand the process, I turned to one of the world's experts in the field, a researcher named Emma Seppälä. When I look back at the calendar, I can see that our conversation began in late January of 2020. At that moment, the threat of COVID-19 loomed larger but remained distant. A paper released in early February in *The Lancet* described the admittance of forty-one people to a hospital in Wuhan. *U.S. News & World Report* carried the headline RISK OF HUMAN-TO-HUMAN TRANSMISSION OF NEW CORONAVIRUS APPEARS POSSIBLE: CHINESE OFFICIALS.

But when I talked with Seppälä in late winter, we were speaking less of real threats, and more of the proverbial lions, the ones that haunt the imagination, and can interfere with creativity. It's a subject she backed into after working with veterans of the ongoing wars in Middle Eastern Gulf states. Oddly enough, her experience with veterans suffering PTSD offers a perfect way of explaining what is happening emotionally and physiologically as creators emerge and begin to hear the voice, the muse.

Seppälä began by telling me a story.

Several years ago, she said, she was talking to a veteran of the war in Afghanistan. He'd served in an intelligence unit, digging information out of captives.

"I was really good," he told Seppälä. "I made a guy shit his pants."

His work may have been vital but, for the moment, that is beside the point. This vet came home and like many who have served, his experience left him in a near permanent state of terror. He felt so confused, praised for what he'd done, left suicidal by it, crushed by the weight of actions that felt necessary to him at the time and yet utterly inhumane.

"I don't sleep at night. I just lie on my sofa and wait until the morning comes," he told Seppälä. "I take Ambien and it only makes things worse."

He'd come to the right person. Seppälä is a specialist who works at Stanford University and Yale University helping vets with PTSD. The experience she's gained in that area has blossomed into her working with some of the world's biggest companies—Google, Apple, Facebook, Ernst & Young, and others. Her work helps people find peace with themselves, become more productive, and, ultimately, more creative. These ideas—of getting beyond misplaced fear and becoming creative—are closely linked, and Seppälä has shown how through anecdote and brain science.

In the case of the intelligence officer who'd served in Afghanistan, Seppälä observed that he learned to breathe. I mean, he knew how to breathe—we all do—but not how to breathe in the way that Seppälä studies it, the method that has extraordinary powers to change how the brain processes information.

––––––

The impact kind of breathing that Seppälä taught researchers involved taking rhythmic breaths in a specific cycle that allows the brain to quickly go into a meditative state. After not very many of these sessions, the soldier began to change, significantly. He started to experience his memories in a new way. Specifically, his memories did not trigger a particular reaction in the body known as the "sympathetic response."

The sympathetic response is a deeply primitive reaction of the body to a threat of danger or a *perceived* threat. Those are two very different things, obviously: a threat of being blown up while checking for roadside bombs in Afghanistan compared to the perceived threat that grips a soldier once he comes home from Afghanistan, is sitting in his living room, hears a car honk outside, and dives under the table fearing a roadside bomb.

Another way to think about this is in very primitive terms that apply to us all, not just to those who have dealt with an acute trauma, like war. A fair analogy compares these threats to lions.

In olden times, if our forebears were threatened by a lion, their bodies would set off a furious fight-or-flight reaction, the sympathetic response. In stark biological terms, this involves the firing of hormones that can provide very important short-term powers. Adrenaline increases, focus heightens, heart rate and blood pressure rise. It's good stuff in a pinch. But this burst of benefits can, as you might imagine, be dangerous and even fatal if prolonged. The chemicals make it hard to sleep, depress the immune system, and put all the emphasis on the external threat, or perceived threat.

That's a great trade-off when you're facing a real lion. But not when the threat isn't real, only perceived, or when your body's primitive reaction outweighs a relatively modest threat. Say, for instance, your boss calls on your cell phone and before you even know what the call is about, you might experience a heavy jolt of these hormones. Then you perceive the conversation as a bigger threat than it might be and the fight-or-flight response grows more intense. The same thing might happen when you and your spouse argue, a child gets a so-so grade, you get sick and miss a few days of work, or get pulled over for speeding.

These threats might have serious consequences but as often as not we can overinterpret them, perceiving more threat than is merited. There is no lion. Maybe not even a lion cub. Still, primitive systems kick in. That is partly because the nature of threats has changed while our primitive response-mechanisms remain largely unchanged. There hasn't been time for our bodies to adapt to the kind of persistent middle ground of low-level threat that might not actually harm us at all. People can get even more overwrought through worry, intensifying this sympathetic response well out of proportion with the actual threat.

This leads to a loss of the sense of proportion. Meaning: The person experiencing the sympathetic response sees greater threat than there is and maybe even perceives a threat that is not there at all.

Seppälä and other researchers posited a hypothesis. What if, they asked, they could short-circuit this powerful primitive response when it is not useful? In other words, they wanted to disentangle the *perception* of threat from the sympathetic response. What if it was possible for a veteran to hear a honking horn for what it was—a honking horn—and not a bomb? What if it was possible to not trigger the lion response when there is no lion—or roadside bomb?

That's what Seppälä and other researchers showed could happen with the breathing and other mindfulness techniques.

Within a few weeks of this simple breathing practice, the veterans began to alter both their physiological response and their perception of threat. They did this by interrupting the sympathetic response. Breathing in this specific way had the effect of slowing the release of these hormones and thus stopping the onset of fight-or-flight.

Then the traumatized soldiers were able to have time to assess the actual circumstances and to calibrate the actual threat. The burst of a car alarm, or the slamming of a door, didn't then trigger an instant sympathetic response that would overtake the soldier's body. He was able to see the external threat for what it was—a harmless noise.

The research shows that this tactic accumulates over time such that the body and mind calm even when the soldier is not performing breathing exercises. This does not mean that the soldiers erased the terrible memories that plagued them. Instead, they are able to pull the past and the present apart.

The soldier who had tortured prisoners for information told Seppälä: "I remember everything, but I can move on." He also started to sleep. "I went to sleep without my meds. I went to sleep before I could remember to take them!" he excitedly told Seppälä. She said the research she and others have done has wide applicability.

These concepts are tied deeply to creativity.

"If you want to innovate, you need psychological safety," she said. "You need to have a feeling of safety, whether at work or at home."

What does safety mean?

Among other things, safety means a person doesn't feel threatened from the outside. Less fear of a lion, spouse, boss. Less fear of external judgment. This is the point where all of this has been heading. Though most of us are fortunate enough not to have had the experience of war trauma, all of us have had the experience of judgment trauma. It begins at a very young age, is the very essence of the teenage years for some of us, and what happens to our brains is precisely what happens to the brains of soldiers: We begin to develop an instinctive fight-or-flight response—even to the sound of our own ideas.

Hey, what about this . . .

Stupid.

Hey, what about that . . .

Stupid.

Here's an idea for a book . . .

People will hate it.

Here's an idea for a business.

Shut it down before it makes you look like an idiot.

These instant sympathetic reactions get even more pronounced when the ideas are deeply personal. This can be true in art, science, or business—an idea that exposes *your* hopes, yearnings, fears, loves, passions may be the scariest of all because judgment of the idea will feel like a judgment of *you*.

And yet, this is precisely what makes an idea unique, singular, powerful. The individual, absent outside noise.

"You must lose your inhibitions," said Kay Kim, the scholar from William & Mary I introduced in an earlier chapter.

She has done some creative research on the subject that I confess I'm not quite sure what to make of, even though she makes a strong case: It involves the connection between sexuality and creativity.

Kim has collected research that shows a correlation between Nobel Prize winners and greater acceptance of, and experimentation with, sexual freedom. Countries like Israel, Switzerland, and the United States, which have a disproportionate share of Nobel winners, also show greater acceptance and embrace of sexual experimentation and of homosexuality. I'm less inclined to comment on the research here than I am to say that, at the least, her observations about eliminating inhibition are consistent with all this other research I'm presenting. It shows that creativity and creative euphoria are built on a foundation of acceptance and embrace of the authentic.

———

As long as I'm on the topic of sex and inhibition, I might as well briefly mention the role of drugs in fostering creativity. Many people have professed that drug use helps them hear their own voices and tap imagination. Does it help?

Who better to discuss the idea with than Carlos Santana, the legendary musician I mentioned in the prologue. He's also legendary for his use of substances. Heck, he started his own cannabis brand. That discussion was in January 2020, again, just as the COVID-19 crisis loomed. At the time, he spoke to me of the mind-expanding powers of marijuana and how central the idea had been to him and a generation of creators, the Beatles, Eric Clapton, Jimi Hendrix, and on and on.

"It helps opening the window for perception and believing that your imagination is the doorway to the future to you," he said. In his case, he said, it helped him transform into a believer in himself. "It takes you away from 'poor little me, I'm just a victim, what can I possibly do?' Because I smoked a joint back then made me realize I could make a living writing the music that I write."

But when I pressed Santana, he conceded that he'd entirely stopped using marijuana from 1972 to 1982 and during that period had been intensely creative. He said he'd found a different tactic: meditation. "It made me higher than any weed in the world," he said. "It gives you clarity into who you are."

Later, when he returned to regularly using weed, he said, it served for him the purpose of a shortcut to the "discipline" of meditating.

This is one man's view.

The science on the subject doesn't much support the idea that drug use and creativity are linked. A paper published in 2016 in the *International Journal of Mental Health and Addiction* explored the sum of major prior works on the subject. The paper concluded: "The studies were unable to show that substance use directly contributed to the growth of creativity or facilitated creative artistic processes."

To the emerging creator, the use of drugs, like sexual inhibition, might indicate some comfort with lack of conformity. But it has not proven to be a gateway to the underlying psychological and physiological mechanisms that foster a creative mind.

Meantime, Seppälä's research shows that the safety that begets creativity comes from eliminating the knee-jerk experience of everyday PTSD—the implicit fear of judgment. This is why ideas come in the shower, or when driving the car, when a person feels disarmed, not threatened, relaxed. Early neurological research, she says, supports the idea that great ideas are generated when "you're awake but super relaxed, when the mind is wandering." This is a state when alpha waves are generated in the brain—between the land of awake and asleep. It's the place where we don't fear external judgment. We are not on guard.

"Innovation, creativity, intuition—it all comes from a place beyond intellect," she said. "Intellect is useful once you have the creative idea. Intellect helps you put it out." But first "your brain has to be primed to have the idea."

Remember the fourth-grade slump?

One way to think about the idea of priming the brain is to allow it to peel back the rigid lessons and external voices that developed during this period. Then, as a person ages, expertise evolves in various areas—whether in hobbies or at work. But the true power of these tools to be used for creation comes from the inspiration, as undiluted as possible. Priming the brain, the way Seppälä thinks about it, is giving it these alpha waves—that moment between sleep and awake, the shower moment—the chance for an aha!

There are dozens of techniques that accomplish the task. This is not that kind of self-help book, as I've mentioned before, so I'll not delve too deeply into specifics.

There are apps that give you guided meditation, and there are others that provide the sound of rain. Some people focus on their breathing. When I perform these exercises, which I do regularly, I think of the words "inhale calm," when I breathe in, and when I breathe out I think "exhale stress," or "exhale fear."

Or I count the number of breaths I take. Sometimes I count up to four and begin again at one. Other times, when my mind is particularly fractured, and thoughts race, I try to count to twenty breaths. Each time I realize that my mind has wandered to a thought other than the number, I start over again at one. After a period of time, usually short, I can make it to twenty while focused on my breaths and my numbers.

These tactics don't make people numb or dumb. They won't take you further from yourself, or eliminate what you feel. They will help a person to make connections between feelings and experiences, ideas and inspiration, without feeling so threatened as to become paralyzed.

There's another crucial reason to employ tactics like these. They help slow down perceptions so that a would-be creator can assess whether the information has value.

It is said all the time: "Life seems to be moving so quickly." People say it mournfully. In reality, I'm not so sure everyone minds so much. The faster time spins, the more we distract and whirl, the easier it is to ignore the authentic experiences, emotions, complexities, and ideas that might cause short-term harm, the terror of an imaginary lion's imaginary razor-sharp claws. My hypothesis here is not a mere stab in the dark: I've written and reported extensively about how the whirl of information, particularly as it comes on mobile devices at breakneck speed, can create compelling and even welcome distractions.

There is no lion, but there is immense value to experiencing the quiet that lets people hear authentic feelings and emotions without fearing what they mean.

Slowing down to hear the sounds of one's own voice is not merely about raw emotion or the ingredients that might typically be associated with art in its many forms. This refers as well to science, logic, even war.

A slowed mind gives a creator access to purer information, ingredients with which to come up with more authentic, specific, new, interesting, creative solutions. The inputs remain in a certain proportion that not only allows a person to create; it also allows the creations to resonate with other people.

Why?

Because a creation in proportion to the inputs of the actual world will connect on the deepest level. This is true in business, art, public policy, and in war.

I learned how powerful these tools can be from General Walter Piatt, who is currently director of the US Army Staff stationed on the Pentagon. He's a decorated combat veteran who commanded the coalition forces in Iraq and led the army's vaunted 10th Mountain Division. Those titles don't fully define him. He's a nonconformist. A poet and author.

"I was asked recently if my soldiers call me General Moonbeam," he told me for an article I wrote for the *New York Times*. The article was about the use of deep breathing, meditation, and other mindfulness used in the military. "There's a stereotype this makes you soft. No, it brings you on point."

That article ran in April 2019. A little bit less than a year later, just prior to the worldwide attack by COVID-19, I checked back in with General Piatt. I told him I was working on a book about creativity and wondered if he saw a connection between his use of mindfulness and creativity.

"There's a huge connection," he said. "It lets you see things as they are and not what you've been trained to believe." He said: "I see it all the time in the Pentagon," which he said is filled with very bright people, some with stark preconceived ideas or fears. "Someone can have the best idea and it can turn everybody off," he said. To be creative, "You have to be open-minded."

To this point in the book, I've described the emergence of multiple creative thinkers in a variety of fields. I've tried to show some of the obstacles that creators confront, and some of the ways that they learn to hear a voice that is authentic to themselves, and how they come to embrace their inner multitudes.

There are other people who are born with such a knack. They get raised with that rare mix of confidence and humility and trust themselves without being arrogant. General Piatt struck me as such a person. But even he learned to take advantage of creativity-enhancing tools to amplify his ability to create, listen to himself, and connect dots without fear of external judgment. And he did it in the fog of war. He listened for ideas and inspirations that would allow him as he once put it to soldiers in his unit, "to win this war without killing one more person."

His point, he told the soldiers, was that it would allow them "to look for ways to win by solving the root causes of the conflict."

"War," he told me, "is man's worst creation. If you put up an emotional shield you'll lose yourself."

I tell his story because it shows that the science I've already described, and that is yet to come in the book, applies to the creator not yet emerged, the one still emerging, and the one already blossomed.

———

Piatt was born in 1961 in Pittsburgh, Pennsylvania, and "wanted to jump out of airplanes so I enlisted in the army." By 2003, he was a battalion commander in Afghanistan, when he struck up a conversation with a sergeant under his command. They'd just been through a "tough fight" to get to a village and the soldier was distressed. He started pouring out his heart.

"He was feeling hatred and dehumanizing the enemy," Piatt told me. "He was a good soldier, and a good guy, and a Christian who believed in God. But he said: 'I can't feel anything but hate.'"

"I was ready to give some advice," Piatt told me, "but before I could say anything, he said: 'But you like 'em, don't you?'"

"That really sparked a wide range of emotions and thoughts because part of me did. I could see the human side. Perhaps I didn't have enough hatred to be the leader, and to order the death of my enemy."

Piatt went and wrote down his thoughts. He said he tried not to judge them. "I was really feeling all these things. I wasn't displacing. I wasn't trying to explain them. I was just accepting."

He used his notebook as part of his fight not to put up the emotional shield. He feared such a shield would cause him to lose his deep appreciation for life, on all sides of conflict.

Creative actions followed.

Not long after that, Piatt and several soldiers were in a vehicle driving down a road when a young boy sprinted up and hurled a grenade at them. No one was hurt. The boy disappeared. But members of the local tribe, ordered to bring the responsible party forward, brought the boy and his father to the soldiers. The members of the tribe told Piatt: "The boy is too young. We'll give you the father."

"I just saw my own dad in that man," Piatt said. Instead of ordering arrest or punishment, he had the boy taken to meet the soldier who had been most directly targeted by the grenade. A dialogue opened up between the soldiers and the family and what became clear was that the boy had thrown the grenade because extremists had told the children of the village they would be taken from their families and put into religious school if they failed to participate.

During a subsequent deployment, Piatt and his company were in a remote base near a local village, in extremely hostile territory. To keep a safe distance from the local village, they'd encircled themselves with wire. A report came in: A grazing sheep had gotten entangled in the wire. The soldiers on the perimeter, per standard operating procedure, had detained the animal's shepherd, a boy. Commander Piatt got the report and went forward.

"We'd arrested the little drummer boy," the commander-turned-general told me. "The boy was scared to death, and the sheep was tied in concertina wire."

The contours of a broader problem surfaced. The villagers were accustomed to allowing their sheep to graze in the area. But the rules of engagement forbade their proximity. Commander Piatt let his mind wander and let the problem percolate and was struck by an idea: The army bought sheep, donkeys, and camels and let them graze the land nearest the wire and worked with the locals to graze a bit farther away. The Afghans, the general said, respected that the army was using the land to graze animals "that we would eventually give to them." In this simple way, a peace was born.

All the while, Piatt wrote stories and poetry, processing. He was a creative on the page and on the field of war, wrestling with complex ideas. Then he discovered a tool he credits with greatly amplifying his ability to hear himself clearly, and hear others.

In 2010, he was introduced to mindfulness by researchers exploring if such tactics could help soldiers. If they learned mindfulness, might they better assess information during life-or-death situations; should they fire a weapon? Should they react, or restrain themselves?

Piatt, already predisposed to trying new things and creative by nature, said he discovered a life-changing tool. "It lets you pay attention and discern what is real and what is present without judgment."

After he'd already begun a regular daily breathing practice—it could amount to eight and a half minutes of breathing a day—he saw results. By way of example, he recalled for a story that took place when he was the force commander in Iraq. He was scheduled to have a meeting with a powerful local tribal leader. He knew in advance it would be a delicate conversation. Before he left by helicopter for the meeting, he sat beneath a palm tree and did his deep-breathing exercises, the very kind that Seppälä describes. The experience, he said, cleared his mind of expectations, outside voices, and allowed him to prepare himself to listen without preconception.

During the meeting, he could feel the authenticity of his responses and the tribal leader's appreciation of them.

"I was not taking notes. I remember every word she was saying. I wasn't forming a response, just listening," he said. When the tribal leader finished, he said, "I talked back to her about every single point, and had to concede on some. I remember the expression on her face: This is someone we can work with."

It was only a few years later that Piatt would move into the Pentagon, where he held a powerful position as director of the US Army Staff. It was the position he held as social unrest gripped the capital. Piatt would go on to write some powerful poetry about the challenges during that period.

I'd underscore the idea that Piatt helps illustrate: creators emerge over time. It's not a one-time deal. Even for those people already prepared to embrace and build on their authenticity and the multitudes within, certain circumstances and techniques can amplify and accelerate creativity. The general also highlights this key takeaway: the way to hear your voice is to quiet the white noise around you. The scream of the internet, the rigidity of preconceived notions, the rules of partisanship, and long since baked-in ideas that certain thoughts and feelings are off limits. Breathing and emptying your brain of those voices can let your own voice break through—along with the harmony of your multitudes.

That's not the only technique, or the end of the journey. Your voice and ideas aren't the same thing. Ideas will come through. One way to discover them—or, rather, to discover what is already inside you—is through mind wandering. It's not as easy as it sounds.

Mind Wandering

Years after I broke through and began to hear inspiration, I looked back to my childhood and realized that I'd been writing stories all along. Many readers are likely already doing a version of this too. It often happens before people go to bed.

Their minds wander, and they begin to tell themselves stories. For example, when I was around ten, I regularly had this fantasy as I lay in bed that I was standing in a sporting-goods store and I had five hundred dollars. In the fantasy, I was told that I had to spend all the money in one hour and I'd roll my cart down the aisle and pick out balls, mitts, basketball hoops, and other things my family couldn't afford to buy with such abandon.

Later, in my teens, I spent a few years regularly having a war fantasy. I'd be in a cabin, armed to the teeth, and trying to fend off a horde of enemies through the sniper holes I'd cunningly crafted in the walls as part of my solo effort to save myself and the world.

In a certain way, I was beginning to pick up seemingly random output from the recesses of my brain. These are where ideas come from if they can be allowed to come across without judgment or fear. In this case, I was relaxed to the point of putting me to sleep and so, by definition, this was the unfiltered me.

I mention this story because readers may relate to the experience of letting their brains wander before bed. I'm not referring to fixation with worry. But a free flow that feels more like riding a magic carpet that steers itself wherever it may go.

This type of mental experience or exercise is one building block beyond the mind-clearing exercise that I described in the prior chapter. The nonjudgmental, meditative state can give rise to mind wandering.

That's good for creativity. As the science shows.

A breakthrough study published in 2017 showed how the simple act of letting the mind wander can yield ideas. The study empaneled a group of fifty-three professional writers and a group of forty-five physicists. Each study subject participated in an email survey aimed at exploring when these creative thinkers experienced their most innovative ideas. Each night, the creators returned a survey that described the most creative idea they'd had that day and then answered several follow-up questions.

"What were you thinking about when the idea occurred to you?" with the options being: "I was thinking about something unrelated to the general idea or problem," or "I was absorbed in the general idea or problem."

A second question probed further, asking: "What were you *doing* when the idea occurred to you?" (italics added by me for emphasis and clarity). The options were "actively pursuing the project," or "pursuing another work-related problem, project, or idea," or "doing something unrelated to work (e.g., paying a bill)."

The study also asked participants to rate the nature of the inspiration. Was it an aha moment? That could be answered with a yes or a no. Subjects also could rate the importance of the idea on a scale from 1 to 7—"low" to "extremely important," and on a similar seven-point scale to rank whether it was slightly creative or extremely creative.

Bottom line: About 20 percent of the ideas came during mind wandering, when the study subject was not engaged in the task at hand. Of note, mind wandering led to an even higher figure—26 percent—of ideas of particularly high value because they provided a creative solution to a problem the subject felt was at an "impasse."

"These findings provide the first direct evidence that a significant proportion of creative individuals' ideas occur while the person was engaged in a particular type of mind wandering: spontaneous task-independent mind wandering."

Plus, the subjects described the thoughts that occurred during mind wandering with a "greater sense of 'aha,'" the research concluded.

Of course, this also means that a huge portion of ideas came when the study subjects were focused on the task at hand—roughly 80 percent of creative ideas came through this directed effort. One of the study's authors is Jonathan Schooler, a leading thinker about the relationship between mind wandering and creativity. He still marvels at the conclusion.

People were creative "when not actively pursuing their ideas—when they were in the shower, while gardening, paying the bills. They were as creative as when they were working, which is pretty startling," he said. "How many things can you be as good at when you're not trying as when you are?"

I asked Schooler if he might offer a concrete example of the phenomenon of mind wandering and creative solution. "The classic example is the tip-of-the-tongue feeling," he said. This occurs when you're trying to remember someone's name and the harder you try, the more desperate and anxious the effort. "If you just let it go, it will come to you."

For those who prefer an example from the world of great creators, Schooler tells a story about Salvador Dalí and Thomas Edison, who he said "stumbled on a similar" technique for finding creative solutions. Each would hold an object in his hands—in Dalí's case a spoon (what else!) and in Edison's a ball bearing—and they would start falling asleep. When they nodded off, the object would fall to the floor, waking them, and "both of them found that they had ideas."

Schooler calls this a "hypnagogic state," a mental place that is between being asleep and wakefulness. Schooler also defines it as the "space between conscious and unconscious."

This is where the connection comes to mind wandering, or, put another way: daydreaming. Awake and asleep, conscious and not.

It's interesting to hear how this plays out in the real world, with a contemporary genius.

Garry Trudeau, the Pulitzer Prize–winning creator of *Doonesbury* (and lots of other great stuff) told me about the value to his creativity of an undirected mind, almost an absent one. The same holds true for his wife, Jane Pauley, an iconic and creative television personality and writer.

"My ideation seems to be at its most powerful in the shower I take immediately upon rising. I once wrote an entire week of strips during a single shower, so I always keep Post-it Notes nearby. Story arcs and bits of dialogue just pop into my head with little effort or prompting, but I doubt that's unusual. Most writers with a routine seem to prefer the morning. When Jane was working on her books, she would rush to her computer upon awakening 'to see what my fingers know.' She once used the shoemaker analogy—spending all day cutting little pieces of leather, only to wake up the next morning to find the finished shoes left behind by elves. You probably know the sleep research that explains nocturnal processing, but it seems the brain, far from resting, is in actuality working the night shift, pinging bits of experience around the brain, and in the case of humor, linking together information in unexpected ways. The fulcrum of humor is surprise—nothing is more disappointing than a joke you see coming—and nothing more delightful than one that snaps your head back. My favorite example, from Sarah Silverman: 'My best friend is Black . . . in this story.' So nighttime, for me, seems to reset my brain so that it's more available to identifying incongruity and integrating it into character."

Trudeau also did not dismiss the value of pressure for creativity, and I think it's well worth acknowledging that the duress of a deadline can have the effect for some people of crystallizing thought. I personally do not like this experience at all, and find that the onset of adrenaline produces less authentic and more forced ideas—ideas that work sometimes, and have to, given the reality of deadline pressure in our world. I have often thought of the ideas that happen on deadline as being able to achieve no more than a B-plus-like grade. I mentioned this to Trudeau.

> Adrenaline for me is a creative accelerant. It forces me to focus and organize my mind. When I was doing the daily strip, I knew exactly how far along I needed to be at any given moment as I approached a deadline. In the early days, that was stressful (especially since I was also a full-time graduate student), but in time, I welcomed the structure—it made sense of my day. And as you point out, this pressure can become linked to quality control. Ideas get stress-tested on the spot. This was complicated by my tendency to do the strips out of order. If I knew the trajectory of the story arc, I plugged in the pieces as the ideas came to me, which often required me to rethink what preceded it. If a Thursday idea came to me first, I'd go with it because there's never enough time to discard a good idea. I'd worry about the Wednesday lead-in later.
>
> Building the aircraft while flying it has been good practice for theatrical work. *Tanner* ['88] was written on the fly—I'd fax pages to the field producer sometimes the night before the scene shot—and the *Alpha House* scripts were delivered only

a week or two before production. The strip prepared me for that kind of pressure, and after a while the actors and crew trusted me to get it done. And I, rightly or not, trusted the ideas to work. I made very few edits or rewrites, just don't seem capable of improving things by circling back. That particular habit of mind comes from years of doing the strip, knowing you can't call a daily back to make it better, that you've only got one shot. The goal in deadline-driven work was once described by my friend Roger Rosenblatt as steady excellence. But for me, steady excellence is more aspirational than practical; of necessity, I mostly reach for good enough.

So it's just that easy, right?
Unfortunately not.
What the mind wandering research shows is that people do not like to let their brains roam without barriers. The reason is fear. It's the same theme that comes up again and again in the story of creativity, and, again, science tells the story.

In 2010, two researchers working at Harvard University began exploring how people feel about and experience mind wandering. They did so by interrupting people at random times of the day by sending texts to cell phone numbers they'd gathered, along with consent to interrupt. They got responses from 2,250 adults.

The text messages they sent asked a handful of questions. One was, "What are you doing right now?" and that question could be answered with a number from 1 to 22 that corresponded to various common, everyday activities—taking a walk, working, grooming/self-care, doing housework, taking care of children, making love. (First off, let's dispense with the joke that for many people sex is not nearly as everyday an activity as they might like. Anyway, this is not that kind of self-help book.) What's of note about making love is that it was by far the least likely time for a study subject's mind to wander. People were, as they say, on task.

That was not the case, though, for so many other activities. A key, high-level finding of the study was that peoples' minds wandered 47 percent of the time on average, at least for all activities except sex.

"The frequency of mind wandering in the real-world sample was considerably higher than is typically seen in laboratory experiments," the research found. "Surprisingly, the nature of people's activities had only a modest impact on whether their minds wandered."

It's a natural activity, part of connecting ideas, and participating in what is sometimes referred to as a "time travel" activity. Mind wandering lets people reconstruct events past and imagine future ones, an act of deep humanity that, as far as we know, doesn't happen among the less evolved.

But the study also found this activity, however natural, makes people very unhappy.

This is the twist.

The very first question the Harvard researchers asked was not about mind wandering but mood. The question was: "How are you feeling right now?" Subjects answered on a 100-point scale from zero, which meant "very bad," to 100, meaning something like "Fantastic!"

Then, after the study subjects were asked what they were doing and whether their mind was wandering, they were asked about the nature of the subject they were thinking about. Had their minds wandered to a "pleasant" subject or a "neutral" one or an "unpleasant" one?

The researchers found that about half the time people's minds wandered to a pleasant topic. In those instances, the study subjects described themselves as being no happier or less happy then when they were not experiencing mind wandering. In other words, a person having a pleasant daydream isn't necessarily a happier person.

Meanwhile, the other half of the time (on average) study subjects described their minds as wandering to a neutral or unpleasant subject. In either case, those people were unhappy.

"In conclusion," the researchers wrote, "a human mind is a wandering mind, and a wandering mind is an unhappy mind. The ability to think about what is not happening is a cognitive achievement that comes at an emotional cost."

Bottom line: People aren't just mind wandering, they're worrying. They're ruminating when their minds take flight.

Schooler reinforced that idea by pointing to a fascinating 2014 study—and in this context the word "fascinating" might be interchangeable with the word "painful." The study aimed to see how comfortable people are being alone with their thoughts. The answer: not comfortable. In fact, people are so uncomfortable that they'd rather give themselves an electric shock than sit quietly for fifteen minutes in a room. In the study, subjects were left alone in a room with a button they could use to shock themselves. This particular test was done after a series of escalating studies exploring how comfortable people were being alone with only their thoughts and after the subjects had said in a questionnaire that they'd rather pay money then be shocked. And, yet, 67 percent of men and 25 percent of women shocked themselves rather than sit quietly for fifteen minutes.

There is a less painful way in which many people avoid letting their minds wander. We entertain ourselves. We stream shows, or send messages back and forth on our devices, creating constant stimulation that allows our attention to hover just a bit above a baseline terrain of self-awareness and discovery, which can be the lifeblood of creativity.

What does this add up to?

People who become creative learn to mind wander without judgment. They let ideas come to them from the recesses of their minds, and sometimes what crosses over into consciousness becomes seed corn or creative solution. They need to be able to do so without fear that the ideas will be a source of worry. In creativity, fear is not the friend of the creator.

That's an idea I've been reinforcing. It comes with a loophole, which I'll describe in the final chapter of this section. The chapter is aptly named: Fear.

Sometimes, it's a great accelerant to creativity, an amplifier of invention almost like no other.

Fear

To this point, I've sought to explain how creators emerge by developing a fearlessness in trusting the ideas and emotions that occur to them.

Sometimes, though, fear is creator's best friend.

Sometimes, there is a lion.

This chapter is aimed at drawing a crucial distinction between fear of self-expression and of external judgment, which debilitates, and fear of authentic threats. These are among the most powerful motivators in all of human creation.

For instance, you have to hand it to smallpox as an evil, murderous, loathsome creation of nature. It was also a force for an even more potent creative response.

Smallpox killed 300 million people in just the twentieth century and untold millions before that. It lurked in every human interaction, cough, and sneeze, every conversation, making people mad with fear at every turn in their lives.

Over centuries, ideas to stop the spread of this contagion sprung like weeds, or hops and barley: One doctor in the eighteenth century tried giving people "twelve small bottles of beer every twenty-four hours" as a treatment, one history recounts. Other ideas, simple Small C's, involved keeping the windows open to avoid spread. The best Little C, called "variolation," involved exposing a person who was not sick and had not suffered smallpox to a small bit of the disease from a ripe pustule to thereby help a person build defenses.

This didn't always work, and there's a good reason: Vaccines, we now know, work only by exposing a person to a weakened version of the disease. With this approach, the person's defenses can build up without being overwhelmed.

We know this in part from Dr. Edward Jenner's Big C creation when he observed that milkmaids did not get smallpox after they'd been exposed to cowpox, which is the bovine version of the disease. That version, it turns out, was just enough like smallpox—and just different enough from it—to inoculate human beings. The world's first vaccine was born. Inspired by fear.

Just as important as the inspiration, though, was who was experiencing it—a person with tendencies we now know to be essential to creativity.

Dr. Jenner was hypercurious. He built hydrogen air balloons, wrote poetry and music, played violin in clubs, made groundbreaking studies of cuckoos (the bird), and helped "classify" animals brought back from a voyage by Captain Cook (credit for these details here to Dr. Stefan Riedel, a pathologist in Boston, Massachusetts, who amassed a concise biography of Dr. Jenner in a medical journal).

Dr. Jenner also was orphaned at the age of five. This kind of childhood trauma, research shows—and I'll elaborate on this later—can lead people to think about and see the world in ways different from those of their peer group.

For the moment, the point is that, when it came to smallpox, Dr. Jenner was afraid of people dying, but not afraid of trying. He made observations, listened to himself, came up with something novel, valuable, and surprising. Medicine from a cow.

By the time the troubles of the pandemic of 2020 hit, the number of vaccines, built on the shoulders of giants like Jenner, had multiplied greatly. The human species could fight chickenpox and diphtheria, measles and mumps, flu and polio, among others. Thanks to Jenner and the motivation of the fear of death, the groundwork had well been laid for a creative explosion after COVID-19 hit as laboratories worldwide attempted to stitch together vaccines in record time.

Fear of authentically dangerous forces doesn't inhibit creativity. The problem is a particular type of fear: the fear of expressing the ideas, particularly the ones that come naturally. This is the key distinction—between fear and doubt.

Doubt can kill creativity, or at least inhibit it. By contrast creativity can be inspired by terror—terror of wanting, of lost opportunity, of imminent or eventual attack, for safety, for your children. These are authentic fears. They are distinctive from the fear of self-expression or the fear of self-exploration, or of the quiet that can bring it.

"Fear can be an initial motivator but when you can't be completely in that state," was how the broader idea was eloquently put to me by Gregory Feist, a highly regarded creativity scholar.

This is why I take some issue with the cliché that "necessity is the mother of invention." The implication is that creativity or innovation gets inspired foremost by some great necessity, or by desperation. In fact, many people face dire, desperate situations and do not create their way out of it. The people who do so are the ones who can hear ideas and have the capacity to pursue them. Fear plays a role, for certain, but it is more of an accelerant or amplifier to the authentic creative drive. It is a reason or excuse to create.

Arguably, it is the most powerful of all reasons for an authentic creator to act. In fact, fear ties us most closely to our genetic forebears, the animals and even cellular organisms with which we share the world. I don't mean to say that cells can feel fear. (So please don't send angry cards and letters suggesting as much, as I fear you might.) I mean to say that the threat of extinction—which is the most primal fear of all—drives change for those predisposed to create.

Creators embrace this fear as one ingredient on the spice rack, as one of the multitudes a creator contains. They tap into fear as an emotion, an underlying state, a thing to be acknowledged or tapped into, watered, tended, drawn from.

One of the best stories I've heard on the subject of using fear to create involves an engineer with General Electric named Doug Dietz.

Dietz was given the task of redesigning a magnetic resonance imaging machine, the MRI, so it would be easier to use with kids. The trouble was that the MRI machine is a giant white tube that requires a person to be slid inside, enveloping them, and allowing radio waves to course through the body to measure what's going on inside. It's a terrific innovation for discovering and diagnosing disease and injury but with a side effect that the person inside the tube can become claustrophobic to the point of feeling extremely alarmed and agitated. Another frightening aspect of the MRI experience for kids: the fiercely loud thumping, clanging, crashing sounds made by the machine.

When Dietz, the engineer with GE, described his task, he started to cry.

"I always kept in my mind that frightened child who was going through cancer or really having some problems," he said in a video made of his experience. "That is such a tough thing for a little one and such a tough thing for a family."

In coming up with a solution, Dietz did not have the option of remaking the MRI machine. It can work only in these tight, seemingly terrifying confined spaces. So Dietz wrestled with what he could change: the perception of the device. The fear.

He decided to figure out how to make the MRI experience . . . fun?

Fun.

Fun!

Dietz did it and without changing the machine at all. It remains a monolithic tube. But it feels very different now because Dietz changed the story, and he gave children a feeling of control. When children go for a scan now, they choose their MRI experience. Would they like to play the part of a pirate or princess, or captain of a submarine? They wear a costume into the scan room, which is decorated as if by the mind of Walt Disney. Pings and whirs? Why, of course! Every pirate faces challenges that require bravery.

"They didn't need a new machine," one creativity pundit told me. "They needed a new story."

Innovative businesspeople are a particularly fascinating group when it comes to fear because many entrepreneurs are optimistic by nature. But they can empathize with fear and capitalize on it.

To that end, some scholars draw a distinction between the way that businesspeople and scientists draw on fear from the way that artists react to it.

Very generally, the artists internalize emotions and wrestle with their meaning through their work, said Mr. Feist, the scholar I mentioned earlier. By contrast, he said, scientists and entrepreneurs might still feel the sting of fear but be a touch more dispassionate. "They're dealing with problems outside of themselves," he said. What the groups have in common is a "borderline irrational faith in their own perspective. They can keep going even when they hear "you're an idiot, this is silly, this is stupid," he said. The doubters are often right, by the way, and many creative ideas flop.

"That's what distinguishes creative people," Mr. Feist said. "The misses don't really faze them."

An interesting example of the power of fear to motivate but not overtake comes from an entrepreneur named Michael Monsky. He's one of the many creators who isn't a household name but whose innovations touch millions of lives.

Several years ago, Monsky was fiercely disturbed by one of the filthier objects people may ever hold: the television remote control in a hotel room. He decided to do something about it.

Raised in New Jersey, Monsky was the son of a news junkie who would bring home the *New York Times*. Monsky would read the paper as a kid and it became a hobby for him to follow the news. For employment, he had a knack with electronics and wound up working in a business that repaired remote controls. It wasn't particularly inspiring, but it was a decent business and good work because many of those millions of televisions in the world have a particular remote control and if the gadget broke then it needed to be repaired or replaced. "I've been in the remote control business I can't remember how long," Monsky told me. "It was before the internet."

Then along came the internet. A friend created a website for Monsky—"The first website I saw was my own. It was a one-page flier that talked about how we had original remotes and told people to call. That was it. And boy did they call."

Once he was captaining his own ship, he began to see where he might take it. Ideas came from the news. One story that really captured his imagination was written just after the turn of the century, and then he started noticing a bunch of contemporary stories about a nasty new kind of bacteria. Around the world, bacteria had begun to develop resistance to antibiotics. You might fairly say that the bacteria had gotten creative in an effort to survive.

"I was reading all those stories. It was like the fourth leading cause of death—more than car accidents and breast cancers—and I remember thinking: What are they doing in healthcare? I was kind of aware of no way to clean a remote off," he said. Like in hospitals, or doctors' offices, or in hotels. "That had me thinking."

"But the thing that put me over the top was that my son got peanut butter in the remote control and I could not get that peanut butter out of there."

It was 2005 when that happened, and the family had moved to Tampa, and Monsky saw his son gum up the remote control, and he flashed on the resistant bacteria. And he was overtaken. Flash of lightning.

"The two ideas married each other in that moment."

Peanut butter and drug-resistant bacteria! (Not peanut butter and chocolate.) He began developing what he called a Clean Remote. It took nearly two years—"I cannot believe how long it took to get a prototype," he said—and in 2007 he had a remote with a kind of plastic, easy-to-clean exterior with the keys beneath the covering. One swipe and away would go the peanut butter and other goop, along with any drug-resistant bacteria left by the last channel surfer.

Monsky happened to have a close connection at Clorox—which has made billions with innovations that help clean our environment of bacteria that justifiably scares us. Monsky wrangled an hour-long meeting with the CEO at the company's headquarters in Oakland, California.

"We were there a week later," Monsky said. "They were in love with it."

Monsky's creation had gotten the backing of one of the world's largest companies. It would be like a musician getting a deal with the biggest record company, a screenwriter landing a two-season deal with Netflix, or a computer programmer having General Motors or BMW decide to back the software for a self-driving car. Monsky could walk into any big company with the endorsement of Clorox, which came with instant credibility and certain huge sales.

"Then the CEO had a massive heart attack," Monsky said. The man left the company.

The incoming chief executive didn't see the value of the Clean Remote partnership. Monsky was no less creative than he had been, but suddenly the world wasn't going to find out about his creation. The company did manage to sell a decent number of Clean Remotes to hospitals. But change is scary, and it is expensive. Hotels didn't want to replace their existing remote controls. The business did not take off. Monsky's own employees pleaded with him to give it up after it became clear that there was not a huge market for remote controls surrounded by a nonporous, easily cleaned membrane.

"Why are you wasting our time and money on this?" he recalled their asking.

Monsky, undaunted, inspired in the way of a creator, pressed on, a lonely quest. He discovered it wasn't just drug-resistant bacteria and food that were on the remote control. "The remote control is the worst thing in a hotel room—30 percent have semen on them," said Charles Gerba, an environmental virologist at the University of Arizona whose own creative journey led him to do all kinds of studies on germs in hotels and how they take root and get carried from room to room.

Every time Monsky presented a sales pitch, he'd use the semen stat—boy, did that gross people out, even hospital-hardened nurses—and he'd talk about MRSA, the drug-resistant infection, and all the other germs. "Every once in a while, I'd say to my team: We might actually be saving some lives here," Monsky said. "I thought it had merit, and I thought our time would come."

It was indeed poised to arrive, as I'll explain later—because Monsky was about to be inundated with requests. That's because he'd had the creative instinct to persevere, and it would yet pay off during the pandemic, as orders poured in from some of the largest hotel chains and healthcare systems around the world.

Meantime, I discovered in writing this book another great story of the way fear motivated a modern-day entrepreneur. The story comes from Silicon Valley, where entrepreneurs have thrived by tapping into peoples' emotional needs and building technology to suit.

Sometimes, these creators hit the jackpot. This is what happened for Michael Lee, who went on a decade-long creative binge after experiencing a commonplace fear: he didn't want to look overweight in his wedding tuxedo.

The story starts in 2003, several months before his wedding to his eventual wife, Amy. Lee is a big fella, six feet three, and weighed 230 pounds at the time. That was too much, he decided, and so he and his eventual wife, Amy, joined 24 Hour Fitness in downtown San Francisco.

A trainer there gave the pair a booklet that listed the calories of three thousand different foods. The pair were supposed to write down their meals and add up the calories.

"I'm a tech guy. I was like, 'There's no way I'm doing this on pen and paper.' I don't think it made it out of the gym."

Right into the trash.

Lee's brief biological sketch will ring familiar as belonging to that of a creator. He was born in Providence, Rhode Island, in 1970, the child of Korean immigrants, his father then at Brown University pursuing a PhD in metallurgy and who later took a job at General Electric in Schenectady in upstate New York—a company and a place rich with creative energy. "It was like this totally random thing where I grew up. There were a ton of PhDs and Nobel Prize winners," Lee said. "I thought that everybody had a PhD."

Family friends hailed from all over the world, and his school was filled with people from places that sounded exotic, like Lithuania. And there was lots of access to computers, donated by GE. Lee learned to program on the computers, learned curiosity from the company he kept, and got permission from his parents to pursue his passions.

By 2004, Lee had moved to San Francisco, and was by now married (slimmer than he'd been). He worked at Palm but kept feeling this itch to pursue his own ideas. As I listened to his story, it didn't seem to me that he realized at the time that he was already building his calorie counter. He thought of that idea as a hobby but it was one that haunted him with constant inspiration. For instance, he realized that many existing calorie counters required users to search each day for the foods they ate, even if they regularly ate the same foods. He had an authentic emotion attached to that experience: I'm too lazy to do that.

"I'm not the only person who suffers from that," he said, laughing. "People eat the same stuff over and over again. People eat the same breakfast every day, literally. That should be super easy to record."

He thought a lot about how people behave, not how they "should" behave.

"Losing weight is so hard. It's just hard. You have to change all these habits, read all this information. The last thing you want is for the tools to help you lose weight to be hard," he told me.

In 2005, Lee launched a website called MyFitnessPal. It did all the things that Lee felt were consistent with making things as easy as possible. He told Amy, who had become the breadwinner, that maybe "it could become a lifestyle business" in which he would monitor the site and handle some customer-service emails and take care of the kids. But Lee worked, and worked. Each new challenge became a new inspiration to learn and solve. The fear he'd look heavy at his wedding—and the recognition that he and others were too lazy to count calories the old-fashioned way—had fallen away, like the boosters of a rocket now soaring into orbit.

"Amy jokes with me all the time: 'You've never worked so hard in your life. What happened to the lifestyle business?'"

It began to grow, and a few waistlines began to shrink. He'd get these notes. *Just so you know, I lost thirty pounds.*

Lee wasn't sure it meant he had a business, not exactly. He was treating it like a hobby. He understood how hard it is for a business to succeed. This is one thing you can say with assurance about a new business creation: It will likely fail—if the measure of success is getting rich. It is the same for all those writers of books. Most won't get read widely, or even purchased. The same is true for all the scientists whose passionately pursued research won't be cited across the globe as world-changing, or win a Nobel Prize.

Businesses' survival is measured by the Bureau of Labor Statistics, and the year that Lee posted his website, 2005, was typical: Of all the 679,000 businesses that started that year, 20 percent were cratered within a year, and half died within five years. They were created by the inspired, the creative, the brave, and liberated. By the numbers, they failed.

Lee eventually dove in and created his business, collaborating with his brother, Albert, a natural networker. After the iPhone came out, "our users kept asking for an app." So they built one. The business grew, and it grew.

In early 2013, *Consumer Reports* named the app as a leading "do-it-yourself diet plan." By now, forty million people had used the technology since Lee had embarked on what he thought might be a hobby. That same year, the brothers sold a part of their business to two of the most prominent groups of venture capitalists, Kleiner Perkins and Accel Partners. These investors in 2013 put $18 million into the company. In addition to the $18 million, which went into the company, Lee and his brother pulled out $20 million in profit.

"Al and I split it," Lee said of his brother. "I remember when they deposited it into our bank account. I had to go to the ATM and look at the receipt. I thought: This is crazy."

Getting crazier.

On February 4, 2015, Under Armour, the sports apparel brand, announced it was acquiring MyFitnessPal, which it called "the largest digital health and fitness community in the world." Now it had eighty million registered users and the capability of counting calories of five million foods and combinations of foods.

Purchase price: $475 million.

I've gotten to know Lee well and I can assure you that he never imagined such a payoff when his venture began. I suspect he didn't want to look overweight at his wedding but also didn't want to work too hard to slim down.

The fear launched him but quickly gave way to inspiration.

By contrast, fear has also inspired much great art. But in the case of art, the process and creation can be more closely hewed to fear itself. That's because the artist might more deeply internalize the emotion in order to wrestle with it.

"Fear" is the name of the first chapter of one of the greatest works ever on the subject of race in America, a book called *Native Son* by Richard Wright that was published in 1940. The fictional narrative tells the story of Bigger Thomas, a twenty-year-old African American on the south side of Chicago, defined by the terror of being Black. His fear hems him in with tight walls, the constraint of having to act a certain way to survive—"yessuh," and "yessum" he says to white people, eyes down—but even then, he cannot possibly be polite enough to help his family rise from its rat-infested one-room apartment. He cannot afford to hate white people, for it serves no purpose, and so he initially turns on his family and friends, at one point making his buddy Gus lick the knife Bigger held at his neck. Then he accidentally, carelessly kills a white woman. He tells himself it was no accident because he realizes he has found freedom. He becomes a new man, one he tells himself is no longer blind like all the Black people around him. He can see the truth. He is free to do as he pleases, able to see the world while he himself is largely invisible to white people. Irving Howe, a literary critic and socialist, is often quoted as saying: "The day *Native Son* appeared American culture was changed forever."

But that's not where this novel began, with an effort to change the world. It began with personal truth, an experience so deep that the plot "fell out, so to speak," Wright wrote. "I had spent years learning about Bigger, what made him, what he meant."

Wright's first published book was, by contrast, more outcome-focused. It was called *Uncle Tom's Children*, and contained short stories with at times idealistic tilts. One ended with whites and Blacks marching together against racism.

The stories showed great writing talent but didn't catch on commercially.

Wright went for raw truth with *Native Son*.

Native Son wasn't pretty, as they say, but it promptly sold 250,000 copies.

This story, on one level, exquisitely depicts the experience of being a Black man in America. There is a coda here, though, that transcends race and that I find particularly captivating in the context of creativity. What Bigger experiences—the abject fear of raw impotence and invisibility—grips many people, well beyond one group. "There were literally millions of him, everywhere," Wright wrote.

This is why the book so resonates, at least for me. What Bigger feels vibrates in the bones the way a great song, or a confession, or an outpouring of grief does. Whatever else its failings (some critics find it not sufficiently literary and some say it is fairly hostile to women) reading it is like watching raw emotion get reassembled into a legible plot, connected in the way of a new form of life.

Rhiannon Giddens had done some groundwork on racial injustice too before the arrival of the year 2020. At times, her motivation was outright terror.

———

Giddens sat in the passenger seat of a Honda Civic in 2017, driving in New Orleans to a zydeco dance with a friend. Her feet were on the dashboard, she and her friend chatting, when a song idea seized her. It was about her nephew, Justin. She feared he'd be killed.

Justin Harrington, her sister Lalenja's son, lived in Greensboro. He was twenty, an artistic soul with aspirations to become an actor and write and perform music, and well beyond his years in terms of introspection and self-expression. When a teen, he had been regular in so many respects. But an African American teen. So he'd had his little moments, like the time he was fifteen and walking down the street after midnight with friends when the cops started tailing them. He told me, "Spencer, my white friend, is telling me to keep walking."

Then another friend got scared and took off running. The cops stopped the boys.

"Are you drinking? Where are the drugs?" an officer asked the boys.

They hadn't been drinking. They had no drugs. The plan for the night was to walk five miles to McDonald's to get a Happy Meal with a toy. The cops let the boys go.

As Rhiannon sat in the car that warm New Orleans night, riffing with her friend, her mind running free, a song popped into her head about the risks to her nephew of being a young man with black skin.

You better get it right the first time.

That was the phrase that struck her, around which she would build the song of the same name. There is little or no margin for error, she thought, when the color of your skin already puts a strike against you in the minds of some people. *You better get it right the first time.*

Two years earlier, after her first solo album, *Tomorrow Is My Turn*, the same NPR reviewer had said the album "reimagines country, soul, gospel, and blues standards. Her musical influences are many but in the face of unbearable grief she, like many travelers forced out of the familiar, relies on the universal."

She was poised for stardom. It was there for the taking, life on the TV show *Nashville*, ever more lucrative record contracts, photo shoots with the stars. But something was not right for Giddens. The acclaim could feel like a burden, and a distraction. What she felt increasingly were the stories of her ancestors. That song "Julie," about the slave, "had been with me for awhile," and there was "Better Get It Right the First Time." These were not the stories that would make her a star. But these were the ones that poured out.

When Giddens writes a song, the words often come together quickly. The rhythms come from traditional places, like call-and-response, verse-verse, chorus. There's not a lot of second-guessing in that initial flurry of creativity. "Sometimes I get an idea and it just goes and it goes," she said. "I look at it in awe sometimes." She doesn't mean that the outcome is good or bad but rather that creations have poured out, from the recesses of her mind. "It's magic."

That's what happened when she wrote "Better Get It Right the First Time."

> Young man was a good man
> Always went to school
> Young man was a good man
> Never played the fool
> Young man was a good man
> Never had no drama
>
> Young man was a good man
> Always took care of his mama
> Young man was a good man
> Hanging with his boys
> Young man was a good man

Didn't know he'd made a choice
Young man was a good man
Only did it twice
Young man was a good man
But now he's paid the price
Better get it right the first time
Better get it right the first time
Better get it right the first time
Better get it right the first time

The words on the page do no justice to the song. It draws its power from Giddens's arrangement, her voice, and a chilling ability to simultaneously communicate empathy, hope, mourning, and defiance. Her voice, like manifest destiny, probes the edges of emotional adventure and boundaries of comfort. When I listen to her songs, I wonder what extraordinary combination of forces could create such a powerful, beautiful, pure sound.

The album on which this song appeared, *Freedom Highway*, was nominated for album of the year by the Americana Music Honors & Awards. "Giddens has emerged as a peerless voice of roots-minded music," one critic wrote of the record.

Sounds great, right? But that kind of critical acclaim is a bit different from the kind of pop sound and story that begets a Country Music Award.

Giddens was breaking away—from external validation. She was hearing herself. Why? What was happening to her?

The answer comes in part from understanding where this raw inspiration comes from in the first place, and what its purpose is. Where do we get this divine-like power to forge new creations? Where does it come from?

What is the origin of the muse?

Greek mythology tells of the Muses, sisters born at Mount Olympus who touch human beings and inspire them to create. The ancient poets disagree about how many Muses there were, but, hey, maybe the ancient poets were touched by different muses as they created their mythology. (We don't judge.)

In the mythology, different Muses inspired different types of creators to produce different types of creations: art, comedy, astronomy, and others.

This is not the actual origin of the muse.

In fact, creativity comes to us from our primitive biology.

This brings us to Book II of creation: The laws of nature.

It comes from the same place as COVID-19, the virus that was poised to cause the pandemic, and the power to overcome these challenges too. All of it comes from nature.

BOOK II

LAWS OF NATURE

Wherein Evolutionary Biologists, a Physicist, a
Theologian, a Virologist, (and a Rock Star) Show Us the
Deeper Principles Propelling the Rise of the Creator.

View from a Microbe

If the idea of being creative makes you feel small, you should see what Andreas Wagner has going on. He watches microbes create. This is evolution, in real time, and it has a lot to tell us about the secrets to creativity.

His laboratory at the University of Zurich whirs with incubators and PCR machines, which amplify DNA, minus-eighty-degree freezers and ice machines (don't ask; cold keeps cells from dividing too quickly when tinkering with the DNA). It's standard mind-blowing microbiology stuff.

But the real action happens in the flasks.

"This is where we perform experimental evolution," Wagner explained. "It is an imminently creative process."

The researchers fill the flasks with bacterial cells. The researchers add simple sugars, which the bacteria like to eat. And off go the microbes, eating and thriving and reproducing.

Then hellfire rains down.

The researchers add antibiotics to the flasks. Antibiotics, it probably goes without saying, kill bacteria, particularly the kind that have been put into the flasks. Death from above!

Can the bacteria create a way to save their own lives?

Not most of them. Most die, quickly. Others manage to reproduce before they die, partly because bacteria reproduce so quickly—every twenty minutes or so. Then most of those new bacteria die.

But in some cases, when bacteria multiply, a mistake takes place: Some of the genes get copied incorrectly from one generation to the next. This is called mutation, obviously. It is an accident, and it often ends badly. The mutated genetic pattern causes the bacteria to die, if say, for instance, a gene that controls an important survival function mutates in a such a way that it no longer works.

But every once in a while, this mutation gives the cell incredible new survival powers, such as the ability to overpower an antibiotic.

Wagner and others have discovered two different types of mutations that lead to such a result.

One of the more typical mutations involves a pump that resides inside these bacterial cells. It's called an efflux pump and it typically pulls material into cells or jettisons materials out. Mutations to the pump can cause the pump "to become hyperactive," Andreas explained. This can save the cell.

"As an antibiotic enters, the pump pumps it right back out," he said.

The microbe lives on!

Another relatively common scenario involves mutations to genes that control chemicals called enzymes that reside inside the bacteria. Typically, the job of these enzymes is to cut, or "cleave," other molecules. They might do this for the purpose of, say, using the molecules for energy.

However, random mutations can occur in the genes that encode these enzymes that cause them to cleave penicillin. This is not the task the genes accomplished when they first went into the flasks. But a handful that mutated to cut penicillin, and therefore kill it, suddenly became the few that survive.

"Evolution discovers mechanisms for neutralizing antibiotics," Wagner said. "That's a form of creativity."

Wagner has devoted his career to proving that creativity can be shown at the most basic molecular level and that what happens there is a roadmap for creativity at large.

He cites a widely accepted definition of "a creative product" as "an original and appropriate solution to a problem."

He sees it every day in his lab.

"Think of life's entire history on the planet as the history of problem solving. Every time organisms evolved a new ability—the ability to fly or see with eyes, or photosynthesize—that was a creative solution to some problem. And you can think of every single one of the species as the end point of a series of creations or innovations."

Life is a survival game. The survivors walk a line between remaining stable enough to withstand existing conditions and flexible enough to cope with new threats, or even get ahead of them.

It's the same balancing act that defines human creativity. It's a parallel that I'm hoping to capture for the reader in the second section of this book, which is aimed at seeing creativity through the eyes of big thinkers who are not normally focused on creativity research. These fields include biology, physics and math, and theology. Among the big thinkers are several powerhouses, including one of the world's foremost evolutionary biologists, Richard Dawkins.

Dawkins wrote a book called *The Selfish Gene*, itself a powerfully influential and creative argument for how genetic forces guide the most fundamental behavior. He held the prestigious position of Professor for Public Understanding of Science at the University of Oxford. He's got a world-class gift for making accessible the most exquisite points of science.

In that spirit, Dawkins described to me the stark similarity of an engineer pumping out ideas for a flying machine, say, an airplane, to a cell reproducing and creating gene mutations. In the case of the cell, mutations come from reproduction and most die and a few thrive, while in the case of the human creator, ideas spew forth and mostly wind up in the trash.

Picture an engineer trying to design something new. "I have an idea!" Quick, before he can reject it, he writes it down. Then he comes up with another one, and then starts another one. His wastepaper basket becomes full of abandoned drawings. Finally, he gets one worthy of a prototype, then he tests it in a wind tunnel, then tweaks, and each of those is a kind of selective process leading to a big mutation with lots of smaller mutations. Then maybe he actually builds a physical model that flies but it crashes, and he tweaks it. That is a kind of Darwinian process.

Dawkins told me that he believes that human creative impulse, like genetic mutation, doesn't initially make a distinction between what will work and what will not. In other words, genes mutate at random, and Dawkins tends to think of creative impulses, at least initially, as a similar process. "A brilliant new idea pops into the mind partly as a random event—random, again, only in the sense that it's not directed toward improvement."

It's as if the random spurts of ideas come themselves from darkness, and the recesses of the subconscious mind.

But human beings bring one important distinction to bear. "We humans, and probably a few other animals, have the power to run a simulation in our heads."

This idea that creativity has a deep analogue in the way our species evolved has been woven through research into the psychology of creativity. Dean Simonton, the researcher I mention throughout, has written "the creative process is essentially Darwinian."

I asked Dawkins if he agreed that Darwinian survival principles could be applied also to art, like writing and music.

Yes, absolutely, he said. With that, he launched into a story about songbirds and sex. You may know a bit about it, but let's get naughty anyway.

The songs of sparrows are among the most studied bird calls in the world. American male birds learn songs from their fathers, creating a veritable copy of the patterns of their calls. For some, though, that template becomes a jumping-off point for additional "trial and error," Dawkins explained. "A young male bird tries warbling and burbling at random and when it hears itself sing a phrase that sounds good to it, it repeats it.

"This seems to me to be a kind of creativity," he said, and by analogy, "Beethoven used to go for long walks and sometimes thought of a good musical phrase. He would write it in a notebook. And if you look at his notebooks, you can see that his melodies started rather dull and he worked on them and the process looked very much like what these birds do."

I'd just briefly interrupt this lesson on bird puberty to give a quick reminder of a point I've made before and will make again: Creativity need not start with explosions of genius. The bird, and Beethoven, tried and erred, played with ideas, abandoned some, built on others. A basic attribute of creators is not the initial quality of their ideas but the sheer quantity of mutation.

In the case of birds, ample additional evidence connects this "artistic" expression to survival and sexual selection. In some experiments, female birds given testosterone wind up learning song when they otherwise might not, again illustrating the connection between song and aspects of gender. Dawkins, in his book *The Greatest Show on Earth*, explained that the ovaries in female canaries and Barbary doves grow when they hear certain "appealing" songs from male birds of the same species.

"Artistic creativity," Dawkins said, "is involved with sexual selection."

Additional validation of these concepts comes from Robert Bilder, a psychology professor at UCLA doing pioneering research on creativity.

Bilder explained to me how a young male zebra finch learns to mimic the songs of older birds and then "introduces novelty into the song."

What fascinates Bilder is precisely why the females are drawn to a bird capable of making a novel and compelling song. Why is that a sign of survival advantage?

Bilder answers the question by stripping away the idea of art or novelty and focusing on a more fundamental definition of what the male birds are doing: They are communicating.

So, he asks, what is the value of communication? And why would there be value in the novelty of a particular sound?

It's a terrific, basic question, born of authentic curiosity and a willingness by Bilder to lose the inhibition that might come from asking something so elementary.

Bilder theorizes that the original value of communication could revolve around trying to unify a group, perhaps for purposes of coordinating around a common goal—"Go kill wild boar to eat!"—or warning a group—"Run! Wild boar that will eat us!"

So part of the value of the novelty of sound, and song, may be that it exhibits some power to motivate. That could come in handy if you're trying to protect offspring.

Even more primitive yet, Bilder said, might be the simple fact that novelty would help a male bird announce its presence—"the goal was to let females know there was a male around, period," and that selected out mute males. The key would be for a bird to differentiate itself, but with a catch: The male song couldn't be so different as to sound weird, nuts, off-key, out of touch.

"They introduce novelty into the song, make it a little different, but not too different," Bilder said.

This idea is sometimes called the "edge of chaos," where a state that is disconnected from order remains tethered to order.

"At the edge of chaos, the states are maximally novel while still connected to states in the ordered regime, and thus are most likely to manifest the combination of novelty and utility that is the hallmark of creativity," Bilder and a co-author wrote in a paper published in 2014. This could be seen as applying to a genetic change, even a cosmic one, like the formation of a universe where new matter forms in ways destined in the short term (relatively speaking) for stability not more chaos.

So what's happening with the singing birds, well, it's happening with us too. Broadly, Wagner said the lesson is that there is a "striking analogy between human creativity and what we see in evolution. It involves convergent and divergent thinking."

Convergent and divergent thinking are key concepts in the world of creativity.

Convergent thinking revolves around ideas that conform. The most pointed definition of the term for convergent thinking is giving the "correct" answer.

Divergent thinking, by contrast, is considered "nonlinear." The answer may not be the straightest line between two points or may not appear to connect two points at all. In that sense, it may be labeled as incorrect.

Who the heck wouldn't want the correct answer?

Microbes facing death by penicillin wouldn't. When they responded to antibiotics in the way they were supposed to, they died. When they diverged from the way in which they were initially programmed—through mutation—they survived.

If you are wondering to yourself, "Wait, bacteria can't think," you are correct. Not to be glib, but this was introduced as an analogy. On the flip side, divergent and convergent "thinking" may not actually involve thinking at all, not the way you may be considering it.

When people create, the process often involves random generation of ideas at a subconscious level. That experience in some ways is as analogous to random mutations in genes as it is to willful, analytical thought. There's more to the analogy: For bacteria, convergent thinking is safe, while divergent thinking is not only risky, it takes resources.

Think back for a moment to the efflux pump that resides inside a bacteria cell. If it performs as it is originally designed to perform, it pumps efficiently, taking in molecules and excreting them in a way honed to perfection by evolution. If it pumps too quickly, the cell wastes precious resources. There's no point in creating a new way, at least not until antibiotics come into the mix. Then the divergent path—the creative one—is not only more efficient, it means life!

For those readers who would rather not choose to live on a razor's edge—death from convergence and death from divergence—evolution teaches that there is a creative middle ground.

"Neutral" is a term for mutations that appear, on the surface, not to have a big impact on the survival of the organism. In fact, Wagner pointed out to me, only about 40 percent of genes have a direct impact on the viability of a species. Genes that are not in that pool can mutate without an apparent survival impact.

In bacteria, for example, a change may occur in the genes that express the efflux pump but that appears to have no impact on the pump. The bacteria goes along, thriving, and then, one day, just as an antibiotic gets introduced, another mutation happens to a gene impacting the pump. This second change, it turns out, works only because of the first change. One divergence built upon an earlier one.

"If you look at human inventions, there are lots of examples," Wagner told me.

Thomas Edison's lightbulb, for instance, required an effective filament and a vacuum that would protect the filament from flaming out. Neither of those two developments have the direct, ultimate impact of the lightbulb itself but, Wagner said, "you have to have a vacuum before you have a filament or it's useless. That's how I think about the impact neutral mutations can have."

Invent a filament!

Or think of the pacemaker, which required multiple developments, including miniaturization of batteries and components, or the device would fit neatly on a tabletop, not inside your body where it can actually do some good.

Create a smaller something!

With regard to the Big C, though, the enduring creation, Wagner offers one more caveat: Biology shows us that this is both possible and quite possibly beyond our control. Sometimes, the creation is the better part of luck and timing. Such was the case with the discovery of the antibiotic, one of the most important findings in human history. Arguably, it happened by accident.

Dr. Alexander Fleming, a Scot, served in the medical corps in World War I. There, he watched many soldiers die of infection. Overall, in the war, several hundred thousand men died of infection.

After the war, Dr. Fleming studied the bacteria that had eaten his fellow soldiers to death. Famously, he came into his lab one day to find that one of his samples, uncovered and sitting under a window, had been contaminated, with mold overtaking the bacteria. Uncovered, contaminated, a sample for the garbage bin, right?

Most people would've tossed it out as a failed experiment. Dr. Fleming did not. Instead he had an aha moment. He could see the power of his accident. The mold, penicillin, became the fruit of arguably the world's single most significant medicine.

Fleming's discovery saved millions of lives, he won a Nobel Prize, and even, presciently, warned in his Nobel Prize acceptance speech that bacteria will learn to fight back if we overuse antibiotics. Today, drug-resistant infections—the very kind being grown in flasks in Switzerland by Andreas Wagner, the evolutionary biologist—present one of the greatest public health threats.

Two lessons about creativity stand out from Fleming's discovery. The first is that the discovery did in fact come from happenstance, much like the way biology itself creates. Dr. Fleming wasn't working with a particular hypothesis that was borne out in the petri dish under the window. A biological event took place that he did not predict. He would say later: "I did not invent penicillin. Nature did that. I only discovered it by accident."

He did, though, help create the conditions that would allow the mutation to take place. He played in the space, the way someone might tinker on the piano, or doodle, or try out business plans on napkins. This is almost a random firing of synapses. So one lesson from biology, borne out by Dr. Fleming, is that great creation can come from an event that appears random, or maybe is random. Such an event becomes a signal, a transmission, a message.

Are you available and able to hear it?

The second lesson is that Dr. Fleming picked up the transmission. He picked up what nature was putting down. He recognized that the accident wasn't meant for the garbage. This is a huge lesson for creativity: Accidents in nature or human invention happen all the time, but they become the stuff of invention only if we recognize them.

Fleming wrote, "When I woke up just after dawn on September 28, 1928, I certainly didn't plan to revolutionize all medicine by discovering the world's first antibiotic, or bacteria killer. But I suppose that was exactly what I did."

Part of creativity on the part of people in multiple fields is being able to pay attention to inputs that others may overlook. Accidents happen. Do they have value?

The world sends signals, sometimes randomly generated. Great creators see the mutation for what it is, or could become.

In this way, divergent thinking doesn't necessarily mean the breaking of natural law but, rather, seeing things for what they are, could be, or have developed into.

That said, is it any surprise that Dr. Fleming's discovery was initially downplayed, even largely dismissed by the scientific community? It took some eleven years for the mass production of penicillin to become the widely appreciated, enormous lifesaver that it was in World War II. The Nobel Prize followed five years later.

Finally, there's a curious coda to this story that shows how hard it is to assess the objective value of a creation. On its face, the discovery of antibiotics appears to be pure bounty for humankind, leading to longer and healthier lives. It is also true that we have used antibiotics so widely that they have now become a health risk. This is happening because the more heavily we use antibiotics, the more we create an environment that benefits bacteria that cannot be killed by antibiotics. They are called "antibiotic-resistant microbes," and they are emerging through a creative process in nature. What happens is that a mutation occurs when a bacteria or fungus reproduces and this mutation then leads to a microbe that isn't killed by antibiotics. In the old days, if there were not antibiotics, this mutated organism would probably just die off because its new form would serve no particular purpose; it would have no survival advantage.

However, in a world saturated with antibiotics, this new creation suddenly becomes the only microbe that can survive, and it begins to reproduce and reproduce. This is a perfect example of an extraordinary new creation that happens by accident and is suited perfectly to the environment. Great for the organism, bad for humankind trying not to die from infection.

A projection, from a study funded by the British government, estimates that by 2050, more people on Earth will die from drug-resistant microbes than will die that year from cancer. This is not necessarily a direct result of Fleming's discovery but, rather, the way in which we have overused antibiotics—often when we don't need them for disease treatment in humans and in livestock for growth promotion—and thus we have created an environment in which even more dangerous bacteria thrive.

To bring this full circle, back to the beginning of the chapter—and Wagner's lab in Switzerland and the creative spirit of the bacteria itself—I'd point out that what is happening now is a kind of arms race between human creativity and the innate creative power of bacteria. They are programmed to survive and so are we. And the result is the escalation of creativity, with ever more refinements.

Simply, the creative urge is biological in origin. It is in us.

And the success of our creations is not only a function of how novel they are or even how "objectively" valuable but also of the environment into which they are unleashed. How hospitable is the terrain?

These biological principles regularly play out in the real world. What follows is one example, and a story of one of the most popular rock bands of all time.

Parable of a Rock Star

On February 21, 2001, U2 won a GRAMMY for the song "Beautiful Day." The next morning, lead singer Bono and the rock band's iconic guitarist known as Edge walked into a meeting at a Morgan Stanley office in Los Angeles. They'd come to meet a man named Roger McNamee.

McNamee had a knack for understanding how to use the internet, would later help found Facebook, and, at the time, was meeting with U2 bandmates to discuss helping them move business and public service operations online.

"So, congrats on the big win," McNamee recalled he said to Bono and Edge when they came into the room.

Bono's response caught McNamee off guard.

"In the music business, we're pop stars and think we're the center of the universe and think our fans are like moons going around us, and that everything revolves around us," McNamee said Bono told him. "That's all BS."

What Bono said next shows that the same trial and error coupled with great timing that saved bacteria in a petri dish in Switzerland also plays out in creativity, including rock music.

McNamee was really thrown, and Bono could see it.

The popularity of music, Bono explained, "is based on hardware."

"First came hi-fi, and the Beatles owned it, then 78s turned to LPs and stereo and that was Pink Floyd, and then came the car stereo and that's album-rock era. You had to like the whole album," McNamee said Bono told him. You couldn't so easily hop around from song to song. This was U2's era, the rock star asserted. Then "we had a long dry period. That was when the subwoofer came. The sub-woofer! We should'a seen it but the hip-hop guys did and we missed it. This song," Bono said about "Beautiful Day," "is us coming back, and trying to meet the technology where it is."

For those less familiar with the technology, the subwoofer took the emphasis off melody and put it more squarely on the beat.

When Bono made the observation, McNamee said, "[I] literally face-palmed myself."

"That's an amazing insight," McNamee said. "I thought: This guy is really effing smart. He's smart not just about creating music but about really thinking about the world he's operating in."

McNamee is no stranger to creativity. He's a persistent divergent thinker, in a good way; he would become an early investor in Face-book and then turn on the company for the way it became a platform for disinformation. He wrote a bestselling book, *Zucked: Waking Up to the Facebook Catastrophe.*

He's a solid musician himself. He started a band called Moonalice that has performed widely, including with some incredible collabo-rators, including the Grateful Dead. In 2004, three years after they first met, McNamee and Bono teamed up to start a Silicon Valley investment firm.

The point is, McNamee knows creativity, and has lived it—in both the technology and music worlds. But in 2001, when U2 came to meet with him, he'd been so busy with the rise of the dot-com, he said, "I could not have named a U2 song."

There was another good reason that McNamee hadn't heard much about the band in the prior few years. U2 had, in the handful of years before the release of the GRAMMY-winning "Beautiful Day," gone through a dry spell.

"With 'Beautiful Day,' they stuck to their thing, recognizing they were never going to be the guys who dominate subwoofers, but trying to find ways to incorporate what people like about the sound," McNamee said.

And Bono concluded to McNamee: "So at least we weren't killed off."

Were Bono a simple bacterium or virus, and the subwoofer a kind of antibiotic or antiviral drug, the creator had found a way to survive, and thrive.

What does it add up to? Evolution, survival, and a "mindless" form of creativity from lower life-forms offer a few concrete lessons for creators and would-be creators. One lesson is to not underestimate the role of the environment—not in terms of whether a person can be creative (which is very much within reach) but in terms of whether that creativity becomes a Big C. For bacteria studied in flasks, the challenge posed by antibiotics provided a kind of perverse opportunity for the mutations that could survive it. They became ultracreative, Big C's. Bono, at least by his accounting, believed U2 owed its great success not exclusively to the ability of the band but also to the environment in which it found itself.

McNamee, the investment whiz and musician, put it succinctly to me: "I cannot overstate the role of dumb luck."

McNamee is seen as a highly creative technology investor. I've been to his mansion to play music and I can attest that he amassed nearly $1 billion investing in technology companies. But he gives the time and place of his creativity more credit than he gives himself. "My career began on the first day of the bull market in 1982," he said. "I happened to be the person who ran the tech thing at the critical moment."

This is not to say that good timing is all that is at play. The product itself—the mutation or new idea—is essential. But what's more influential than the product itself in determining how well a creation is received into the world is the relationship between the creation and the environment. A creator can control only part of the relationship, just as a microbe is responsible for mutation but not the time and place in which the creative twist occurs.

So that's a view from evolutionary biology, and rock and roll. Another set of key insights come from the world of math and physics, and a big thinker who discovered natural laws that appear to govern innovation.

Enter a Physicist

Long before *Time* magazine named Geoffrey West one of the one hundred most influential people in the world in 2006, he was a curious kid in London riding a domestic roller coaster.

When West was eight years old, his dad came home with a huge stack of money.

"Here, son. Go and take a look at this and count it," West recalled he'd said. "It was like he'd robbed a bank or something."

Not theft, gambling. West's dad was a "professional gambler," which is more or less an oxymoron, since the whole game is rigged for people to lose their wages. West's father bet on horses, dogs, cars, sometimes football (soccer, in the American vernacular). The day he won big seared a memory into West. "But it was in marked contrast to the more usual thing when he would come home having lost a lot of money."

West was very reserved and there was huge tension between his parents. "My mother did not like gambling."

West turned for solace to the precision of math, and the stars. When he was eleven or twelve years old, he recalls, hopped up on a love of math, he read a homework problem that asked: "If you're standing on the top of a high cliff, how far away is the horizon?" And West figured out the formula, which had something to do with the height of the cliff and the radius of the Earth.

"I thought: My God, this is extraordinary," he said. The answer was "encoded in some mystical language about the world around us that is really true, something that corresponds to reality."

His mind reeled.

"I would never have put it this explicitly but effectively: Maybe the whole world is like this."

Maybe the Earth, the universe, life, could be explained by math.

Maybe creativity.

Woven through this book, as you hear stories of great thinkers, I hope a theme emerges: These creators tend to exhibit extraordinary curiosity, humility, an openness to discussion and ideas, romps of conversation, and interests in their own lives that go in different directions. On one level, that might sound obvious. The venerable and now-deceased Stephen Hawking, I heard from one of his closest working companions, showed relentless curiosity.

That was true of West too. We commenced talking and lost track of time as we went back and forth, moving ideas like chess pieces that could be returned to their original places without penalty. His voice rose and fell and rose more with excitement, punctuated with the occasional f-bomb, not used in any profane sense but only to express the profound shock he'd experienced at discovery.

West left his dysfunctional home for college, became a theoretical physicist, studied quarks and string theory and dark matter. But he's prone to letting the world open up to him, as creators do, and his authentic interest turned to a different question: How does life work? Was there math to explain the underlying laws of creation?

"I migrated unwittingly from fundamental physics to biology," he said, sounding a bit surprised himself by the transformation. He'd moved by that point from Cambridge to Stanford. "Was there a way of showing that all organisms are actually manifestations of the same kind of underlying mathematics?"

Questions like:

- **WHY IS** it you're going to be dead within fifty or one hundred years? "Where the fuck does one hundred years come from?" he said to me with a kind of awe.
- **WHY SLEEP** for eight hours a night?
- **WHY ARE** some cities more creative than others?

"One of the hardest things is: What is the question? Creating the right question is often a large part of the problem," West told me.

One key question that West focused on has to do with the common math that connects all forms of life. Is there a math formula, and what is it? West, trying to answer this question, made a huge discovery: As life-forms get larger, they use energy more efficiently and at a rate that is consistent across organisms. To put this another way, the bigger an organism is, "the less energy is needed per cell or gram of tissue" for it to survive.

In other words, a mouse requires far more energy per cell to survive than does a dog, and a dog needs much more per cell than an elephant. The formula shows that when you double the size of an organism, it needs 75 percent less energy per cell.

"It doesn't matter how much the size, you double anything, you need just 75 percent more," he said. "There is extraordinary regularity in what seems like a totally random system. And what's more extraordinary is that it's not true of just mammals; it's true of all animals and all plants, all insects and all fish. They follow the same law. And here's what's even more amazing: That's just the metabolic rate; anything you measure about animals has the same scaling characteristics."

How big the heart needs to be, or the kidneys and how their system works to flush toxins from the body. All of it governed by scaling formulas that West developed and that a piece in *The New York Times Magazine* in 2010 called "one of the most contentious and influential papers in modern biology."

Some critics found flaws. Like in the crayfish; it didn't seem to follow the same rules. Big deal, West said; every rule has exceptions. Looking for the flaws, he told the magazine reporter: "That's not science. That's just taking notes."

West makes a key point, at least when it comes to creativity. If people wait to be perfect, exactly 100 percent right, they will never venture.

So I repeat one of the most fundamental laws of innovation:

PERFECTIONISM IS PUBLIC ENEMY #1 OF CREATIVITY.

West got tired of arguing about the core truth of his work, and whether there might be an exception for bottom-feeders (the critics, the crustaceans, or both) and he turned to a new challenge: the math behind cities. That's how he and his peers discovered their own law of creativity.

He looked at cities as he did organisms. What did they consume, and produce? He and another pioneering researcher, a theoretical physicist named Luís Bettencourt, found more compelling math. They found that when cities get bigger, just like biological organisms, they need less infrastructure per person—and these greater efficiencies have a linear progression. The key figure is 15 percent.

If a city doubles in size—if it goes up 100 percent in population—it requires only 85 percent increase in the sewage infrastructure, for example, or 85 percent more of the gas stations or grocery stores to support this growing number of people. West says this is true of any city, anywhere in the world, when it doubles. There is a magic number.

There is a crucial corollary. When you double the size of a city, the amount of what that city produces goes up by a factor of 115 percent. Pollution, crime, economic output—all of it goes up by 115 percent.

To put that another way: Each person in a city that has doubled is 15 percent more productive than a person living in a city half the size. Why might this be? People are around each other, sharing resources, pooling physical and intellectual capital, experiencing the proverbial and literal economies of scale.

And it turns out this goes for ideas too.

Creativity follows the mathematical models of biology and municipality. You double a city and the number of patents go up by 115 percent. It's as if each person has 15 percent more ideas than if living in a city half the size.

"The underlying mechanism of that is that in bigger cities you have more people, obviously," West told me. "Therefore, you have possibility and actuality of more interactions per unit time. It is the exchange of information, ideas, whatever in those social networks, giving rise to all socioeconomic activity."

He pointed out that the density brings not just volume of people but breadth of ideas. The people who walk the streets muttering to themselves, the mentally ill, "these outliers—the homeless—they provide and expand the boundary," he said. "They provide an ambience and atmosphere, a culture where anything can happen."

This just makes so much sense. You have more people and they bump into each other and they start discussing ideas, and those ideas compete and are refined and there are more aha moments. And, boom, you have, in various periods, Silicon Valley, Florence, Jerusalem, Manhattan, Babylon, Detroit, Berlin, Paris, Amsterdam, Moscow, Melbourne, and on and on.

"It's no accident that all great ideas and all innovations take place in an urban environment," West said. "It's a rare occurrence that you have the Newton phenomenon."

Newton phenomenon?

It was the summer of 1665 (who can forget it?), and the bubonic plague swept London. Isaac Newton left Trinity College in Cambridge for the countryside. There, at age twenty-three, he built the foundations of calculus and, one of the great Big C's of all time, the theory of universal gravity, illustrated by the legend of the apple falling on his head from a tree. (Hey, sometimes great discoveries happen in the suburbs!)

Newton himself, though, traced the concept to connections made by others, and he is credited for putting into English an epigram that preceded him, when he said: "If I have seen further, it is by standing on the shoulders of Giants."

Bacteria do something similar, remarkably enough. I learned about it in the year before COVID-19 hit. The story has much to say about West's insights, but also about how the world might be changing too.

In 2019, the *New York Times* published a series of stories on drug-resistant infections. My job was to lead the reporting and writing about it, along with a colleague. Our first story was about a terrible fungus called *Candida auris*. The fungus has evolved to evade antifungal medications. It is spreading throughout the globe.

For a long time, it had been thought that the way microbes develop defenses to drugs, like antifungals, was through the laborious math of random mutation.

But what researchers have discovered recently is that these powerful defenses against fungal medications can happen in a way that is different from evolution. It can happen when one fungus passes the defense tools to another fungus that doesn't have them. This is called "horizontal gene transfer." It is a form of cooperation. It happens, in essence, when a fungus that is in trouble calls out for help and a fungus that has already evolved or obtained defenses passes them over.

This happens when the fungi are in close proximity to each other. They are, in effect, touching, and the molecules pass between them.

This leads to a direct analogy to the way humans, living in denser conditions, share the underlying ideas that lead to a shared platform for further innovation.

But that very series of developments also shows how human beings might be evolving beyond the need for such proximity.

I, and my fellow reporters and a *New York Times* video crew, were distributed around the country. We traveled for the story about *Candida auris*, and I spoke to experts by phone and internet audio from all over the world—Russia and Britain, China, Brazil, Spain, South Africa and Malawi, Canada, Israel—and to researchers all over the United States.

The stories in our series were read by people across the globe. The accompanying video, which was nominated for two Emmys, was among the most watched of the year, with more than one million views. It was shot in part in my living room by two producers who lived in New York and then one of them moved overseas.

Our ability to cooperate using technology almost entirely eliminated the physical space between us, and the ability to share the information across the globe led to public policy change—such as efforts to protect against drug-resistant infection—in places around the world we'd never visited and likely never will.

We did not have to rub shoulders like microbes doing horizontal gene transfer. This was knowledge transfer over great distance.

"The internet in some senses frees us from space," West said. That was true earlier of the telephone and the railroad.

"This," West said, "speeds it up."

Know this: the noise of the world can make it hard for a creator to hear their authentic voice. But a major driver of that noise is technology that lets us connect, work together, learn about ideas. The power of technology, harnessed, can be electrifying.

Real-world examples abound, and they help to illuminate a changing world when it comes to geography and proximity, and some of the underlying math of creativity.

The story of Justin Sandercoe is very much the story of how a creator (and his own authentic muse) forged a new path using technology.

A Funny Thing Happened on the Way to a Platinum Record

(PARABLE OF A ROCK STAR, PART II)

Sandercoe sat in the backyard garden of his London flat in midsummer 2012. He lazily took in the sun, his brain in the off position—or so it seemed. The guitar teacher had made a ritual of clearing his mind, letting it go blank, for rest and recharge, particularly since his website had become such an unexpected hit.

Thousands tuned in each month now to take free guitar lessons from JustinGuitar.com. Empathic and unassuming, Sandercoe has a particularly clear way of expressing basic concepts. He sits in front of the camera, often with a cap on his head, encouraging, nurturing, pushing along hobbyists, would-be rockers, a far-flung student group clicking in by the hour and from around the globe.

What a change from when he was a kid, isolated on the island of Tasmania. Born in 1974, he fell in love with guitar at the age of six. He learned not from the internet, of course, which didn't exist at the time, but from records and the radio, piecing together his tutorials without the extraordinary wellspring provided by computers. Today, an aspiring guitarist in the most remote island nation, has access to the world's library of teaching tools, plus teachers themselves, connections, and an outlet to be heard by fans, or potential fans.

As Sandercoe taught, he continued to pursue his passion of writing and recording music, though not gaining any particular notoriety. He created for himself, a band, self-published. Not a bad life, a working man making a decent living, builder of his own creative lifestyle.

Then, sunbathing that summer afternoon in 2012, the three words struck him.

Turn to Tell.

These words came without warning, expectation, or effort. Justin had not been trying to write a song. He sprung from his chair.

Turn to Tell.

These were lyrics, he was sure, and they held meaning. Justin ran into the house, looking for a pen or pencil, a piece of paper. Words poured out.

> *I turn to tell her things*
> *I still make tea for two*
> *I keep the kitchen clean*
> *The way she'd want me to*

Then came the sounds. "The melody appeared in my head." He scrambled to find a guitar. "I couldn't find one," he told me. "The first thing I saw was a bass—in the bedroom—so I composed on that."

The frantic process lasted less than an hour. It had come from nowhere, it seemed—"sunbathing in my backyard with no thoughts of writing music at all," Sandercoe told me.

Not long after Sandercoe recorded it, he shared his song with one of his students. The name Katie Melua may mean something to some readers. She's a sensation, particularly in Britain. In 2006, she'd become one of England's bestselling artists. She took music lessons from Justin. She and her music team heard "Turn to Tell." They loved it. She recorded it. Sandercoe would have a song on her new record, which turned into a platinum album.

Not long afterward, Justin's phone rang. The caller introduced himself—a name Justin recognized, as anyone in the world of music might. "In my fantasies," Sandercoe said, "it was the one person I'd most hoped to hear from." The caller was the head of Sony Publishing in the UK.

"I heard that song you wrote for Katie," the record executive said. "I want to offer you a record deal. Can you come and have a talk with me?"

"I was over the moon. " Justin said he thought, "I've won the lottery ticket. This is the whole thing."

Some days later, Sandercoe sat in the office of the industry giant and played his songs. All the inspirations from all the years, the songs he'd willed and the ones that had come more easily, none, though, quite as mysteriously as "Turn to Tell." The executive listened and took in the collection. He leaned in.

"They're okay," the executive said. "Do you have any more like the other one?"

Did Justin have more like the one that became a hit? He did not, at least according to the record executive on that day.

"That was more or less the end of that," Justin told me. "That was the end of that particular story."

But it was only the beginning of Sandercoe's story.

The Parable of Justin is about what happened after that meeting.

Nowadays, he teaches some thirty thousand students a month. His lessons remain free. He takes donations. He makes a good living, and has renown—as a world-class guitar instructor—the world over. A columnist for the *Independent,* a newspaper in Britain, called him "one of the most influential teachers in guitar history."

A Funny Thing Happened to Justin on the Way to His Platinum Record: He created a thriving, innovative, inspiring venture, supported a creative lifestyle, and got a song performed by a chart-topping artist. What Sandercoe has created is not the rock star life that some might idealize as the pinnacle of musical creation, although there has been some notoriety mixed in. It's bigger than that. He's shaped an entire life around creativity, and brought it to the masses.

His story again reinforces the idea that creativity is not someone else's idea of what a creative life looks like—or what a creative product should be. The best one-paragraph story I heard on that subject came from a close family friend. He was in law school years ago and he wondered if he was creative. So he bought an easel and a set of paints and went into his backyard and started painting. After a couple of hours he thought: This is so stupid. I hate this. I'm not creative.

He threw out the paints and easel and never looked back.

He went on to make tens of millions of dollars in real estate, maybe $100 million. He did so through a totally different kind of creativity, though he maintains to this day that he isn't creative, because his creative take on real estate transactions doesn't fit how some people view creativity.

And Sandercoe thought creativity was a platinum album, when instead it was becoming a beloved, deeply satisfied, and highly creative stay-at-home guitar teacher.

But there's a more pointed reason I tell Sandercoe's story. It has to do less with the age of a creator and more with the age we find ourselves in. We live in Jerusalem no longer.

This book started in Jerusalem, one of the early examples in human history of how a close-knit, relatively highly populated place became an idea machine. It was an innovation town, and its major product line was religion. Ideas emerged and were refined like so many people standing on stones and preaching. The people spoke, listened, refined, shared, and created some of the most lasting ideas this world has ever generated.

The world since saw communities like these emerge, congregations of the curious, in Florence, Russia, Paris, Chinese dynasties and ancient, enduring medical techniques, and on and on. The research from the Santa Fe Institute proves that the density of population directly correlates with new ideas. More people, with more spices in their individual spice racks of emotion and experience, mixing together, sharing and learning recipes, building and creating.

Then along came the internet. It is effectively a quantum change in the way ideas get expressed, shared, heard, viewed. The value of physical proximity has become far less significant in the way we collaborate.

The numbers of patents given to collaborators across borders have soared.

Some 142,932 were applied for in 2018, a figure that rose from 99,000 in 1999. No wonder.

People are collaborating across borders, building new ideas, developing in one place, manufacturing in another. Yes, much of the innovation still happens in some centers, but the possibilities have soared for creation at a distance.

My children became huge fans of an internet sensation named Charli D'Amelio. She reached one hundred million followers on TikTok by the age of sixteen. She dances, adding her personality and authenticity to short and charismatic performances. Some people might not perceive of this as particularly creative, but she put herself into the world, took a risk, and influenced people to make their own creations. Her astronomical reach from her own home made a mockery of the geographic limitations of old.

This reality became all the more palpable during the COVID-19 pandemic. Not only did people begin working from home—and not in collective offices—they were required to do so. Then some began to move altogether away from the towns where their offices were located. They moved nearer to extended family, or to regions of the country or world where they felt more comfortable, more at ease, more authentic.

One of the greatest exoduses from any city was from San Francisco. Rents plummeted as young techies—once tied to the region by the demands of employers—went looking for more comfortable, less expensive confines. The world was, to borrow a wonky word, "decentralizing." Creativity decentralized with it.

The *New York Times*, which once had told me that I would be fired if I didn't move back to New York, encouraged employees to make sure they found comfortable and safe places to live. It encouraged people to be all over the country and the world in order to find the inputs that would yield the most creative and powerful stories.

This was the New Jerusalem. Everyplace.

In this analogy, the whole world now is the New Israel. Israel means wrestling with God, or creation. It can be done from everyplace.

Geoffrey West, the big thinker I introduced a chapter ago, offers some reason for doubt about a side-effect of creativity from technology and the rapid pace of change it has introduced. He calls the problem "a speeding up of time."

"You know it in your own life. Life has speeded up, there's no question. So you have to innovate faster and faster," he said. "This is not a sustainable system. The system is going to collapse."

Greater social networks leading to greater innovation and then developments with side effects that require even greater innovation, paces of change that we herald but that threaten to break us.

"At some stage, we won't be able to adapt fast enough to the changes driven by this extraordinary process driven by social network," he said.

This is a staggering tension—between the problems that grow from a connected world and the creations that solve the problems and create new challenges.

I offered West a competing vision, however. I see reason for hope. Two reasons, actually.

The first reason has to do with you, me, each of us, a world of individuals who possess an untapped resource. Specifically, we have vast unmined creative forces that will come not from networking but from using the skill sets to create so many of us have kept at arm's length. Creativity is a function of social networking, sure, but it is hugely a product of individual power built upon the lucid, quieted mind, the one that I'm humbly promising is inside of you already.

There's more to that idea.

When I look at our world, I can't help but feel this very notion at play as we, collectively, take in all the news and information the internet throws at us, then spit out our own versions—creating a cacophony. What this adds up to is a formidable amount of external focus. What did that CNN host say? What did that Fox host say? What did the president say? What did the majority leader say? What did my neighbor say?

I am so ticked off! I will tweet, post, cajole, insult, take my own energy and put it into the supercollider, spinning up the chaos.

This can be anathema to creativity. That's because creativity would have us listen to ourselves, our own muses, not the external voices. What if you could become more creative while also quieting the pace of the world—simply by turning down the volume on the outside?

What if we have contributed to entropy by failing to take advantage of the one most essential resource at our fingertips: the exquisite divine silence of creativity?

I proposed this to West and he gave me a solid hearing. And I gained a bit more of his attention with the second reason for hope. It has to do with leadership.

Over time, over the years, leaders have arisen. Men and women with Great Big C ideas, huge vision, courage—Martin Luther King, Jr., or Martin Luther—you'll hear about him shortly—Winston Churchill, Mother Theresa, Indira Gandhi.

My wholehearted belief is that the chaos will be reinterpreted at some point, by some great new leader, who will reframe the way we see the world.

Yes, yes, West said.

"The great innovation we need is a leader," he said. "The big unknown, the huge unknown" is if and when. But, he said, "It's happened a number of times in human history."

A Big C is coming.

It is almost inevitable, based on history.

And now a word from God.

God

The story of creativity and religion starts in the Middle Ages. It is considered politically incorrect to call them the Dark Ages, suggesting that the world was culturally backward. But life could be dark.

"No arts; no letters; no society; and, which is worst of all, continual fear," Thomas Hobbes, the philosopher, later wrote about the lot of man. "And danger of violent death: and the life of man, solitary, poor, nasty, brutish, and short."

Get born, maybe survive childbirth (which might not be survived by your mother), live in poverty, hope to live long enough to die of the black plague. A period of great disarray and chaos that makes the COVID-19 outbreak look like Disneyland on a balmy weekday without too many crowds and with a fast pass.

The world remained chaotic and bleak, but the rise of the Holy Roman Empire—where the church held sway—created some structure.

"The Roman Catholic Church is the only thing holding things together," said Scott Cormode. He's a professor of leadership at Fuller Seminary, one of the world's most highly regarded learning institutions for ministers. Cormode is obsessed with creativity and leadership—and for what turns someone into Martin Luther, Martin Luther King, Jr., Moses, Jesus, Confucius, Mohammed, or a person whose ideas warp the way we look at the world into a new way of seeing things. These are people who create the product of a new reality.

He really likes to talk about it.

"You're in trouble. You just asked a professor to speak about something he just wrote a book about—innovation in the church," he said. "This is not going to go well for you. I'm going to go on and on."

He sounded just like a creator. He's developed a model for understanding creative leadership that links the Reformation to the personal computer and Silicon Valley.

This chapter is about how religious thinking has influenced human creativity.

Before elaborating, I feel duty bound to share my bias about religion.

I am an agnostic. I do not know if there is a God. I accept that I sorely lack the wisdom to understand our origins. Who can say what is out there? When I told this to Richard Dawkins, who is vehemently atheistic, he expressed a touch of frustration with me because he said that I must at least accept also that there is no more evidence for the presence of a God then there is for, say, a giant teapot pouring us into existence. On this point, I concede: I've not been presented with convincing evidence of the presence of one God, or many gods—as millions of people believe in different cultures.

For now, know this: It is also beyond dispute that major religions define the human experience, and their texts are among the most influential creations. Their leaders are titans of creativity, and so the issue for me is what they teach us about how to think about innovation, not faith. This section endorses no particular religion or belief system. I hope you'll read it with an open mind. Whether you believe in God or not, Cormode offers a powerful construct for seeing the creative process behind some of most powerful ideas in the history of human existence

What follows is the perspective of a theologian on creativity.

———

So, back to the Reformation—one of the great product innovations of all time.

Prior to that point, Judaism had emerged, let's say, around 2000 B.C., Hinduism about five hundred years later, Confucianism a thousand years after that, followed shortly by Buddhism; in the Middle East and Europe, Judaism is fractured by a variety of forces, most seismically by the birth of Jesus, who some people see as the Son of God, which gives rise to Christianity, which gets fractured by a variety of forces but becomes dominated by the Roman Catholic Church, an Anglican ideal spread across the western part of the world.

As I noted, during this early modern period in Europe and the West, the Roman Catholic Church provided glue, a source of continuity amid the chaos. "All-powerful" is how multiple historical texts describe the church in and around 1500. The law of the land. "The Holy Roman Empire."

Holy and also corrupt. This is not heresy; just fact. "The corruption of the church was well known and several attempts had been made to reform the church," reads a history from the Khan Academy, which I mention both to give credit where it is due and also as another periodic aside to point out a further example of the network effect that provides so many resources for learning and creativity across the globe. At one point, the history notes, three popes ruled simultaneously, reflecting inner power struggles. "Popes and cardinals often lived more like kings than spiritual leaders."

The issue really hit home for people around an idea called "indulgences." This was a teaching of the church that allowed people to receive less punishment for their sins by doing charitable and other good acts. But the system became highly corrupted. Church leaders basically doled out forgiveness to people who gave land or money to the institution. Indulgences meant "You got to heaven more quickly," the Khan Academy history puts it simply.

"Then along comes the Renaissance," Cormode said. This is the transition into the fifteenth and sixteenth centuries, when the Middle Ages begat what historians call the beginning of modernity.

Leonardo da Vinci, Michelangelo, a storyteller by the name of William Shakespeare, Galileo, and Johannes Gutenberg, who gave us the printing press, which was the internet before the internet— spreading information with a speed previously unthinkable. New ideas, producing new ideas, mutations forming and spreading and finding ecological niches.

Wasn't the Renaissance a secular phenomenon? It wasn't really bound by a particular field—religion, astronomy, art. It was a period, not unlike this modern one, when the pace of ideas and creative energy took flight and spread and spread. As I've already discussed, creativity can be infectious, and it had become so during the Renaissance, mutations colliding and combining.

When it came to the church, the circumstances had been primed for innovation with an existing product that had spawned widespread dissatisfaction. At that moment in time, the church was not user-friendly. The papacy might have been working for some, and doing some wonderful things, but not for all. Most important, people felt the corruption in their bones, their souls—why did the rich and connected get to heaven before the commoner?

If you think of religion as a product, this one was not meeting consumer demand.

Enter a monk named Martin Luther.

Luther was deeply dissatisfied by the indulgences and felt that same dissatisfaction among other people. But if he wanted to remake the product, he had a major problem on his hands. He had to overhaul the religious experience without appearing to overhaul the religion itself.

It's hard to overstate the significance of this challenge or how commonplace this kind of challenge is in the history of creative leadership. Luther had to come up with a new idea that would be palatable to the masses (who believed in the Bible as a sacred text, and Christianity as essential to their eternal souls) while making fundamental change.

"We are happily and inextricably tied to the past. So what does innovation look like?" Cormode asked. When people talk about Big C creativity, Cormode said, "they talk about burning the boat and that the best way to innovate into the future is to abandon the past."

Martin Luther did not have that luxury.

"Our credibility is built on the fact that we're never going to stop talking about Jesus and the Bible," Cormode said.

So Martin Luther pulled off an extraordinary act of creativity in leadership. He re-created the past.

The version of Christianity that Martin Luther and his peers were born into revolved around the power of priests. They were believed to be intermediaries between God and human beings. The church, and the priests, interpreted the Bible.

The Bible was the Word of God, a holy text, unassailable.

Martin Luther, as a Christian, couldn't attack the Bible.

But his great insight was that he could attack how the Bible had been interpreted. God can't be flawed, of course, but human beings can misunderstand what God meant. To pull the priests out of the picture—to undermine their power base—he had to prove that they misunderstood the Bible.

Martin Luther's creative inspiration is that the Bible is absolutely correct and that the church had gotten it wrong. The interpretation has been mistaken all along.

The essence of his revision comes from a passage in the Letter to the Romans.

The passage reads: "There is no distinction: for all have sinned and fall short of the glory of God, and are justified by his grace as a gift, through the redemption that is in Christ Jesus."

Martin Luther anchored his re-reading of this passage to mean that human beings are redeemed by "his grace as gift." It's a freebie from Jesus Christ. No priest needed!

"It's the key insight that will trigger the reformation," Cormode said. "It's by faith alone and it doesn't require a priest to do it. It's a free gift from God."

That doesn't sound so profound, looking back. That seems as reasonable a way to read the text as any other.

"You know," Cormode said, "it's one of those moments when somebody says something and you realize nobody thought of it that way."

Martin Luther reformed the Christian religion by giving it a new story.

What he created was one of the world's most embraced products—a reformed version of religion that was much more palatable to many people than the prior version.

There are analogues in many religions. Think about what happened when Jesus came along in the first place. He was a Jew but Judaism, as a product design, had some real challenges for its consumers. The Old Testament, the user manual for Judaism, tells Jews that they are the Chosen People but that they must follow a very clear set of rules in order for God to return to Earth. It's an idea that means that only some people on Earth get to be included (the Chosen People) but also that they are Chosen only if they can very closely follow a set of difficult rules.

The innovation of Jesus doesn't scrap these ideas—he couldn't just toss away the foundation—but he offered a powerful new product: himself. He said that the rules in the Old Testament were too hard to follow because human beings were never able to be that perfect to begin with. In other words, he reconceptualized the old interpretation of religion by defining "Original Sin." He didn't create a new idea from whole cloth; he stitched it from highly accepted material. In fact, the account of the original sin he refers to—the man and woman in the garden eating the fruit from the tree of the knowledge of good and evil—appears just pages into the Bible, in chapter three of Genesis (and the chapters of the book are short!).

Then Jesus offered a powerful plot twist based on the Old Testament witness: His death allowed people to be Chosen whether or not they could follow every rule of the Old Testament. They just have to believe in him. Oh, and there's more to this new product: It is available to everyone, not just the Chosen People.

This, arguably, is among the single greatest Big C concepts in the history of the world. I mean, you could make a case for the wheel, or agriculture, domestication of animals, vaccines, sewage treatment, any of these, as the most seminal, but the innovation of the enduring religions, whether or not *you* believe in one, undeniably has become the lens through which billions of people see reality.

There is a main point to drive home in this chapter. It is about what religion and theology tell us about the essential nature of creativity: It is often extremely effective when it connects the past to the present and helps guide the future. The most powerful new ideas don't necessarily break the mold. Creativity often happens within confines. Consider Joseph Smith, who introduced the world to Mormonism and was a man of extraordinary creativity.

The legend tells that, walking in the woods early in the 1800s, Smith had an audience with God and Jesus Christ, and "the Savior told him to join none of the churches then in existence because they were teaching incorrect doctrines," according to the official biography of the Church of Jesus Christ of Latter Day Saints, the religion that Smith would go on to establish. The period in which Smith found himself was fecund for religious ideas, a new land with a relatively open view of religious freedom that not only allowed for new concepts to emerge but also, through tough competition and widespread discussion, helped refine ideas to their most desirable iterations.

"As more and more Americans migrated to the open lands on the western frontiers of the country, various denominations competed for converts. The period was marked by a resurgence of religious conversion, perhaps best illustrated by camp meetings, with their fiery sermons and displays of spiritual fervor," the collection of papers recounts. "Methodist circuit-riding preachers and Baptist ministers took their populist message to the people in remote regions, and both movements saw enormous growth. Other denominations, including Presbyterianism, worked to keep up. Into this religious "war of words," as he later called it, stepped fourteen-year-old Joseph Smith.

But Smith, like Martin Luther, might well have failed if he had broken altogether with long-standing beliefs. He needed to be sufficiently consistent with the existing creation so as not to lose adherents, while also proving new enough to gather others.

He said he found the answer buried on a hill near Palmyra, New York. Directed there by an angel, Smith purportedly found gold plates engraved in ancient Egyptian that were lost scripture, the eventual Book of Mormon, equal in its authority to the Old and New Testaments. This was what Smith used to establish the Church of Jesus Christ of Latter Day Saints. The ideas that Smith created were particularly alluring for American pilgrims facing an open, hostile expanse and so many choices. Smith offered them stability and simplicity.

"It sought to cut through the confusing welter of warring sects and denominations and restore the simplicity of the early church by resting itself on a few clearly revealed, authoritative truths," according to a history written by Donald Scott, a former Dean of Social Science and Professor of History at Queens College/City University of New York. He continued about Mormonism: "Above all, it provided desperately desired structure for lives beset by unpredictability, disorder, and change. It gave its adherents enormous social, psychological, and economic support."

Religion offers many examples of Small C's that seek to rewrite rules to accommodate discomfort and to disconnect with changing conditions. Witness the Kosher smartphone.

Orthodox Jews have wrestled with the implications of the popularity of the cell phone. On one hand, it is virtually impossible these days to function in the modern economy, or to communicate, without one of these devices. It also has functions the Rabbis consider wholly objectionable, like an internet browser, which might supply distracting or heretical information from the outside world.

Their Small C innovation is called a Kosher smartphone. I kid you not. This device is a regular smartphone stripped of many of its functions. It is a largely app-less gadget that provides basic modern conveniences. Ideas like the Kosher phone allow for the embrace of the new without abandoning strictures of the faith.

"One of the biggest problems is when we feel trapped between two poles—you have to choose between A and B," Cormode said. "Then leaders come along and say you can have A and B."

Or, in another Small C example, Orthodox Jews grappled with a rule that tells them not to do manual work on the Sabbath—not to "carry" or use their hands. So how were they to turn on the lights on Saturday morning? The rabbinical interpretation was to allow the use of lights that turn on and off automatically. The rabbis also allow toilet paper to be pre-ripped on the day before Sabbath so that people can use the restroom.

These are Small C inspirations that allow religion to maintain a certain consistency—one that its adherents find acceptable.

You can see all kinds of other examples in the Judeo-Christian religions (and in modern versions of Islam)—the reformed version of these religions—in which new interpretations run afoul of the older teachings.

For people who are not religious, these prior passages about creativity connect to life in a very powerful way. The type of creativity the passages describe touches virtually everyone in a constitutional democracy, and in the interpretation of law governing hundreds of millions of people in the world.

On March 4 of 1801, Thomas Jefferson took the oath of office and became president of the United States. He'd defeated an archrival, John Adams. It had been a brutal, ugly, nasty campaign, the kind that we tend to think of as modern and media-sparked, but this one took its place in the history books for good reason.

Prior to Jefferson's taking over as president, Adams had signed the Judiciary Act of 1801, a law passed by Congress that gave expanded authority to the president to appoint judges. Adams delighted in this law because he used its powers to try to stack the courts with like-minded thinkers before he left office.

One of the newly appointed was William Marbury, who was to be seated as justice of the peace in the District of Columbia. He needed only to go through the process, which entailed having the secretary of state deliver his appointment to the Senate for confirmation.

Ah, but there was a complication.

After Jefferson took office, his new secretary of state, James Madison, didn't want to deliver the appointment to the Senate. Why would he? This would be like one modern president naming Clarence Thomas and an incoming one preferring Ruth Bader Ginsburg, or the other way around.

Marbury, the man who would be judge, sued, demanding the appointment he'd been given by Adams prior to Jefferson's taking office.

The problem for the United States Supreme Court here is hard to overstate and was much more significant than the dispute itself: The case held the possibility of bringing down the court. Why? Because if the court found exclusively for Jefferson or for Adams, the whole institution might have been seen as illegitimate, a raw political tool. To stay relevant, the court needed a creative stroke of genius, and it got one.

The chief justice at the time was John Marshall. "Marshall's great talent was his legal creativity, which takes hard work for a layperson or lawyer to appreciate," wrote Garrett Epps, a modern-day Supreme Court reporter for *The Atlantic*.

"If the Supreme Court ruled against Marbury, it would be admitting that Jefferson's partisan purge was lawful. If it ruled against Jefferson, the new president would gleefully tear up the (appointment) order. There was no clear law that gave the court the power to issue orders to the president, and Marshall had no means of enforcing such an order. The Jeffersonian Congress could accuse Marshall of overreaching—and impeach him," Epps wrote.

"But the chief justice proved too wily for Jefferson and Congress."

Epic creativity ensued in what many have been called the single most important ruling in US constitutional law.

Marshall found for everybody—not just for supporters of the Adams camp or supporters of the Jefferson camp but also for a camp people didn't fully grasp had a stake: the Supreme Court itself.

Marshall wrote in his opinion that, in fact, Jefferson did not have the right to take away Marbury's position. This was Marbury's livelihood, his job, and depriving him of it was the same as tyranny. This made the Adams camp happy.

Marshall also wrote, though, that the Supreme Court was not technically the place where the dispute needed to be settled, and that the court lacked the Congressional authority to force Jefferson to make Marbury a judge. This made the Jefferson camp sufficiently satisfied that there was no partisan bias in the Supreme Court.

More than any of that, though, Marshall cemented the role of the court in the United States in the most creative and backhanded fashion: It looked like he was saying that the court had limited authority but, in the same breath, he was also saying that the court had the authority to review these cases. He had created one of the most important concepts in all of law: "judicial review."

Marshall had found a way out of a bind that appeared to force him to choose between A and B. He created a new story. And that story gave the Supreme Court the power to choose thereafter between A and B over and over and over again.

All of the examples I cite here capture the remarkable intersection of creativity and conformity, Big C innovations that nonetheless seem close enough to their creators and adherents to appeal to a sense of familiarity.

This type of thinking—the familiar and the new, drawn from jurisprudence and theology—show the slow, plodding progress in American race relations. On the cusp of a new challenge, we had been there before.

The story starts just shortly after Abraham Lincoln, creative to his core in convincing a racist and entrenched federal government to change, led the nation through a Civil War that was followed after his death by the adoption, in 1868, of the Fourteenth Amendment to the US Constitution. This legislation ended slavery. But African Americans, while not in chains (mostly), were not free or treated equally by any stretch.

Consider so-called Jim Crow laws, largely in the south, that mandated segregation of the races. In 1892, an African American man, Homer Plessy, was arrested after he would not give his seat on a train in New Orleans to a white man. His defense went all the way to the Supreme Court based on the "equal protection law," written into the Fourteenth Amendment that gives all citizens equal protection under the law.

In 1896, Plessy's case made it to the Supreme Court, which demonstrated how far the United States had yet to go by ruling 8-1 against the African American. The language of the opinion boggles the mind but the reason for including it here is to explain the creative thinking that had to follow. The court wrote that the Fourteenth Amendment was meant to enforce the "equality of the two races before the law, but in the nature of things it could not have been intended to abolish distinctions based on color, or to endorse social, as distinguished from political, equality," and it went on: "If one race be inferior to the other socially, the Constitution of the United States cannot put them upon the same plane."

This grotesque ruling, nearly unanimous with only one dissent, made glaring the system of racism that would echo until the present, but also set the stage for the creativity to follow. How would a nation of laws and precedent create its way out of so heinous a principle?

Then came a series of Supreme Court decisions, each built upon the same kind of creative pattern of thinking that pervades creativity in religious thought: The new ideas were built around a reframing of the past so that it would permit progress.

In 1933, a pioneering lawyer named Thurgood Marshall, grandson of a slave, decided to challenge the practice by the University of Maryland Law School of rejecting Black applicants who were as well-qualified academically, or more qualified, than white applicants who were accepted to the law school. Marshall's creative argument didn't directly challenge the idea of "separate but equal." After all, the Plessy case had essentially given an outright embrace of the idea that two races could be separated for political or social reasons as long as treatment was equal. It's that last part that Marshall attacked. He said that "Black" law schools his client could attend were grossly inferior to the University of Maryland, and therefore they were not "equal" at all. Marshall and his client won in federal appeals court in 1936 and the client ultimately graduated from the University of Maryland Law School.

Another baby step, using related creativity, came two years later. In 1938, the US Supreme Court ruled that a Black man could attend the University of Missouri Law School because there was no Black law school in the state. This wasn't sweeping away systemic racism in any meaningful way—not even remotely. This was not within a million miles of being enough. It was instead making a racist system comfortable by creating a future that didn't diverge so quickly from the past as to make the new ideas wholly unpalatable to a nation with yet so many bigots.

In 1950, Marshall used a similar argument to secure a victory over the University of Texas Law School. The Supreme Court agreed unanimously: the systems of legal education were separate but not equal. Simultaneously, the Supreme Court ruled in another case that an African American man who had been admitted to a doctoral program at the University of Oklahoma was made to sit apart from his white peers and to eat at a separate lunch table, and these restrictions made it impossible for the man to learn equally.

Then came the big daddy.

Brown v. Board of Education. A complex consolidation of multiple cases, the case—with Marshall arguing on behalf of Brown—involved whether public schools could continue segregating Black and white children. The court initially was divided. Amazing, right? Less than seventy-five years ago, and the decision wasn't clear-cut. Then one of the justices died, replaced by Chief Justice Earl Warren. In 1954, he revisited the decision. Separate education systems, he concluded, were inherently unequal. Marshall's creative thinking was built on the ideas of a pantheon of scholars. Years of one Small C attack after another on a racist system culminated in a Gigantic C.

All of it came through the kind of creativity that jurisprudence has in common with that of religion: convergent thinking with the past, to bring along those tied to precedent for whatever reason, and enough divergent thinking to create a future more in keeping with how the modern world works.

This sounds like the stuff of mere social policy or the creativity of new ideas.

In point of fact, this very balancing act provides the foundation for many creations in every field, including the biological ones, and developments that are not at all for the benefit of society, as were those of Marshall.

There is a coda to this chapter. It contains several paragraphs I suspect could elicit the most contentious response to anything I write in these pages. A new study suggests that deeply religious people are less likely to be creative than people who aren't devoted to a monotheistic God.

Wait! Before you start screaming at me things like "what about the Sistine Chapel!" (along with everything you just wrote in this chapter about religion and creativity), I think it's worth considering the implications of this fascinating new study.

It was co-authored by Jack Goncalo, the highly imaginative thinker about creativity I wrote about earlier and who illuminated how people can associate creativity with vomit. That core notion—that creativity is scary—is relevant to a new study he and two fellow scientists did about the impact of strong religious belief on creativity. Their paper, which was peer-reviewed and published in 2021, used multiple measures to explore this idea. For instance, they found that in states where more people express strong religious beliefs there has been lower patent output than in states with a less religious population. The study has many potential limitations, the authors acknowledge, given all the factors that go into the development of new ideas that lead to patents. However, they also accounted for many of those factors, like income and education levels.

That was just one of six studies they did. Others looked more at the individual level. For instance, several studies asked subjects about their religious beliefs or even had them think about the God they believe in, and then asked them to undertake tests that measure creativity. Such tests explore how many ideas a subject can come up with that relates to a particular word or concept—or, in other words, show how able someone is to come up with new ideas and connect dots among ideas. This is an accepted way to measure creativity. Nonreligious people performed better.

The authors posit three reasons why, with each reason supported by and drawn from prior research:

"Believers' passive followership mindset, in which they look at the world through a prism of God as the all powerful, all seeing, and all knowing leader, might inhibit creativity because it entails legitimately accepting God as inherently superior and therefore viewing one's own role as someone who carries out orders without question," the paper reads. "This passive demeanor runs counter to advancing creative ideas which require independent thought—even rebelliousness and a willingness to break rules."

A second broad reason that the deeply faithful might prove less creative is because "passive followership toward God not only discourages independent thinking but it might also prioritize the established worldview, making it less likely that people will be able to generate solutions that depart from or challenge the existing socio-cognitive lens."

There's one more factor, the authors theorize: "Finally, believers' sense of passive followership toward God affords them with a sense of certainty. Feelings of certainty may be comforting but not necessarily advantageous in the creative process—a process that demands a willingness to accept the legitimacy of potentially contradictory perspectives."

As I digested all of this, I realized it was easier for me to think about it without thinking about the idea of religion—which is so heavy with deep personal meaning—and to think about it instead in terms of "worldview." If someone has a particularly hard-and-fast worldview, it limits the ability to consider information that falls outside that worldview. That doesn't feel to me like a particularly controversial statement.

If I extend that logic to religion, the point isn't that people who are deeply religions aren't, or can't be, creative. It depends instead on what sort of worldview is held by the religious person. Some people may believe that every single word of the Bible is true and that certain thoughts and behaviors are so sinful as to be unthinkable. This would, of course, limit the person's ability to develop ideas built on these "sinful" considerations.

However, Goncalo gave me an example of a religious worldview that might be much more conducive to creativity: a person who thinks that their God encourages creative thought and discovery. That type of person, Goncalo told me, might actually be inspired to create by this worldview. It is not an orthodox view of religion, but there seems to me to be so many different ways that people interpret religion and integrate it into their lives that it certainly leaves room for religion and creativity to coexist.

This is a point that the authors themselves make forcefully in their conclusion.

"We do not mean to suggest that believers are necessarily less creative. Indeed, historically, some of the most creative individuals—

from Galileo to Max Planck—were devout believers. Our findings, however, do seem to suggest that while believers can think of God and be creative, it might be prudent they not do both at the same time," the paper concludes. "This conclusion dovetails nicely with the observation made by the famous astronomer, Father Angelo Secchi, who had stated that: "When I study astronomy, I forget my priesthood and when I perform my priestly duties I forget astronomy."

All of this discussion about religion underscores a larger point, which is that all creations exist in a certain context. A big takeaway for me is that the ideas that stick around the ones that strike a powerful balance between being novel, and being relevant. This is true for changes in religion—that mix the new and the accepted—and it is true for biology, whereupon the emergence of a new organism (or even species) can only survive if it has sufficient commonality with what already exists.

This brings us to the doorstep of the pandemic, and to the study of virology. It may not seem like a perspective that belongs in a book about creativity. But nothing could be further from the truth.

COVID-19 was a terrific creation from the standpoint that it matched novelty with conformity. It was new in key ways, and familiar enough to integrate into our bodies and feed on them.

This was one creative virus, with mass-market appeal.

Pandemic

"Viruses are super sloppy. They make mistakes. They don't care about anything," Dr. Paul Duprex, director for the Center for Vaccine Research at the University of Pittsburgh, told me.

The prelude had passed. The pandemic had hit.

Thanksgiving of 2019, a time of relatively peaceful ignorance of the coming trouble, was followed by a Christmas season and New Year with whispers of viral spread in China. I've previously noted the dribbling of coverage in the news in early January. Then, on January 24 of 2020, *The Lancet*, one of the world's most respected scientific journals, wrote of 835 confirmed cases in Wuhan, with 93 percent hospitalized, and twenty-five others already dead. The paper reported nine "exported cases," in, among other places, Thailand, the United States, Japan, and Korea. Symptoms included dry cough and fever. The lungs appeared to be under attack.

Dr. Duprex would eventually be among those eminent scientists to receive millions of dollars of government funding to develop a vaccine against the deadly virus. He marveled to me at the way viruses get created, and the differences in creative methodologies between the work of vaccine makers and that of COVID-19 itself.

Viruses, he pointed out, are extremely creative in the sense that they introduce an incredible amount of novelty into the world. When Dr. Duprex said "they don't care about anything," what he meant was that they introduce through random mutation billions of different combinations, obviously without forethought, but therein is a strategy of its own. The individual virus that mutates usually dies.

After all, it is different from the virus line that survived the pressures of time and circumstance.

On the flip side, a virtually infinite number of mistakes are introduced into the world—"a swarm," Dr. Duprex said, "the popping out of ideas, probing, sequence after sequence. Constantly poking around for new heights, new reservoirs. Most of it goes too far."

It's almost as if, he said, creativity comes at no particular cost to the virus. "They operate in the billions." By contrast, "We pay for creation. We don't want a million pieces of art."

Another way to think about this is that human beings typically create with some sense of the cost. Simply put, we have ideas and almost simultaneously ask of each one: Is this a *good* idea?

If it is not, many of us will not waste time dealing with it. We are most definitely on the other side of the spectrum from a virus, which doesn't ask at all. But we're also so far removed that we very frequently kill potentially good ideas because we fear they will take more resources than they are worth to pursue. This is PIMS, Premature Idea Murder Syndrome, which is a term I've invented that is probably barely worth the resources I put into it.

The pandemic has much to teach us along these lines. A creation that sweeps the globe—in this case, a nefarious, evil, deadly disease—is not easy to predict until it is tested in the environment. This particular creation took hold through a new genetic combination that happened to be a perfect fit for the world in which it was introduced. At another time in history, this creation might well have died on the vine, as they say.

The article in *The Lancet,* published on January 24, 2020, noted that three weeks earlier, scientists in China had isolated the genetic sequence of the virus.

This viral mutation combined the genetics of a bat with those of a human, thereby presenting the human immune system with a novel threat it had not before experienced. It particularly preyed on the lungs, which are arguably the most vulnerable of all organs for a handful of reasons, but chiefly because they are more exposed to the outside world through constant inhalation than any other organ in the body. The virus happened to remain dormant inside people for up to two weeks before they knew they were infected, leaving them asymptomatic to carry and spread the virus's genes from one person to the next across shared surfaces, through handshakes and hugs or a cough or sneeze.

These particular mechanisms put previous deadly diseases into some perspective. HIV was much, much harder to transmit—only through exchange of blood and other bodily fluids. Ebola didn't do itself any favors because it killed its hosts so quickly that it gravely limited how effectively it could be transmitted.

Meanwhile, not only did the unhappy accident of COVID-19 solve for these inefficiencies, it also happened at the right time in history. Human beings, living in close contact with one another in an increasingly dense world, also lived in closer contact with animals—in this case bats, or animals that had become carriers and were sold in public markets—could easily become infected by nature and infect one another. In turn, the great innovations of air travel and trains, subways, buses, and other mass transit, made it possible for this creation to spread worldwide over the course of mere hours. All while the afflicted were asymptomatic, the unknowing ferries of death.

There's more: This disease, it became clear, also preyed upon the aging population, as do many illnesses, but this one in particular did so at a time in history when many nations—the United States, Italy, Japan, Germany—had grown top-heavy with older people, the elderly and the infirm. Why did the virus assail particularly the elderly?

In part because of a kind of loophole it found in the human immune system.

———

As the disease first began to appear, doctors and scientists noted the emergence of a dry cough. This was curious in a way. Many diseases of the lung include a wet cough. This wetness comes from the production of mucus. Mucus is produced as part of an immune-system response. The sneezing and the production of mucus that gets coughed from the lungs are part of a lubricating process to jettison viruses or bacteria from the body.

This was different somehow. What we knew at the time was that the lungs appeared to be under attack in a particularly effective way, through a virus that was either new altogether or new to human beings.

To understand what it was doing—why it "caught on"—it helps to understand the delicate relationship between the immune system and the lungs, a particularly delicate organ even by the standards of human organs.

The lungs are the only internal organ directly exposed to the outside. This allows us to breathe. We inhale, and air comes in, and we extract oxygen that gets transferred through tiny air sacs in our lungs into our blood, which carries it to the rest of our body. Carbon monoxide gets transferred out and exhaled. This exchange is so essential to our survival that its absence for even a couple of minutes can kill us. That is not true of food or water; both are also essential, but we can go days without eating or drinking

The lungs, open to the world for good reason, pose a real challenge for the immune system. Our internal defense system must allow the exchange to go on, and therefore needs to give some berth to the lungs to work. This means, for instance, that we can breathe in some toxins—such as smoke from a wildfire—without setting off a pervasive immune-system response. If the immune system went nuts each time we inhaled a foreign particle, it would create all kinds of challenges. On the other hand, if the lungs come under sustained and brutal attack, the immune system has to react strongly to repel an attack and keep us breathing.

The defense of the lungs is a delicate balancing act. And COVID-19 seemed to thwart that stasis, particularly in the elderly and infirm. In some people in this group, with aging lungs, the immune system appeared to flip out. After initially failing to kill off the infection, the immune system effectively freaked over the attack on this precious organ and wound up reacting too zealously. Immune system signaling cells screamed "attack, attack," and not just in the lungs. Multiple organs in the body became enflamed. This, in its most extreme form, is called a "cytokine storm."

One reason immune systems overreacted could be in part that human beings hadn't seen this virus before. It was called initially a "novel coronavirus."

This all added up to make it essentially creative. It was novel—to us, at least—and it had value, meaning that it found a way to thrive in its environment. Its timing was superb, given the density of the world's population and the easy movement of people across borders.

On February 23, the *New York Times* reported: "Europe confronted its first major outbreak of the coronavirus as an eruption of more than 150 cases in Italy prompted officials on Sunday to lock down at least 10 days."

Until that point, only five cases had been reported in Italy. "The worrisome spike," the *Times* wrote, "shattered the sense of safety and distance that much of the continent had felt in recent months even as the virus has infected more than 78,000 worldwide and killed more than 2,400, nearly all in China."

That very same day, the United States would be forced to confront a second extraordinary challenge.

———

On February 23, Ahmaud Arbery went for a jog. It took him to a tree-lined neighborhood in Georgia called Satilla Shores. That's where he was trailed by three white men. They cornered Arbery. One of the men shot the jogger. In cold blood. Unlike many past murders, this one was caught on camera. A thirty-second cell phone video showed Arbery's desperate attempt to evade his hunters. No arrests were initially made, nor recommended. The case sat dormant, seemingly with no hope of justice being served. Ultimately, all three men were found guilty of nearly every charge.

Hundreds of miles away, on May 25 in Minneapolis, George Floyd died after being pinned to the ground by police, the officer's knee on Floyd's neck disrupting his breathing for eight minutes. Floyd called out for his mother before he died. This took place in Minnesota after a store owner called police and accused Floyd of passing a counterfeit twenty-dollar bill. This unjust death was, like Arbery's, recorded on a cell phone.

The death, and the video, set off protests, one after another, furious calls for justice. The anger intensified with revelations of the Arbery killing, for which no arrest had yet been made. Names of other murdered Black men and women, like Breonna Taylor, surfaced or resurfaced.

More demands for change. An outpouring, one city after the next, like the country had not before seen. It was a creation of a movement.

After all these years, why did demands for social change crescendo at that moment? The movement wasn't new. Grieving mothers of dead Black men had pleaded for years for change. Pastors and community leaders begged someone to listen. The calls stirred some interest. Nothing like this. That's because the timing was right.

What happened next is a powerful, real-time example of how what matters when it comes to creative change is not just the idea for change but the terrain where the change occurs.

The timing was right.

The technology was right.

It was the era of the mobile phone.

The terrible videos created on these wondrous devices (and on the body cameras of police themselves) provided unequivocal evidence for what African American men had said for years—that they had been subject to discrimination, unwarranted violence, murder.

The videos also showed unmistakably what researchers have long proven in the lab: that the subconscious power of systemic racism allowed some police officers to feel so threatened that they overreacted. The subconscious bias helps explain the disconnect of police officers—hired and empowered with guns to protect health and safety—turning the idea of justice and protection of public safety on its head.

Technology had provided proof of the systemic and viral nature of this deadly discrimination.

The timing was right for an old idea to surface as a new movement, a new creation. There was another aspect of the timing that allowed the movement to thrive.

It was the coronavirus itself. That's right: the rise of the pandemic helped create conditions that led to social change.

I first heard this observation from a brilliant creator named Darrin Bell. In 2019, he was the first African American to win the Pulitzer Prize for editorial cartooning. His Pulitzer award cited his "beautiful and daring editorial cartoons that took on issues affecting disenfranchised communities, calling out lies, hypocrisy, and fraud."

I knew Bell well. For a decade, starting in 2001, he and I had teamed up on a syndicated daily comic strip called *Rudy Park*. We came up with ideas together; I wrote, and he drew. I've rarely known such a creative soul and a deep, deliberate thinker. So when I called Bell as these issues were unfolding, I should have expected he'd hit me in the teeth with some authenticity.

He talked of remembering, as a teen, where he'd been when he watched the Rodney King video on March 3, 1991—"the first in-progress beating we ever saw," Bell said.

"Older people were saying it was just an exception, but it was really formative." He grew up in Los Angeles and he knew it wasn't anomalous at all. It also was not so commonplace for him to see on video—the validation for the world of what Bell and his peers knew to be so. Then, after Bell, came the generation who began to see it more regularly—the brutal incidences captured by video. "Generations younger than me saw them rapid-fire, one after the other," Bell told me. "It's hard to overstate how important this was that it happened when they were in their single digits."

He likened it to the way young kids would see Westerns or World War II movies and want to join the military. A generation of youth had their reality shaped by the media on their phones. "They know that it's going on all the time and they were frustrated that older people didn't care about it. They recorded it and they shared it."

Then came Arbery and Floyd and people had time on their hands to focus on what was happening and take to the streets in protest, Bell told me.

"This was their world and all of a sudden they had no school and nothing else to do," he said.

He didn't want to sound cynical, but what he saw happening was that many Americans, locked inside and watching the news, found themselves unable to escape evidence that otherwise might have slipped from view in a healthier and more economically vibrant time. People would have been commuting, going to their offices, attending college classes, playing professional sports. The cell phone videos of murder met with a moment in time, an ecological niche, that allowed people to digest, reflect, react—and to act on years of simmering anger, authentic feelings of injustice validated by the phone.

Now was the time the idea of confronting systemic racism—dating to *Native Son* and earlier—that had become so resonant and found such a powerful niche because the environmental conditions were ripe.

The two creations were linked, the virus and the social movement—the kind of unexpected, unpredictable nature of creation and response.

Human beings began to respond.

Nature's Call-and-Response

In an epic sense, nature's accidental creation, combined with undeniable video evidence of systemic racism, set off a creation of determined ferocity, the will of mankind conjuring under duress.

This was a time when the creation of the nonhuman world and that of humans were not distantly analogous in character but almost identical. The virus emerged by mutation, but then set off a furious combining of ideas, communications, and science across borders, the putting together of puzzle pieces like splices of genes, as scientists and policy makers, innovators, entrepreneurs, and artists with philanthropic leanings sought to stand the ground.

A good friend and fellow *New York Times* reporter named Andrew Jacobs wrote a story about a surge in creativity around ventilator technology.

The creativity was happening in every part of life—starting with medicine, and an explosion of ideas among doctors. They are considered to be highly rule-oriented, and fairly so. These are the people, don't forget, who decided it was a good idea when they were freshmen in college to wake up at 6 a.m. to walk across campus to get to organic chemistry class, where they would memorize and regurgitate how compounds interact. Then they followed a highly regimented path through medical school, fellowships, and to the doctor's office, where you'd want them matching your symptoms or disease against known fact patterns, not going all free-range with creative interpretations.

This doesn't mean doctors aren't creative. Please. It just means that they've often chosen a path that requires them to subvert those impulses to very crucial, very practical analyses.

Fear of COVID-19 unleashed their inspiration. Jacobs wrote:

But fears of a ventilator shortage have unleashed a wave of experimentation at hospitals around the country that is leading to some promising alternatives to help sustain patients.

Doctors at North Shore University Hospital on Long Island have been using machines designed for people with sleep apnea to keep scores of coronavirus patients breathing, and engineers at New York University have transformed hooded hair salon dryers into personal negative pressure chambers that deliver oxygen and limit the spread of aerosolized virus, lowering the infection risks for health care workers and other patients.

Pulmonologists across the country have been turning to a remarkably simple intervention: flipping patients onto their stomachs, which markedly improves oxygen levels for those in respiratory distress.

Doctors say these and other ad hoc interventions have allowed many hospitals to weather the surge of desperately ill patients in recent weeks, and may have helped stave off the dire ventilator shortages and rationing that some had feared but have not come to pass.

"Some of these are battlefield interventions that we would not normally use in hospitals, but this crisis has been an incredible spur for creativity and collaboration," said Dr. Greg Martin, a pulmonologist in Atlanta and the president-elect of the Society of Critical Care Medicine. "The beauty of this is that we're learning a lot and hopefully some of this will translate to things we can use in the future."

The innovations crystallized a collective period of awesome creativity—fueled by cooperation across borders, which is a particular kind of group openness, a furious connecting of dots accelerated by extraordinary fear so powerful that it forced people to abandon the plague of doubt. Almost every facet of our lives underwent some adaption fueled by creativity. Examples abound.

———

On March 30, 2020, Dr. Sonali Wilborn sat at a desk in Ann Arbor, Michigan, listening to yet another Zoom call, struck by inspiration. She suddenly knew how to help people with COVID-19 die humanely.

"People thought I was crazy," Dr. Wilborn said.

Dr. Wilborn, an internist by training, had found a sense of purpose when she began focusing on palliative care and hospice. She helped people die in better ways. During the COVID-19 pandemic, people were dying more badly than they had in years: without even being able to see friends and family. Last moments were being spent alone, in isolation, in beds in intensive care units or in nursing homes that could not, or would not, allow visitors. No one wanted to risk further spread of this terrible virus.

Agonizing stories followed, and images of family members gathered outside nursing homes peering through windows to say hello, or goodbye, to a parent or grandparent, uncle or aunt. At other times, a ventilated person in the final throes of life pleaded with his or her eyes to get a glimpse by cell phone—through FaceTime or some other powerful innovation—of a son or daughter, a grandchild.

One of these people was named Willie (for privacy reasons, no last name is used here). He lived in New Orleans, and Dr. Wilborn heard about him on a Zoom call in her Michigan home. Dr. Wilborn, in addition to her other work, had taken on the role of chief medical officer of Heart of Hospice, an organization that helped bring the idea of hospice and palliative care to sixteen regions in the southern part of the United States. The vision, the organization says, is to "transform end-of-life care."

Willie needed change. In an ICU bed, he would soon die without any contact from his family, including his son, from whom Willie had been estranged for more than a decade. He pleaded for intimacy.

Ordinarily, it takes eighteen months to get a new inpatient hospice unit up and running. There's a lot of red tape, and there are major safety and medical issues. There are real estate questions, and on and on.

Dr. Wilborn told the team they had to create a new type of inpatient hospice unit, one that would be safe to prevent the spread of COVID-19 and allow the droves of dying to see their families.

The team worked tirelessly and created a "pop-up" hospice inpatient unit, decked it out with safety equipment so that family members could visit patients in individual rooms, wearing the best protective equipment, and say goodbye. It took eight days.

Willie went there and died after saying hello and goodbye to his son. By the fall of 2020, when I first wrote these words, the hospice unit had served eighty-nine people who might otherwise have died without human touch or interaction.

Dr. Wilborn did not invent hospice, or PPE (personal protective equipment). She connected some dots and fewer people died alone. It was a terrific example of pandemic-inspired creativity, one that would lead to other organizations taking similar steps.

Creativity came from people of all ages—aging scholars and young, determined innovators. In March of 2020—right after the pandemic emerged—a seventeen-year-old from the state of Washington built a website that scoured the internet for accurate information and reported on the status of the pandemic and its response.

Marvel at it! Contemplate all the creativity that led to the point at which the virus could be identified, captured, and described, broken down into bits of DNA, battled with vaccines. This became the creative tension in its essence—disruption and response, call-and-response.

In this case, with the help of a seventeen-year-old.

The creativity came from all corners, in so many aspects of life, technology, medicine. The moment lent itself to trying these ideas. They made a difference. I particularly love the story of Tina Syer, who was astounded by an idea while driving down the highway, just south of San Francisco, on the night of March 19. It was just days after it became clear that the United States would not escape COVID-19, and many cities began lockdowns.

This meant that the doors would close in Syer's little corner of the world—the Boys & Girls Club of the Peninsula. The Boys & Girls Club, in general, has long served less fortunate communities. The branch where Syer worked as executive and the chief fundraiser served a particularly overlooked niche: the invisible poor of Silicon Valley, in the area around Palo Alto, California, one of the richest regions of the world—Stanford University, the venture-capital hub known as Sand Hill Road, Google and Facebook and Tesla and all the rest.

So, no surprise, the income gap soared in the region where 75 percent of the wealth was held by 13 percent of the population, according to a think tank called Joint Venture Silicon Valley. At the other end of the spectrum, some of the poorest lived in and around a small city called East Palo Alto, which was literally and proverbially across the tracks (actual railroad tracks) from Palo Alto. The residents could be invisible in multiple ways: They worked as the housekeepers and gardeners, the bussers in restaurants, the janitors—the employees meant not to be seen or heard. And many are undocumented, from Latin America, so are part of the dirty secret of cheap labor. But labor they did—extremely hardworking families—some with multiple jobs to earn the rent. And that's where the Boys & Girls Club came in, taking care of the children in the afternoons, teaching academic skills, serving snacks and some dinners, and providing a huge source of support.

Then came the pandemic. And as Syer drove down the highway from her home in San Francisco to the Boys & Girls Club, she realized she'd be going for the last time for a long time: Under state lockdown, the chapter would have to shut its doors.

As she drove, she thought: "The kids don't have the safe space of going to school, and they don't have schools where they get breakfast and lunch and they don't have clubs where they're getting dinner."

And then she thought: "Wait, we have clubhouses where we have wonderful kitchens!"

The Boys & Girls Club had been serving 350 meals a night to the young people while they did their homework and had a place other than their latchkey homes to hang out. Syer was relatively new to the organization, so what she had was an aha moment but without much certainty or influence to turn it into anything more.

But it was a strong enough spark that when she turned it over to the organization, a remarkable creation took hold. I wrote a story about it for the *New York Times*:

PALO ALTO, Calif.—Andres Pantoja, an up-and-coming Silicon Valley sous chef, spent his pre-pandemic evenings delicately preparing the $115 plate of lamb chops and deboning the $42 Psari Plaki whole fish at a fashionable restaurant here. It is frantic work serving 200 upscale meals a night.

His new gig is proving way more chaotic, though—making thousands of free meals that seem priceless to those being served: the gardeners, janitors, construction workers, housekeepers and others who have seen their meager income dwindle further as the coronavirus ravages the economy. Mr. Pantoja has become part of a large-scale effort to help feed the poorest families in a region with one of the nation's widest income gaps.

Call it tech-to-table, a Silicon Valley effort to feed the hungry engineered by a local Boys & Girls Clubs chapter. The organization's chief executive, Peter Fortenbaugh, a Harvard M.B.A., employed his background working at McKinsey & Co.

and lots of connections to turn what had been an education-centric program for underprivileged students into one of the busiest takeout operations in the Bay Area.

Two sites serve more than 2,000 free meals a night, one in East Palo Alto, and the other in Redwood City, where Mr. Pantoja runs the show with exuberance.

"Jambalaya tonight: Chicken, andouille sausage, some shrimp," he said on a recent night, as one of his fellow chefs stirred in the rice. The seasonings? "So many things: paprika, cumin, chili powder. The rest is a secret blend."

This week, the group served its 100,000th meal, spending now $30,000 a week. A recent infusion of $218,000 came in from a bike fund-raiser, 784 participants with a quarantine twist.

Food insecurity—a mild term for terror of being hungry—has become central to the COVID-19 story as job losses grow chronic. So go the stories from the people lined up starting at 4 p.m. outside the two Boys & Girls Club sites: a house cleaner with four children whose income has dropped to $110 a week from $400; a 57-year-old janitor who lost his job when Macy's shut and lives in a home with seven people, none now employed; a mother of three whose husband, a painter, gets only occasional jobs now.

"The owners of the houses don't want him to come near them," said the woman, who is undocumented and gave only her first name, Josefina, to avoid trouble from immigration officials. She and others described the food as particularly helpful, given that rent has to come first.

A few weeks after the *New York Times* published the article I'd written, I learned that the community meals program had gotten over half a million dollars in new donations.

Syer's aha moment caught on in her organization, inspired the brass there, the rank-and-file, local chefs, and inspired me enough to write an article and excited my editors enough to publish it, and it built on the shoulders of the giants who had created the *New York Times*, and the innovators who took the newspaper and made it a success online, and they, in turn, had relied on the creators of the internet, and all of it led to more help for Syer and the Boys & Girls Club: more money donations. This is a modest example of the creativity cascade spawned by urgency, fueled by fear, and then tapping into a well of authenticity and individual spark.

And across the country, the battle waged in the streets for the future of race relations. Leaders emerged and voices rang out. People began to float a spectrum of systemic changes to address the relations between police and poor and minority communities.

One idea came from Justin Harrington.

He's the nephew of Rhiannon Giddens.

He's in his early twenties and had spent most of the quarantine in his bedroom in Greensboro, North Carolina, working on an album. "I was just going to create," he said. "Isolated from everything."

It was energizing, and then depressing. He missed other people. He couldn't take his album to the stage. And the early protests didn't inspire him. He felt like he'd seen it before, people taking to the streets in years past, making hay for a few days, returning to their lives, defeated by the enormity of it all, and the weight of the system.

Then, one Saturday in mid-May, he watched on Instagram a video of protests in downtown Greensboro. So he and his mother, Lalenja, packed their van with masks and water and other supplies to support the protestors. "At the front, I see my friends leading the march. The people who had been working underground on their mics. It was like a switch turned on for me. I thought: This is what I'm supposed to do."

A muse overtook him, as it had many in the nation. In his case, he'd wind up on the front lines, with a creation of his own aimed at mixing policy and art. It would lead to a powerful impact.

A similar spirit was overtaking Giddens herself. Early in the first week of June 2020, she sat at the kitchen table in her part-time home in Ireland. On her MacBook Pro, she pulled up Twitter. That morning, a fan had tweeted praise for a heralded song called "Cry No More" that Giddens had written and performed in 2015. Her inspiration had been the murder of nine African American church members killed in a mass shooting in Charleston, South Carolina.

Giddens watched the song on YouTube.

"I looked at it and thought: 'oh shit,' and the idea hit right then."

She followed the overpowering muse where it took her: a vision for a new version of the song, bigger and grander. She could picture and hear Yo-Yo Ma playing cello, with accompanying dance from Misty Copeland, the first African American ever promoted to principal dancer by the American Ballet Theater. Giddens began to reach out, from her distant perch, using technology that allows far-flung collaboration as never before.

An explosion of creativity came in response to the challenges facing the world, and the United States.

What unites these stories is that they came from the great power of the human mind to innovate. Increasingly, we have developed an understanding of how the mind works when it comes to creativity.

Time for a glimpse inside a creator's brain, and other physiology.

This is Book III.

BOOK III

NEUROLOGY, PHYSIOLOGY, PERSONALITY, CHRONOLOGY, AND (THE NEW) GEOGRAPHY

The Brain

"How many things can you think of to do with a brick?"

The question was posed to me by Roger Beaty, a neuroscientist at Penn State. He was giving me the "alternative-use test," or at least one standard question from it.

The test, which helps define the field of creativity, was devised by a scholar named Joy Paul Guilford (called J.P. by friends and followers) in 1967. The test was aimed at measuring a person's ability to develop divergent thoughts.

"How many things can you think of to do with a brick?"

Or a paper clip, a pen, a shoe?

These questions are aimed at identifying four qualities that Guilford associated with creativity. One is **fluency**, a concept I described earlier and which is really just a fancy word for quantity. How many ideas can a person come up with?

A brick could be used as a doorstop, thrown through a window, put under a tire to keep a car from rolling down a steep hill, and so on.

A second category is **originality.**

"The brick could be ground down to a red paste, mixed with water, and used for paint," I told Roger Beaty, the neuroscientist, after I'd listed a handful of other ideas for the brick.

This particular idea seemed to get his attention. It might be an example of originality, but it also contains aspects of the two other attributes that J.P. associated with creativity. One is **flexibility**, a measure of the different kinds of categories a person came up with— paint is different than a doorstop. The final category is **detail**—red paint made from a crushed brick mixed with water is a description with a fair amount of specificity.

Beaty had an idea. He decided to administer the test with a twist: The person taking the test would be lying inside a real-time magnetic resonance imaging (MRI) scanner that formed images of the inside of the study subject's brain.

This chapter is about what he and others have discovered about the brain of creators. It fits into a larger section of the book about the physiological and emotional attributes of creative people. I begin with the brain.

Beaty was in Greensboro, North Carolina, at the time, working on a graduate degree, when he got his idea. He came upon found gold: a brain scanner, "collecting dust" in a room. The service contracts alone on these machines run into the six figures. This one was being underused. Beaty set out to change that. He wound up scanning the brains of around 170 people while they took a timed alternative use test. Generally speaking, the scanners measure blood flow in the brain as a way of showing what regions of the brain are, in effect, working harder at any given time.

Did the blood-flow patterns in the brains of those who had higher scores on divergent thinking tests look any different than the brains of those who came up with fewer, novel ideas?

Beaty looked at the results and felt he'd made a powerful discovery.

"Those who did better," he said, "had stronger connections between regions of three subnetworks of the brain."

These three subnetworks are called the default network, the executive control network, and the salience network.

The default network in the brain appears to be most active when a person is not particularly focused: at rest, zoning out, mind wandering, thinking about past events or future ones.

The executive control network is the most evolved part of the human mind. It is involved in complex decision making, focus, and directing of attention.

The salience network plays a filtering function—"picking up on something that's relevant or interesting or that you need to attend to."

In Beaty's construction, connectivity was heightened among these networks in people who performed well on creativity tests. It suggested to him that the default network allowed for the cropping up of ideas, the salience network helped sift through the networks for the most potentially relevant ones, and the final processing was accomplished by the executive control part of the brain involved in deep focus.

My simpleminded way of thinking about it is seeing the brain as a gold-mining operation. One part of the brain digs up tons of stuff— rocks and minerals and fossils and gunk and some hunks of gold. One part of the brain sifts for those pieces that might be gold. One part of the brain takes the ones with the most potential, polishes them and melts the best nugget and shapes it into a ring, and takes it to market.

The work by Beaty is part of a surge in the efforts to map the brains of people thought to be creative.

It is extremely controversial.

Considered nonsense, by some.

"Full of crap. Has no value," I was told by the long-time creativity scholar named Arne Dietrich I mentioned in this book's first chapter. He authored the book *How Creativity Happens in the Brain*, in which he explains that the complexity of creativity currently exceeds our ability to map it in the brain. "I cannot think of a mental faculty so central to the human condition for which we have so little understanding as to how brains do it."

And in a 2018 paper, Dietrich wrote: "The neuroscientific study of creativity is adrift from the rest of the psychological sciences and finds itself in a theoretical arid zone that has perhaps no equal in psychology."

I am introducing the neuroscience of creativity in this way to underscore two main points: There is extraordinary potential for the field of neuroscience when it comes to understanding creativity, but the science is very embryonic and therefore might mislead. It is partly for these reasons that I did not make the neuroscience a core foundation of this book. That might have sounded sexy, but it would have overstated the depth of the embryonic field of research.

So this chapter is intended to explain what scientists know, don't know, and why the prospects are so tantalizing. Dietrich himself, despite being known as a respected skeptic in the field, leaves the possibilities open.

Dietrich spent his early childhood in Northern Germany until his family moved to the United States when he was a teen. He attended college and graduate school at the University of Georgia, captivated by creativity and consciousness, and spent many hours doing freakishly long exercise workouts. He participated in multiple Iron Man competitions and regularly completed runs in excess of twenty miles just to train.

It was after one of these jogs—a twenty-one-miler in the woods in Central Georgia in 2001—that Dietrich says he was thunderstruck by an idea. It had to do with where creative germs originate in the brain, or, rather, where they *don't* occur. Dietrich felt certain that the ideas were flowing when the prefrontal cortex was experiencing a lull. This idea is increasingly well accepted but, at the time, Dietrich found the idea scary enough that he was afraid to discuss it publicly. With good reason: The prefrontal cortex is, as I've said, the most evolved part of the human brain. It is what separates us from the beasts, as it were.

"It took me years to work it out—to make sure professionally I was not missing something catastrophic," he told me.

In 2003, he felt confident enough to come forward. He published a paper that introduced the "transient hypofrontality theory."

The important part of the word is the prefix "hypo." It means "under." Like "hypotensive" means low blood pressure. It is the opposite of hyper.

Transient hypofrontality. A temporary slowing down of the most advanced parts of the brain would lead to the generation of more creative ideas.

On its face, this Does. Not. Compute.

Could it be that creativity has its origins in less evolved parts of the brain?

Over time, it has become clear from evidence I've already shared in this book that Dietrich was on to something. Ideas generated in meditative states—less directed and less rigid states, the ones that might hold our morality in check or hew us to rules and laws—seem to be consistent with the childlike capacity to be more fluent with the generation of ideas.

This doesn't mean that multiple parts of the brain can't be involved, as Beaty proposes. But what really shook Dietrich was that creativity is "fully and embedded and distributed" in the brain.

This is partly why Dietrich came to step back from the idea that neuroscience, despite its rapid evolution, held imminent answers to how creativity works. The idea was ultimately too narrow, not that the goal was misplaced. Imagine, Dietrich says, if you could actually understand what parts of the brain led to brilliant innovation?

"It's a complete game changer—for any country, for any military, for any company. You could not only foster creativity but move the lever that in and of itself could enhance this process," Dietrich said to me. I spoke to him by Skype from his home in Lebanon, where he is a professor at the American University of Beirut; once again, the power of networking at play in the sharing of ideas.

Also of note, Dietrich, while he believes much about neurology remains missing, does believe that the ultimate answers draw from evolutionary biology. "That is to say, brains produce mental models that simulate the consequences of generate-and-test trials that are then fed into the variation process," he wrote. "Once we have accepted the evolutionary paradigm, we have a clear way forward."

Some combination of neural connections generate ideas and snippets of ideas that creators connect into bigger thoughts that get assessed by rigors of analytics and intellect. These are not parts of the brain that are the domain of the few, he writes. "Obviously, creative people are not a special class of prophets."

Meantime, if Dietrich remains highly dubious of the progress on the neuroimaging front and Beaty believes a map is already taking shape, there is a kind of middle ground developing in neuroscience.

Neuroscientists studying creativity are taking modest steps that provide clues but not a complete picture.

A small study at the University of Iowa explored the brains of seven accomplished creators: four artists (three authors and a filmmaker) and three scientists (a neuroscientist and two molecular biologists).

While these various creators were in the MRI brain scanner, they performed a task aimed at revealing their creative impulses. The task involved the creators being shown a common word—chosen from various nouns and verbs—and the creator's job was to whisper the first thing that came to mind. The premise was that accomplished creators would respond in ways known to reflect creativity, imagination, the connection of disparate ideas.

To allow a comparison, the same seven creators were slid into a scanner and then shown a two-digit number. Their job was merely to repeat the number, a task that was aimed at showing the brain in a less creative state.

What the scanner disclosed was that the brains of the study subjects were more active when they responded with a word of their own invention rather than repeating a two-digit number. This is not a surprise. After all, the brain undertook a heavier task when it had to respond with a word.

The second basic conclusion was that when the artists and scientists were asked to come up with a word, their brains showed activation in similar areas. In particular, they lit up in the default network, a part of the brain involved in less directed activity. This is what Dietrich had theorized: Scientists and artists, creative in different ways, each showed heightened activity when creating in a part of the brain known for downtime and not active analysis.

Another refined and fascinating study found provocative implications when comparing the brains of people who had made significant creative achievements—Big C creators in their fields—with people who hadn't had such achievements but were very smart.

The study was part of the Big C Project at UCLA. Researchers recruited high-achievers in creative fields, people like painters, sculptors, photographers, and those from scientific fields, including biology, chemistry, and math. Their creative achievement was marked by various measures of productivity and influence. A second group was recruited: the Smart Comparison Group—people with high educational attainment and IQ. There were altogether 107 study subjects.

These subjects had their brains scanned while they were engaging in various tasks, including a group of tasks associated with creativity. These were the "divergent-thinking" tasks. The study found that both groups used similar parts of the brain while working on a creative activity, but the creators showed less activity in these parts of the brain.

The creators needed less brain power.

Of note, both groups were able to produce similar results. But the people in the Smart Comparison Group had to work harder.

"This kind of effect, observed as less activation within the same neural network, is often considered to reflect increased 'efficiency,'" reads the paper, which was published in 2018 in the journal *Neuropsychologia*.

The study helps explain why some people might be more inclined to creativity than others: It comes more easily to them. The brain feels less taxed in people who create more naturally. This helps explain why various businesses get segmented among people who gravitate to the more creative side of the business (screenwriting versus running the movie studio, or writing software code versus running logistics for a major company). All the tasks require some creativity, but the act of coming up with ideas from whole cloth might well come more easily to some.

This also doesn't rule out creativity for others. The activity just might require more work.

Broadly, what I find so valuable about research like this is that it begins to break down the neuroscience of creativity into smaller chunks—idea generation, processing, and so forth.

The more that develops, the more it seems like, seems even inevitable, that these maps will emerge. Then, as Dietrich hypothesizes, it might be possible to develop behavioral techniques that spur great creativity by strengthening activity or capacity in certain parts of the brain, and their relationships.

For now, it might be fair to conjecture very broadly that ideas are generated in one area of the brain, and then they are assessed in a second process or network in the brain. The significance of this idea is that it heavily underscores the connection between the way human beings create and the way more primitive organisms mutate and evolve.

In the basic cellular model, mutations occur at a genetic level, often causing an organism to die for want of viability in our world. Some survive. Some thrive. The ones that thrive do so by being tested in the physical world.

A precise analogy appears to exist inside our brains.

Ideas come to us through our default networks. They stream from the subconscious, in times of quiet, moments of inspiration, experiences of raw emotion, states of authenticity. They appear to us, often not so much willed but allowed and permitted. These are almost like mutations, new forms of ideas, slight variations on what has come before. Mutations on the prior knowledge.

Then we process the ideas more actively, through the intellectual networks of our brains, the control tower and its partner regions of the brain.

This assessment of ideas that have sprung up is, again, precisely analogous to the idea of a mutation being tested by the physical world. Our own minds create both the mutation and the initial ecological environment against which to test it. Our brains become the rugged terrain where a creation gets raked through the heat and cold of experience, the slippery and jagged upward slope of prior knowledge, the freezing oceanic and shark-infested depths of reality. All of that can happen in an eyeblink, or a few minutes, a week.

"I've got an idea!" I'll tell my wife, not infrequently.

"Sleep on it."

The mutation had appeared, and I'd heralded it as the next brilliant product of the Wright Brothers. And on my wife's lofty counsel I slept on it and let it get processed.

"You know that idea I had the other day?" I'd return to her. "It doesn't make any sense."

Insert wry and knowing spousal smile here.

Mutation had sprung, run across coals of the rough ecology of my experience, and tossed on the heap of dead inspirations.

Yet some make it through that process. Prolific creators seem to have a knack for generating more mutations, assessing them effectively enough to take them to the next environmental challenge: the real world itself. The world outside the analytical networks. These become ideas that, in the biological analogy, have survived several generations. They have a chance to flourish outside the brain. They become any number of innovations: the business idea that gets pitched to investors; a song posed to the rest of the band; the book pitched to an agent or a news story given to an editor; the research idea written into a grant.

Or the script idea that would become a movie, or television show. Which brings me to a telling story I heard from Judd Apatow, a highly popular maker of soulful comedies. He's not a neuroscientist, but you could have fooled me.

It is important to note that Apatow's skill travels in a tight elevator packed with comedy, sorrow, discomfort, and authenticity. His creations wrestle with real things, recognizable characters, near-universal emotions, marital conversations taken word-for-word from our own bedrooms. Maybe that is the definition of great comedy, and he has done it over and again: *The 40-Year-old Virgin*, *Knocked Up*, *This Is 40*, *Funny People*, and multiple television shows, including *Freaks and Geeks*, a story of awkward adolescence that had a short commercial run but was beloved by its audience and critics. "*Freaks and Geeks*," a New York *Daily News* review reads, "is tapping into something primal: adolescents' hunger to begin to understand themselves and their world. *Freaks and Geeks* is too honest to offer answers. But it affirms the value and the universality of asking the questions."

Credit Apatow with hearing his voice, and letting it loose, starting with a stand-up career that began in high school coupled with a dedication and ambition that led him within a decade after graduation to write for *The Larry Sanders Show*, where he was mentored by that brilliant HBO show's lead, Garry Shandling.

Which brings me to this brief parable about the brain shared by Apatow.

Movies and television shows are, at their core, acts of creative collaboration. Directors, actors, cinematographers, writers. Sometimes dozens of writers. These shows are created in writers' rooms, which are strange and beautiful places, churning with ideas, emotions—often raw—storytelling, griping, insults, jokes, ideas, ideas, ideas.

"It does become a giant brain that's firing all over the place," Apatow told me.

The writers' room is a kind of real-world analogue for the neuroscience of creativity. When the room works, comfort levels become so high that ideas flow as if the people sitting around the table had fused into a single brain, personal fears faded, giving way to a raw, unfiltered explosion of stream of consciousness. It's like the whole room was one person having a creative explosion while on a jog or in the shower. A great writers' room is like the brain's default network—except it is multiple default networks, building on each other.

Idea. Response. Idea. Great. Idea. Yuck. Idea. Are you kidding? Idea. That gives me another idea! Yeah, and what if we . . .

"A person will pitch something that won't be funny, but make someone remember something that will be funny, which wakes up someone who is half-asleep and who insults something in that story, and then someone realizes that insult might be a point of view," Apatow said. "A lot of my profession is about being open to strange connections. It's hard to know where these ideas come from and what they mean to us. It's about trying to get into the flow, get rid of that critical voice, see what bubbles up."

Then the show's head writer, or showrunner, takes notes, tries to gently steer, gathers the output of the collective brain into the day's work of a superconnected default network.

But.

The writers in the room also play the role of the prefrontal cortex. They reject ideas, sometimes within moments of the ideas being expressed. This is the call-and-response of creativity. And if the responses are too rigid, unforgiving, or if even one single voice becomes too oppressive, it can act just like a prefrontal cortex of individuals who are repressing their ideas, subverting their authenticity to clichés or to easily accepted ideas, to raw commercial sensibility.

"A room killer," Apatow described this person. "This personality is so strong, it shuts down the whole room."

The Larry Sanders Show, widely beloved and critically acclaimed, had a kind of broken creative brain. The reason, Apatow explained, was that writers tried to channel Shandling's genius, and voice—without him in the room, in part because he was so busy—"The room was trying to anticipate what he would like and not like," Apatow said.

The room's prefrontal cortex became highly critical of ideas, fearing they'd not meet with approval, and if Shandling "read a bad script he'd get very upset," and "he would go into a very negative place.

"That energy would get back to the room. People were worried about getting into trouble. They didn't want to disappoint. Some people got nervous. They wondered if they were good enough to be in the room," Apatow said. This is completely consistent with the way to ruin creativity: by shooting for perfectionism, and outside ideals. "The next thing you know, it all gets a little bit harder, neurotic, and at times, toxic."

This is a brain that is given permission to create and still fights against itself because the outside voice overtakes the flow of ideas.

For a contrast, Apatow offered a different example: the writer's room for a show called *Crashing*, another HBO project with a comedian at its center, this one a semi-autobiography of Pete Holmes, a stand-up comic and neurotic. His own presence in the writers' room helped but, more than that, Holmes is supremely open, almost to a fault.

"Pete is very chatty; he loves to entertain—even when riffing he tries to entertain. He gets a kick out of cracking up the room," Apatow said. "The environment is joyful and sometimes annoying. 'We get it Pete, we don't need to hear another hilarious story from your life,' and the room might suddenly turn on him in a hilarious way, and Pete might be hysterical." Holmes would start laughing with them, at himself, at the situation. "It feels safe in that place. And great things can happen."

In a room like this, where people share with such abandon, lots of bad ideas are voiced too, and they get filtered out. There also, though, can be bad ideas that offend. Unlike a writer sitting alone who filters the ideas before anyone hears them, the writers' room can work only by removing the filter between default network and mouth. Apatow himself has faced mild criticism for lack of political correctness. When I spoke to him, I hadn't realized that and, to his credit, he himself brought up the challenge of dealing with ideas that people grapple with inside, that are authentic to a person's experience and maybe many peoples' experiences, and yet can be explosive.

By way of an example, many white people see people with dark skins as more likely to be associated with crime than white people. This is clear, undeniable, and innovative science that I'll describe in the next chapter. But what happens in a writers' room if someone acknowledges being afraid of a Black person walking down the street?

Should that be spoken? How should it be spoken? It is possible to think of many other examples, involving lots of tribalism.

"You want everyone to feel like they can be very deep and reveal themselves—the good and the bad, to take what comes up," Apatow said. "A lot of times you will go down a dead end and someone will embarrass themselves. They'll tell you something that they think will be helpful and it's just shameful. It might be the worst story you've ever heard and the whole room will talk about it the next five years."

In a way, the airing of those ideas might help a process of healing, of eliminating through the airing of baseless stereotype. Giving light to darkness.

Without question, it helps to have diversity in the room. Who knows what good could come of plot twists and character narrations that take these ideas and add in what the African American fears of the white person, or whatever other social context might help explain the greater truths.

Apatow has a bottom line when it comes to the people with whom he likes to share a room—and a brain.

"It's all about having people who have a good heart—to be surrounded by people with kind hearts who are offering up the good and the bad in their life experience."

The sum of the stories and science of the brain is that they broadly reinforce the idea that ideas and innovations percolate from parts of the brain associated with more relaxed states, and then get assessed by the more intellectual or analytical parts. This notion reinforces the value of letting the brain wander, of giving it freedom to conjure from the imagination, without judging what comes up, and then allowing the more logical parts of the brain to put those ideas through the paces.

But this brain science is still very definitely emerging. We have much to learn.

We're doing better with the eyes. Some of the most surprising research I learned about for this book comes from researchers studying creativity and vision.

What people create comes from what they see. Literally.

The Eyes Have It

A scientific paper that appeared in August of 2019 in a journal called *Neuroimage* captures one of the most important concepts to date in the scholarship of creativity. The paper describes how creators see the world—not philosophically, but literally. Specifically, it shows that creative people actually see more material in the world around them, picking up and dwelling on information that others who are less creative miss.

This revelatory study—its own act of creativity—helps explain multiple facets of the creative experience, including why and how creators have more material to draw on when they are building a business, making a medicine, painting at the easel, and crafting a song at the guitar or piano. It helps explain the value of travel and new experience, of conversations with people who think differently, and of leaving a bubble of information that wraps many. The more you see, and the more you are trained to see, the more you can create.

What you create depends on what you see.

"Creative individuals seem to see the world differently, to notice what others overlook and find meaning in what others deem irrelevant," the paper begins.

What follows is what they discovered.

At the University of California at Santa Barbara, eighty-eight undergraduates were given a sheet of paper with four boxes. The boxes contained lines in a vague pattern. The study subjects were given ten minutes to report what images they saw in the lines. In creativity research, this is called "the incomplete figures task."

The test is a subset of the Torrance Test of Creative Thinking I introduced a chapter ago. The responses from the eighty-eight study subjects were assessed independently by two different experienced creative scorers. The scorers' assessments largely overlapped, giving the researchers a clear sense of where all the study subjects placed on a creativity spectrum.

The study subjects were also assessed on several other scales. One was a questionnaire designed to measure curiosity—or "the desire to acquire new knowledge," as the trait is sometimes described, or "a drive to know, or to explore." To complement this questionnaire, the subjects were asked how often they undertake "day-to-day" artistic behaviors, like creating an original poem or picture.

The subjects were also scored on a third scale. This is where things get interesting. This scale measures a person's propensity to magical or delusional thinking. This is a personality characteristic that falls under the heading of the fancy word "schizotypy."

In the scholarly literature, it has a very broad set of definitions that revolve around the idea of detaching to some extent from reality. In extreme forms, schizotypy manifests as schizophrenia. In more mild forms, which appear not so uncommon, people can have modest and occasional delusions, or, even more blandly, can be visual thinkers or magical thinkers. Some literature describes people who are deeply religious as having schizotypy tendencies because they believe in stories that have no clear basis in reality or that cannot be supported by physical evidence. In other words, this personality trait is not so narrow as the daunting word itself—schizotypy— might suggest. And it might well have positive attributes, according to a growing body of science.

To assess where people fall on the spectrum, the subjects were given a test called "an oddball task." This involved having the study subjects listen to various auditory tones and then measuring whether study subjects identified related sounds and how quickly they made those connections, as opposed to identifying unrelated sounds; to put it another way, whether they saw connections that were not clearly, objectively related to one another.

In sum, the researchers assessed the study subjects based on three personality factors: creativity, curiosity, and proneness to magical or delusional thinking.

Then came the part that really captures the imagination: The researchers evaluated how the study subjects see the world, literally. What information do these creative types spend time looking at, and for how long?

Study subjects sat roughly two feet from a seventeen-inch computer screen. In increments of eight seconds, they were shown twenty pictures. These included a relatively random array of "natural indoor and outdoor scenes," for example, "a bicycle lying on the grass, a bathroom with assorted objects on the countertop."

The study subjects then were shown twenty-two different images, "lively in color and content," including "bright-colored lizards or skydivers."

Finally, the subjects were shown twenty abstract images, like impressionist and surreal art.

During the process, the researchers used sophisticated eye-tracking software to measure the number of places that study subjects looked, and how long they focused on a particular region. This test, the paper noted, "is a way to quantify the complexity of individuals' fixation patterns and captures how much individuals explored the images." It created a spectrum of responses from "a more ordered or systemic gaze pattern," and a "more random, unpredictable, and exploratory scanning pattern."

The researchers found that the way people looked at these images connected closely to the three personality measures.

- SUBJECTS WHO scored more highly on the creativity test tended to look at more regions of an image and spend more time on those regions.
- THE SAME positive correlation was made between more curious subjects and their tendency to look at more areas of images and spend more time on those regions.
- THOSE WITH higher magical thinking—tending to making connections that may not be logical—led people to look at fewer places with less fixation.

So what?

"We could venture to say," the research noted, "that creative and highly curious individuals see the world differently in a quite literal sense."

It is hard to overstate the importance of this finding in the pursuit of understanding creativity.

In earlier parts of this book, I described the way that rigid thinking is anathema to creativity, in part because it limits the ability to tap into the authenticity of individual creative sparks. People who learn that there are precise ways to behave and think are less likely to see the multitudes inside themselves that provide access to more creative material, additional ingredients in their Spice Rack of Creativity.

But what is so intriguing about this recent research is that it suggests that more rigid thinkers also blind themselves, physically, to the material that surrounds them in the physical world. They don't even take in information that might be relevant to a solution or a creation. This means that the ability to create gets further limited by the number of ingredients—the pallet of colors, set of experiences—that a person can draw from. That a person can *see*.

The more people see, the more they can create, the more experiences and ingredients they possess to draw from.

This happens with rigid thinking that includes, importantly, overly simplistic bias, stereotype, preconception, and misconception. When such thinking occurs, when a creator becomes blind to an authentic experience, it may be impossible to create anything of resonance.

What do I mean?

Imagine a simple example of a scientist who lacks enough experience to know about how certain chemicals interact. That person may well not see connections between two ideas because one of the ideas remains invisible.

Or a television writer might continue to write one clichéd or unoriginal idea after another by relying on watching other peoples' ideas on the screen, or drawing on what has been seen previously as marketable or acceptable, in effect regurgitating that which the writer has seen before.

By definition, it can be hard to be novel or surprising, two core aspects of creativity, if a would-be creator is narrowed by seeing few things or by failing to see things as they are.

Garry Trudeau, the creator of *Doonesbury*, and arguably someone whose name and ideas are Big C enough to stand the test of time, described to me a bit about how he came to see more than perhaps did some of his peers as a result of feeling like an outsider.

"I was short, shy, and unathletic, and had few friends during the seven years I spent in boarding school. But being on the outside looking in can make you a better noticer than those admitted to the party, a better observer of the games people play to preserve their status, and, of course, more empathetic toward those who have none," he told me. "I had zero self-confidence during those years, but—and this is what saved me—I never doubted my self-worth for a moment. I was a well-loved child—had a rich and happy early childhood—and I believed my mother's frequent declarations of how special I was. I had every expectation of life working out."

Trudeau exhibits an invaluable balance: the confidence to allow himself to see and express those feelings of discomfort that are the stuff of great creativity.

By contrast, I've heard it said by one of the wisest editors I've never met—a longtime top editor at the *New York Times*—that many reporters he's worked with in his life are too insecure at their core to allow themselves to make observations they fear may cause them to look stupid or weak. The editor calls this failing "expertitis" and he told me that one reason that journalism can lack for original storytelling and reporting is that some reporters decline to truly listen to what they are hearing, to internalize the breadth of opinions from a breadth of sources. In the case of this lesson, the metaphor was "hearing," not "seeing," but it serves the same end.

Almost certainly the best story I heard about the value of vision to creativity—and one of the best stories I heard overall in reporting for this book—comes from Jennifer Eberhardt. She's a Stanford professor and MacArthur Genius Award winner who got to see race relations in America through the eyes of a child.

The story took place in 2017, as Eberhardt sat next to her five-year-old son.

"Mommy," her son said, "that man looks like daddy."

Eberhardt looked around the plane, wondering to whom the boy could be referring.

"Which man?"

The boy pointed closer to the middle of the plane.

She settled on the only possibility, an African American man, the one person who shared the skin color of the Eberhardt family. But the man looked nothing like Eberhardt's husband, the boy's father. Eberhardt felt her blood pressure rise as she thought about how to handle this delicate conversation with her son. Not all Black people look alike. Before she could respond to him, though, it got worse.

"Mommy," the boy said, "I hope that man doesn't rob the plane."

Eberhardt saw stars. Confusion, anger, insight, a connection with all those people experiencing fear of the other. And terror for the world her son was inheriting.

This core fear, this pure emotional spark, helped lead to powerful, creative science that I'll describe here to underscore how she took a personal moment of inspiration and then proved that her experience was not isolated. Many people feel what her son felt, and see what he saw.

Eberhardt's proof of how and why this is happening would go on to be an important contribution in 2020 as the nation grappled with videos showing the murders of African American men at the hands of white men who were sometimes civilian citizens and other times police officers.

Eberhardt embarked on novel studies to show the deep nature of bias around race—in order to determine scientifically whether this conversation involving systemic racism is merely observed and hypothesized or can be demonstrated scientifically.

In one study by Eberhardt and her colleagues, study subjects—white male students from Stanford University and the University of California at Berkeley—sat at computer monitors while being shown blips of images, indistinguishable, lightning-fast. Some of the images, shown to some participants, included white faces and Black ones. Those participants then were asked to make determinations about the identity of an object that began to appear on the screen.

The object could be a pocket watch or a penny, a stapler, or a telephone. It could be a gun or a knife. In each case, the object appeared slowly, ill-formed and grainy at first and impossible to discern, and then increasingly clear. The participants pressed a button to indicate when they could identify the object.

After the participants saw a Black face, they tended to be much quicker at being able to discern a gun or a knife.

"Black prime faces dramatically reduced the number of frames needed to accurately detect crime-related objects." Not only that, the study showed that exposure to white faces, in a control group, actually slowed identification of a crime-related object. That finding shows the profound difference in the associations between skin color and crime.

In the same paper, published in the *Journal of Personality and Social Psychology*, Eberhardt and her co-researchers intensified the significance of the findings with a second experiment. This one utilized a similar demographic of subjects and computer modeling but in this case first exposed the subjects to fleeting images of crime-related objects—like guns and knives. The subjects were then shown images of Black and white men at frame rates too fast for them to process consciously but enabling subconscious recognition. The study found that when subjects were shown objects related to crime, they saw Black faces more readily than white ones.

"Not only are Blacks thought of as criminal, but also crime is thought of as Black," the study concluded.

In a third study, published in the same journal, the scientists examined the biases of police officers. They did so by working with an urban police department that serves more than 100,000 citizens. More than three-quarters of the officers, 76 percent, where white and 86 percent were male. The study found that the officers, when prompted first with words associated with crime (violent, arrest, shoot, capture, chase) made significantly faster subconscious associations with Black faces. Not just that: The police officers were more likely to recall the Black faces in memory tests and also to "falsely" remember the Black faces as more stereotypically Black—darker skin, larger lips.

"Thoughts of violent crime led to a systematic distortion of the Black image," the research found.

In the context of creativity, this group of studies, and others by Dr. Eberhardt, were obviously not the first to show the phenomenon of subconscious bias. They built on other creations, though, and added their own creative twist, in particular by showing that subconscious bias works in two directions—images of crime prompt study subjects to make associations with Black people while images of Black people prompt study subjects to make associations with crime. This is how creations get built—one on the next, each a stop that leads to the precipice of a Big C, one that might change the world.

Drawing on the research, Eberhardt has begun offering simple ideas to help diminish our subconscious bias. The ideas begin by understanding what our brains are doing, and then taking a moment to actively process our biases so that we can see the world more clearly, and more truly.

There are several reasons I'm telling you this story, and only one of them has to do with citing an example about how Eberhardt found creative inspiration by drawing on primal fear—the terror, for example, that her son could be killed by someone overcome with bias. A second is that Eberhardt essentially predicted the future.

"When ordinary civilians seek to prevent violent crime in their neighborhoods, how likely is it that a Black face will draw their attention?" Eberhardt and her colleagues wrote.

Eberhardt's work is essential in that it helps demonstrate how our own biases and what I'll call "false fears" can greatly interfere with creative processes.

———————

Bias exists for good reason. It helps to save mental resources. Think how much less brain power the world would require if there were easy shortcuts that let you judge people just by looking at them. If it were possible to tell with just a glance whether someone presented opportunity or threat, it would cut down greatly on the time commitment of knowing how to interact with that person. It is easy to see how prejudices climb into your psyche—African Americans are like this, Catholics are like that, Jews are like this, the French are like that, and Democrats and Republicans get simplified into respective buckets. People can become prone not only to see "others" in a particular light but also to embrace their own tribe with undue optimism. Many different problems come from this, some of them deadly, but I won't dwell on all of that here. I want to focus for a moment on the idea that bias creates false fear that inhibits creativity. The trouble is that the creation of great works—scientific or artistic—often comes from seeing things as they are, not as you've been told they are, or as you've been told they should be.

Here, I can offer a brief personal testimony to the value of trading the accepted point of view—which saves time and energy—and making the longer-term investment in going the other way.

I mentioned earlier that I began to hear my own voice after I had a good, old-fashioned emotional collapse in my late twenties. I started to trust what I saw and felt more than I ever had before. I turned down a posting for the *New York Times* and managed to stay in San Francisco but still work for the paper. That meant that I was asked to cover the wonders of technology. What a moment! What innovation! What wealth!

This was the bulk of the coverage I was assigned to provide. What was Steve Jobs's next brilliant idea? What would we automate next? Would the microwave soon take voice commands?

As I'd gotten more comfortable accepting that what I felt was okay, reliable, something to draw on, I began to notice behaviors in myself that had me looking differently at technology. For instance, I'd be in the car driving and find myself itching to call somebody—anybody—even if it were someone I wasn't all that interested in talking to under normal circumstances. Why was that? If I ran out of people I ordinarily liked talking to, I'd start going down listings in the phone book. Why?

I nearly was involved in a wreck when looking down at my phone for directions. That made my compulsion to use the phone in the car particularly odd.

It wasn't just in the car. I'd watch my urge to check my device ramp up at interesting times. During one period, I noticed that I tended to check sports scores on the phone in the moments right after a tense interaction with my wife (I don't mean we were having a fight, but she might say, "Did you take out the trash?" and I'd notice in myself a small tic of irritation and then I'd check the Giants score. What was I doing? Escaping?)

Why, when I went to the airport or another public place, couldn't I catch anyone's eye anymore? Faces were down, entranced.

What hold did this device have on me, and maybe on other people too?

I wasn't at all alone in making these observations; a number of people were asking questions, watching their own behavior, hearing their own voices. My voice was paired with a set of circumstances that allowed me to create: a position with the *New York Times*, a great deal of experience telling stories and interviewing scientists, and, crucially, a high-level editor, the one who despised "expertitis," and who loved the "smart-dumb question."

He launched me on a monthslong look at this simple question:

What happens when people take a phone into a car ? Isn't that a bad idea?

This might seem so obvious now but it wasn't at the time, in 2009. It may be why when the story about distracted driving was published, in July, it led to a huge response. The editor at the top of the paper who was responsible for building multiple-part series asked me: "What else do you have in your notebook?"

Plenty. What followed was an all-consuming, six-month period of ecstatic journalism, of muse and opportunity, in which I got permission from the most powerful journalistic institution on Earth to pursue stories that connected dots in science, policy, the emotions of families who lost loved ones to distracted drivers, and the voices of the drivers themselves who killed while texting or using the phone. Stories kept coming together until they became one giant story, one that returned to the very beginning of the cell phone, which was not called the cell phone at all, but the "car phone," engineered for use by drivers even as its creators buried science they knew showed how dangerously distracting their new creation would be. All the while, I was given increasing faith from the paper to trust in my own storytelling instincts.

At the end of the year, when we were asked to put together a submission for a Pulitzer Prize, we discovered that the phrase "distracted driving" had been added to the dictionary during that period. President Barack Obama had signed an executive order, a copy of which hangs on my wall, preventing federal employees from texting while driving. States passed laws banning the practice.

All of it happened because of a huge collective effort, the weight of the paper and its amassed talent and influence. But in basic ways, I could trace the series back to the fact that I'd learned to listen and to see—in myself and in others, with a kind of raw authenticity I now understand attends much of creativity, in any field.

This brings me back to Eberhardt, whose work on helping people see the world more clearly goes to the very heart of creativity—both of the individual creator and creative enterprises and the country as a whole.

The individual creator who makes assumptions about people—something that can occur regardless of political or ideological positions—limits what the creator can draw from.

A person with an elite sensibility might not listen to the amazing idea or observation of someone less educated or who doesn't come from a fancy school. The person who didn't attend a fancy school may tune out the wisdom of someone who studied at an elite university.

The Republican might ignore the idea from the Democrat and the reverse, and so too the pauper and the billionaire, people from different religious faiths, genders, sexual orientations, etc., etc., and on forever. The observations and ideas from any number of people could be the stuff of an individual creator's spice rack of emotion and experience, or the stuff of a corporation's next great product development and marketing campaign, but not if it is ignored for want of being seen in the first place.

I happened to hear this idea uttered with particular clarity on a sports radio program, a venue from which we might not expect to receive such concise wisdom.

It was early September 2020, and by then there had been twenty-eight million infected worldwide and 905,000 deaths from the terrible creation called the novel coronavirus, or COVID-19. In San Francisco, where I live, we were in a kind of double quarantine, not just because of the virus, but because wildfires had caused ash to fall with such density that the air was dangerous to breathe. Social unrest gripped the streets.

I got into the car and the radio happened to be tuned to a sports talk show in which the host interviewed a man named Arik Armstead, a defensive lineman for the San Francisco 49ers and team co-captain. Armstead had become vocal of late in discussing social issues gripping the country and had creatively used his platform in press conferences. In the radio call I heard, the host asked the giant lineman to describe why he so mourned bias in the world.

"We are missing out," Armstead said, "on our full potential."

The sentence really hammers home this key notion: the more closed-minded we are to ideas—whether they come from one side of the aisle or the other or a person from one group or another—the less able we are as individuals to be creative. And the less we can create as a society.

It's hard to be open-minded. It's hardly impossible. It's not beyond any of us.

There's more good news for those who aspire to creativity. It doesn't require genius. In fact, the personality-traits that lend to inspiration and execution can be developed. They don't depend on a characteristic I just assumed, when I started this book, to be key to creativity: a high IQ.

It makes me feel so much better to know that being just plain smart is overrated.

Personality

When I began researching for this book, I held an assumption that I suspect is widespread: People who are smart are more likely to be creative. As I look back, I confess that I'm not sure what I thought I meant by "smart." Maybe I had IQ in mind. I had much to learn.

"One of the more common-sense and intuitive conclusions concerning intelligence and creativity is that high level intelligence is synonymous with creative genius," reads a 2003 paper in the *Journal of Research in Personality*. That paper won the journal's award for best article that year, and with good reason: It dispelled the myth of intelligence as the chief personality trait among creators. It is also highly valuable in that it looked at multiple bodies of research to draw its conclusion.

A co-author of that study, Gregory Feist, a professor of psychology at San Jose State University who I mentioned earlier in this book, has since shown in multiple ways that intelligence gets a creator only so far. As a preface, he takes pains to define what intelligence means in the first place, or how it is generally perceived.

Intelligence is fairly associated with problem solving and the speed of doing it, abstract reasoning, and, broadly, the capacity to process information. It is a component of creativity, to a point.

The 2003 paper that Feist co-wrote draws evidence from a handful of studies. Earlier in the book, I mentioned one of them, having to do with one of the most extensive "life-span" studies ever done that considered 1,500 students starting in 1921. The students had high

IQs, an average of 147, but that didn't predict future creative achievement, even when they were observed over decades.

Other studies have found similar results, yielding a basic relationship between intelligence and creativity that should be highly encouraging for those of us (present company included) who have average intelligence: People with an IQ that is above average are not likelier than people with an average IQ to achieve creatively.

In fact, above an IQ of 115-120, "the relationship becomes essentially zero," the 2003 paper reads. It notes that this has been called the "threshold theory," meaning that a person need rise above only a certain threshold of intelligence to become extremely creative. "In summary, instead of being twin or even sibling constructs, intelligence and creativity may be more like cousins."

Subsequent research has refined the thinking. A 2013 paper from scholars in Austria found that the IQ threshold for some creative thinking, namely generation of ideas, was much lower, below 100. But for overall creativity measures, the threshold for creativity of 120, the average, has prevailed.

It is noteworthy that some research shows that a better predictor than test-measured intelligence of whether someone will achieve creatively is whether outsiders *perceive* or report a person to be intelligent. "Observer-rated intellect at age twenty-seven," the 2003 paper co-written by Feist noted. And he wrote that "Potential for creative achievement can be evaluated explicitly by asking people closest to potential creators."

This finding relates to several studies that begin to inch toward the type of personalities that are more likely to be creative than those personalities that are merely highly intelligent as measured by scores.

The Westinghouse Science Talent Search, for fifty-seven years beginning in 1942, rewarded students for original research papers and scientific presentations. People who fared well in the study wound up faring disproportionately well in creative fields, and they include Nobel Prize winners. The science competition was taken over by a new sponsor, Intel, in 1988. Then, in a twist that shows a changing world, it was again rebranded several years ago, this time by Regeneron. That was the company whose drug was used in 2020 to help fight COVID-19, including when it attacked President Trump.

A related study found that young scientists who produce a lot of papers are likely to continue to be more productive, and have greater creative accomplishment, than peers who are not as productive early in their careers.

The importance of noting the predictive nature of early creative achievement as a measure of future creative achievement is that it begins to bridge the gap to a broader set of personality traits that characterize creativity. What does this particular predictor suggest?

For one thing, it puts the emphasis on doing, on action, and on the simple act of perseverance. Is a question compelling enough to spur someone to create? How much does a person care about the question, and not just the answer?

To me, this leads to one of the core defining principles that separates a merely intelligent person from a creator, which I mentioned in this book's opening:

An intelligent person answers a question.

A creative person comes up with the question in the first place, and then answers it.

A handful of personality characteristics have been shown to complement intelligence in leading someone to want to ask questions, pursue answers, and even be unsatisfied with simply answering the question in one pat fashion. The most significant trait is known in the literature as "openness."

In a 2013 article titled "The Creative Person in Science," Feist and a co-author studied the personalities of 145 scholars from major research universities in the United States. The study looked at the scientists' creative achievement, as measured by productivity and impact, and then compared that to various personality traits as reported in a questionnaire.

The most striking variable was openness, which Feist and his co-author characterized as "the need for variety, change, and novelty," with the study finding that "scientists who have wide imagination, who are curious, and open to new experiences tend to be more creative than their conventional and down-to-earth colleagues."

The idea of openness can be read in a variety of ways. It describes someone who is curious, as the authors note, but also someone who might view the idea of failure differently than someone who is less open. In one respect, the value of being open or curious outweighs the outcome in the minds of some highly creative people to the point that the creators become relatively blinded by the outcome. But there is more at play, given that the creators are, in fact, achieving creatively.

The finding by Feist in this study conforms to broader work in a field of creativity scholarship that actually has a personality trait that is named: "openness/intellect."

When I first read this term, it left me confused. That's because intellect seems like one thing and openness something else. What it took my average intellect a bit to grasp is that the research lumps these two ideas together as a single, related personality trait because they both relate to the way a person processes, or tends to process, information.

"Openness," the literature says, "reflects the tendency toward engagement with aesthetic and sensory information (in both perception and imagination)." By contrast, "Intellect reflects the tendency toward engagement with abstract and intellectual information."

There are a lot of other types of language that might be used here. An open person might tend to feel with his heart and an intellectual one with her head; an open person might be more flexible and an intellectual one more rigid; an open one might entertain the possibility of multiple right answers and an intellectual one see only the precise right answer.

What the literature says is that prolific and effective creators tend to see an overlap and function highly in these two areas. That means that they blur skills, or tendencies, that might be heavily weighted in others to one side or the other.

For instance, at the far extreme of the spectrum of intellect, a person with a massive IQ might be able to understand extremely complex ideas. The thinking is concrete, rigid, and very, very smart in the way of a great test taker.

On the other end of the spectrum, where openness is at its most extreme, is a condition called "apophenia." This is the tendency of a person to make connections between unrelated ideas, a concept loosely related to schizophrenia. Less extreme under the heading of openness is fantasy and even "absorption" into an unreal or imagined place.

It is worth noting that openness doesn't require one to shed all inhibitions. It requires the consideration of ideas and a willingness to explore those ideas, experiences, and feelings. This is a key distinction and it allows for a person to draw some lines. The creative person is not, as some readers might be inferring, left to flounder in a world without rules. In fact, the more deeply I got to know Giddens, the more I came to understand that she picked and chose how and what to share with her listeners, and even with herself.

"There's a really guarded piece of myself," she said. "I am creative and I create things," but, she told me, there are parts of her that she still isn't comfortable incorporating actively into her work. "How much do I want to disturb that—what I went through as a child? I really don't know. It's scary and it's why I haven't fussed with it. It is a scary place to think about."

She's found her comfort zone.

So has her sister—and in a way that speaks to the limitations of intelligence as it is often measured.

Giddens' sister, Lalenja Harrington, is the director of Academic Programming Development & Evaluation for Beyond Academics at the University of North Carolina at Greensboro, where I could practically hear her voice without the use of the phone from my home office in San Francisco. She is so passionate about what she sees, and what she has seen: people unfairly written off because they have intellectual disabilities.

"I try to provide multiple ways to engage with them. It is so fucking important for us as a human race," she said in one of a handful of enlightening conversations. She is giving these students a college education that was never before available. "I resist this idea that there's one standard way, or a standard approach to sharing information."

This is what a creator sounds like—open, willing to take risk, determined. (By way of example, Harrington admonished me that students with intellectual disabilities "are written off because of arbitrary standards of intelligence that are anchored in white supremacy." She was referring to measures like IQ.) She, like her sister, exists in the middle of the spectrum of insights and openness that researchers call "innovation/imagination."

It is a balance struck between openness to the world with analytical capacity to contextualize what the creator sees.

Meanwhile, the work done by Feist also shows a connection between creativity and another personality type: neuroticism.

———

The 2013 paper about scientists and creativity describes neuroticism as the tendency to feel more anxiety and sadness, but also more emotional sensitivity and vulnerability. The influence of this personality type on creativity is less than that of openness, but is still statistically significant. Interestingly, and I think fairly, Feist and his co-author see a link between the idea of neuroticism and openness in that both represent a lower "threshold" for allowing in information—whether from the outside or the inside.

"The openness to experience and predisposition to sadness may lower the threshold for finding solutions that are both novel and original," their paper notes.

In an interview, Feist said that "openness is definitely the predictor of creativity in art and science," and he explicitly mentioned "openness to experience."

In support of this point, I'd offer the reader powerful testimony from a creator I mentioned early in the book named Mark Romanek. He's among the most celebrated music-video directors. Part of what makes Romanek so effective is that he hears and sees things so acutely. This can be a liability too. "As I take in stimulation, it's exhausting," he said. "You know sometimes when you turn your laptop on and you hear it revving. There's a high-pitch sound and it seems hot and you're afraid it might crash? That's how my brain is most of the time."

He told me he has Asperger Syndrome, which can cause people to become socially awkward and highly absorbed.

The information that Romanek takes in, while it can stymie him, can also provide him incredible richness for creation. One of the best music videos I've ever seen is one that Romanek directed of Johnny Cash covering, beautifully, a song written by Trent Reznor titled "Hurt." At the time, Cash's health was fading and he would die within a year. Plans to shoot the video had to be amended so that Romanek, rather than shooting the video he had scripted in a Los

Angeles studio, wound up flying to Tennessee at the last minute with a cinematographer, camera operator, and no plan at all. With just a few days to shoot on the fly, Romanek used this superpower of his to draw from the surroundings to create a brilliant homage to Cash and mortality. (Pro tip: watch this!)

On the question of being open to new experience, I asked Feist if it would be enough for someone to experience the world through, say, watching Netflix shows of all kinds. After all, so much of the world comes to us through a screen. Would that be the same as having physical experiences?

"Direct interaction with people is the obvious difference," he said. That experience, he argued, forces someone to truly confront habits and assumptions. He said this is particularly true with experiences like travel that can open a mind by confronting it with concrete challenges to basic ways of thinking. "It's a willingness to be confused and not understand and not know. That's really the quality of highly creative people. The willingness to jump into the unknown. They take pleasure in not understanding rather than withdrawing from it."

A final piece of this personality puzzle comes in the form of the trait of "confidence." It's a very interesting word to consider in this context because what Feist and other researchers mean when they refer to a confident creator is not that the creator is confident in all that he, or she, or they know. But, rather, that the creator is confident enough to be willing to be uncertain—but then confident enough to settle on an answer authentic to a particular creative approach.

"You have ideas and a vision and a way of thinking that is kind of unique," he said. "You may get pushback and criticism but you're open enough and confident enough to stick with it."

It's a razor's edge of confidence, a willingness to take in new information without being threatened but also to hold the line when a new idea feels authentic and powerful enough to be in the world.

For would-be creators, I tend to think of this as more good news. Creativity depends less on raw intellect, which arguably cannot be learned, and more on the combination of at least some intellect with a high level of openness. Another word for this could be curiosity. One way I sum up the difference for myself between intellect and creativity is through a simple test. Someone with great intellect may well find a single, clear answer to a question—an answer that meets all the tests for logic. A creative person might find some real value in exploring different answers, or even coming up with a new question altogether. In fact, great creators often are open to finding creative solutions, or new ways of thinking about things, from unexpected places.

It's a perfect transition to the stories of two great creators whose personalities have more in common than might meet the eye: James Allison, who won a Nobel Prize for helping to cure cancer, and Steve Kerr, the coach of the Golden State Warriors.

Kerr's tale begins on January 8, 2015, in Cleveland (as so many great tales do).

The Coach and the Diamond Head

It was on this night that the Golden State Warriors played in game four of the NBA Championship series at Quicken Loans Arena. Their opponent was the Cleveland Cavaliers, led by LeBron James, by all accounts sharing legendary status with the likes of Michael Jordan, Kobe Bryant, and other players who, not coincidentally, married openness to ideas with searing intellect. LeBron and the Cavaliers were ahead in the series two games to one.

A magical Warriors season appeared to be in trouble. Kerr was in his first year as the Warriors head coach and had guided the team to sixty-nine wins, one of the highest numbers of victories in NBA history. He had great gifts in All-Stars Klay Thompson and Draymond Green and, above all, Steph Curry. But Kerr received well-deserved wide praise for bringing it all together. That year, he won Coach of the Year.

But now they were losing the series, against one of the greatest players ever, and playing away from home.

They needed an idea. Something creative. Or they were going to lose the championship and feel they had squandered the series.

Kerr found an idea. In an unlikely place.

Before I describe what happened, it helps to explain why: Kerr, like great creators, contains multitudes, and is exceedingly open in a jock culture that can be very closed.

For a professional basketball coach, Kerr is some kind of nerd. As a kid, he was an introvert. He read nonstop. He picked up intellectual curiosity from his father, a scholar who became president of American University in Beirut. That was the position Malcolm Kerr held when Islamic Jihadist assassins gunned down the eminent professor outside his office door. His crime: trying to find creative solutions to support peace in the region.

It was particularly cruel because Kerr's father strove to understand all sides, to listen. To underscore the point, I borrow here a passage from a spectacular article written by one of the *New York Times*'s most creative writers, John Branch, who profiled Steve Kerr. Branch wrote:

> "The truly civilized man is marked by empathy," Malcolm Kerr wrote in a foreword to a collection of essays called "By his recognition that the thought and understanding of men of other cultures may differ sharply from his own, that what seems natural to him may appear grotesque to others."

Malcom Kerr's murder happened during Kerr's first year playing basketball at the University of Arizona. His father's assassination didn't seem to dim Kerr's worldview or make of him a fanatic. Over time, his perspective broadened. He became more empathic, coming to decry the conditions that lead to hateful tribalism, looking at the individual and not the group. It wasn't always easy. In a horrific moment, the fans at a rival university, Arizona State, chanted "PLO" to taunt Kerr during a game.

"It's really simple to demonize Muslims because of our anger over 9/11, but it's obviously so much more complex than that," Kerr told Branch for his article. "The vast majority of Muslims are peace-loving people, just like the vast majority of Christians and Buddhists and Jews and any other religion. People are people."

Kerr had not been heavily recruited in college. In fact, lore has it that when Kerr tried out at the University of Arizona, the wife of the coach—who was in the stands watching—said to her husband: "You're going to give *that guy* a scholarship?"

In life and basketball, Kerr became a student, hard knocks school all the way. He persevered like a Westinghouse Science prodigy but with a basketball. A particularly creative type of leader began to take shape.

After graduating from Arizona, and despite a slight frame and modest speed, he wound up in the NBA, where he established and still holds the record for highest percentage lifetime shooting from three-point range. He didn't score a lot of points—on average six a game—but he was accurate when he did shoot, especially when it counted. He wound up playing with a guy named Michael Jordan and was a bit player on a Chicago Bulls team that won—count 'em— six NBA Championship rings.

By the time Kerr got hired to coach the Golden State Warriors in the spring of 2014, he'd become a curious mix of a grown-up introvert who remained both insecure, in that there was a lot that he didn't know about the world, and deeply confident inwardly that he could somehow figure stuff out. He consistently engaged with the world—to learn but without the kind of chip on his shoulder that often accompanies jock culture.

At press conferences, Kerr told me that he sometimes would be so open and unfiltered that he'd wonder: "Did I just screw that up?"

"There's a level of self-awareness that can blend into self-consciousness but the confidence the game has given me has helped me to become a coach."

At the time of Kerr's hiring, a veteran sports reporter named Monte Poole talked to a fellow sports reporter who had known Kerr as a high school classmate. "He said: Kerr's such a great dude. He said: He's just genuine. He's open and he's honest and he's also got a sense of humor. He can be sarcastic.

"Our conversations tend to revolve as much around social issues, politics, books, and just life beyond basketball," Poole said. He recalled a moment just before the COVID-19 outbreak, when the Warriors were struggling through the early part of a tough 2019 season, beset by injuries. Kerr held a brief news conference and "He started walking away, and I caught up to him to ask him a question," Poole recalled, "and he said: 'Well, what do you think?'"

"About what?" Poole said.

"Bernie, Joe, Klobuchar, Kamala?" Kerr responded. He wanted to talk politics. "I talked to David West, and David likes Bernie." (David West was a long-time All-Star, no longer on the team at that time.)

When I reached Kerr on the phone to talk about creativity, I frankly was surprised by how candid he was when he and I first started speaking, talking about the insecurity of his youth that gave him a lifelong humility.

"I'm an open person," he said. "I listen to everybody's opinion and I value people's opinions and some of that is probably born from the awareness and understanding that nobody has all the answers. It is closely related to being insecure about not knowing something."

Not to be mistaken for a shrinking violet. People close to Kerr told me about his intensely competitive side, his loathing for losing. (There once was a famous shoving match he had with Michael Jordan in which he refused to back down after feeling bullied by the larger man and star.) But Kerr's strength doesn't come across as pride or hubris. He is so strong, in fact, he can show his curiosity without feeling weakened by it or feeling perceived as being seen as weak. And that is the very balance of intellect and openness that returns me to what was then Quicken Loans Arena in Cleveland. The Warriors, after their magical season, were down 2-1 games to LeBron James and his Cavaliers in the NBA Finals, where the first team to win four games is christened champion.

"It was perilous," Poole said of that fourth game. "They were ready to be good, but there was no certainty they'd be champions."

Just before tip-off of that pivotal game four, one of the TV announcers described a conversation with Kerr. "Kerr said: 'We lost two in a row; we're going to look at everything,'" the announcer explained.

That's no small thing to do after you've done things one way for a long time and it's worked so well.

What was so problematic about the Cavaliers and what could the Warriors do about it? Was it just that they faced a team with LeBron James?

Where would the answer come from?

Kerr and his senior staff looked for answers.

That's when one of the staff noticed something. It wasn't a senior coach. It was a lower-level assistant, named Nick U'ren, who was twenty-eight at the time.

His job with the team was to watch videotape of prior games and put together sequences for the Warriors coaches and players to watch. The video included watching videotape of prior series, including of the Warriors and the Cavaliers, but also the way other teams in the past had played against LeBron.

He noticed a pattern. Teams that beat the Cavaliers and LeBron used a different kind of lineup than the one that the Warriors had used all year. They'd tended to use smaller, quicker players at certain positions.

Sitting in his hotel room, U'ren, the video assistant, had an idea. Maybe the Warriors needed to change their starting lineup so that they could guard LeBron James differently. Yes, yes! He was certain, the more he thought about it. The Warriors needed to change out their starting center, a beloved teammate named Andrew Bogut, who was also cherished by the ownership of the Warriors.

He thought they should instead start a wily veteran named Andre Iguodala, shorter than a traditional center like Bogut, but strong, and as savvy as they come. Iguodala was typically the first Warrior to come off the bench and play during the game, so it wasn't a huge change, but one at an extremely high-risk moment.

"I knew it was going to work," U'ren told me. "I didn't have the data. I don't know why."

I could hear the inspiration in his voice, even years later. And a touch of terror. Who was he to suggest such a change? He texted an assistant coach at 3 a.m. The next day that coach broached the idea with Kerr.

It resonated.

"It was a very good suggestion," Kerr told me. "What made it unique was that Nick was a first-year coach, a video coordinator. It changed everything. It changed the whole series."

The Warriors won the game, and the series, and Iguodala—the guy who became a last-minute starter—was named Most Valuable Player. In a press conference after they won, Kerr explained what had happened, and unsolicited, Kerr gave U'ren credit.

"Sometimes you see people in power in positions of power and they seem to have all the answers, and I don't have all the answers," Kerr told me.

I should be very plain here: Kerr coached the team to a championship and this decision, while key, was part of a much bigger context, put into play by some of the best to ever lace 'em up, and some exquisitely executed basketball.

The thing to take away from this story is that Kerr was able to hear and seize on the right idea at the right moment. He did so because of a powerful combination of intellect and openness, illustrated by such humility that Kerr ultimately shared it publicly; he subverted his ego and his own need for control—which are the opposite of openness—such that he could consider many possibilities. The Warriors subsequently have won two more championships, and from everyone I spoke to, the success owes to Kerr's balance of brains and humility, along with, of course, Steph Curry and other All-Stars. That's whom Kerr credits. "We wouldn't be having this conversation," he said, "if we didn't have great talent.

"Our job is to put them in the best position," he said. "There has to be some humility."

Typical. Take a bow, coach.

This idea of blurring sharp intellect with a willingness to consider all manner of solutions carries across subjects and creators.

The very notion is so powerfully embodied in the person most singularly responsible for developing new cancer therapies. His name is James Allison. Growing tens of thousands of people owe their lives to the discoveries of this Nobel Prize winner, and his openness to different solutions. Of all the creators I've had the privilege to speak with as a journalist and for this book in particular, I would argue none has made a Big C discovery as significant as the one Allison made.

"The common thought people have of the way science works is that you have a hypothesis and you design an experiment to test it," Allison told me. "Then you look at the data and see what it tells you about the hypothesis.

"If you do that, it can be interesting, but not very interesting."

He prefers a more open-ended method.

"What you've got to do when you get the data is look at it like a many-faceted crystal—look at it one way, and another way, and it may well tell you a different question that has little to do with the question you're asking."

This is Allison's way of describing the fact that great science comes from erasing a kind of stereotype or preconceived notion that can plague science as much as anything else. In fact, medical discoveries have been littered with pushback from people with preconceived notions over and over throughout history. The field is, no pun intended, not immune to unscientific thinking.

"Sometimes, you just have to get away from everybody. I take some pride in the fact that I don't think I read as many journal papers as other people," Allison told a science writer named Claudia Dreifus for a piece in *Quanta Magazine*. When he did read papers: "Some of the experiments weren't even understandable," he told her. "I'd think, 'Either I'm too stupid to understand this, or nobody knows what they're talking about. I'm just going to sit down and figure out something logical to me, making certain assumptions and predictions, and just do it.'"

Allison, born in 1948, grew up in a small town in Texas and was nicknamed "Diamond Head" by his brother for his stubborn resolve and independent thinking; he lost his mother to cancer when he was a boy, fought with his high school math teacher because Allison refused to accept the certainty of the existence of God, and today wears long, unkempt white hair, and, when not making discoveries, plays a mean blues harmonica.

Allison's Nobel-winning discovery came when helping shatter ordained ideas of how people think about cancer and then proving he was right. He didn't do it to be stubborn. He followed his innate curiosity and his gut reaction that the traditional way of seeing the relationship between cancer and the immune system did not add up.

The long-standing idea had been that cancers develop inside of people and grow because the immune system—our internal defense mechanisms—doesn't recognize the tumor as being a malignant growth. In the parlance of immunology, scientists thought the immune system didn't see the cancer as "non-self" and therefore didn't attack as it might otherwise attack bacteria or viruses or other organisms that are non-self.

The result of this kind of thinking was that cancer treatments were built by essentially ignoring the role of the immune system and attacking the cancer. This meant using chemotherapy and radiation that tried to destroy the cancer. These treatments are blunt force attacks with all kinds of collateral damage, including destroying lots of healthy tissue, wreaking havoc on the patient on the theory that scorching the Earth was the only way to save it.

But cancer treatment has undergone a quantum shift in recent years, in no small part thanks to Allison. Today, the biggest-selling drugs in the world stimulate the immune system to attack the cancer because, it turns out, our defenders can and do recognize these growths inside of us.

And then the cancer sends a signal to turn the immune system off.

I've chronicled much more of Allison's role in this discovery and his remarkable journey in a book I wrote about the immune system, and I'll briefly summarize that here: Allison in the 1990s homed in on a molecule called CTLA-4. In simple terms, this molecule exists on the surface of immune cells. That fact alone is a bit mind-blowing: So many creations had led Allison to the point where he, and other researchers, could examine and play with molecules on the surface of immune cells. The shoulders of giants.

Allison in his experiments noticed that the effectiveness of the immune system depended on what kind of signal CTLA-4 received from other molecules. If CTLA-4 was stimulated such that it began to proliferate, the strangest thing happened: the immune system stopped attacking.

"I thought, we gotta figure out what CTLA-4 does," Allison told me.

Through a painstaking process, he discovered exactly what it does: It is part of the immune system's braking function. That means that the immune system can recognize cancer, show up, and then— whoa—the cancer can send a signal to tell the immune system to stand down.

Now why might this be? Why would the immune system have a braking system? Isn't it supposed to be perpetually in attack mode?

"CTLA-4 is there to protect you from being killed by yourself," Allison told me for my prior book on the immune system.

What he understood was that the immune system is a razor-sharp double-edged sword. Too little immune system reaction leaves you open to disease but too much leaves a person open to autoimmune disorders and rampant immune response that can be as devastating as any disease.

What cancer was doing, Allison realized, was taking advantage of this signaling system to put the brakes on the immune system. And Allison then figured out how: He discovered the way to turn off the brakes by changing the signal. In one of the most chilling (in a good way) stories I've ever heard told, Allison recounted how he performed an experiment that involved changing the signals and then came into the laboratory one morning to see what had happened to cancer-ridden mice who'd been treated by his experimental procedure. Their tumors had disappeared.

His work, done roughly simultaneously with complementary work by a Japanese scientist named Tasuku Honjo, won them equal shares of the 2018 Nobel Prize in Medicine. Instead of attacking the cancer, as had been the way of the world, they tinkered with the immune system.

The pair, the Nobel Prize citation reads, "established an entirely new principle for cancer therapy."

Would you believe this story connects us back to COVID-19, and the pandemic savaging the world in the fall of 2020 as I write these words? By now, the death toll has climbed above one million worldwide and above 200,000 in the United States. That viral organic creation has become a total wrecking ball, a razor-sharp scythe swinging through humanity with gruesome efficiency and unconscious disregard for its toll.

There was some good news. The world began to create back.

Researchers were getting better at figuring out treatments to dampen the mortal effects of this disease on the lungs.

They did so in part by building on the work of Allison and his generation of creative thinkers about how the immune system worked.

What they found out, after the early days of the pandemic, was that much of the suffering, including many deaths, came from an overreaction of the immune system to COVID-19. That may sound nuts. After all, a reasonable assumption was that the immune cells were failing to react enough to the novel coronavirus to keep it from taking over human lungs. The reality was more complex.

In many cases, the immune system felt so swamped by the disease that it fired off an almost-hysterical response. Attack! Go Nuclear! Masses of signals from proteins in the body sent hordes of immune cells, some of which were contributing to the flooding of the lungs. Some of the most effective treatments involved tamping down the immune system, to keep too much fluid—including immune cells—from clogging our delicate breathing apparatus.

Plus, vaccines and medicines were being developed—built on the same kinds of ideas Allison came up with.

Just prior to the election in the United States in November of 2020, President Trump contracted COVID-19. He was given several different drugs to slow the infection. One was a particular kind of drug called a monoclonal antibody. (The maker of the drug, Regeneron, is the inheritor of the Westinghouse contest.) It's a complicated drug, but the simple explanation is that it sought to tinker with the immune response in ways not unlike those Allison pioneered. The point is not that Allison's discoveries led directly to the medicines that would be created in response to COVID-19. Rather, the conceptual leap that Allison made had a huge impact on the development of many drugs that followed, including those incredible innovations during the pandemic.

A second drug taken by the president—and many others suffering with COVID-19—was a steroid. Trump took it early on when he was coughing and experiencing shortness of breath. That drug tamps down the immune system to lessen inflammation and prevent lung clogging, among other potentially deadly effects of an imbalanced immune response to the virus.

Meanwhile, Allison's discoveries also point to the way that particular discoveries make a mark at particular periods in history. They arise built on the discoveries that came before but also in response to the demands and environment in which they occur. And they came relatively late in Allison's life—he won the Nobel Prize at age seventy, and the work he'd done for it spanned several decades prior. No spring chicken.

Which raises one of the handful of final questions I let my curiosity ponder: How old is a creator?

Age

On several occasions, I've referred to a researcher named Dean Simonton. In creativity scholarship, he found a great niche: He examined clear, demonstrable facts from the lives of creative geniuses—Einstein, Picasso, Freud, Edison, Bach. How many papers did they write or patents did they acquire? What were their specific habits?

He looked at empirical evidence in a field that, as you now know, can be slippery with subtle social science.

One of the questions Simonton asked is: At what age were these great creators most productive?

In 2016, Simonton wrote an article for *Scientific American* titled "Does Creativity Decline with Age?"

"This question has attracted scientific research for more than a century," Simonton wrote, then added: "I can offer a confident answer: not quite!"

His article went on to note that a person's peak creativity generally corresponds with peak productivity. That makes considerable common sense in that productivity relies on energy, and no matter how inspired you are, it can be hard to follow through if you need more naps. Some careers, Simonton wrote, like those of historians and philosophers, appear to suffer no perceptible decline in creativity. Maybe, with each passing year, the creators tucked under their belts more history and philosophy from which to draw, and perhaps it takes less effort to write a history than to, say, perform a rock concert.

I'm also struck that historians and some other scientists—like journalists—get the benefit of drawing from external information. And I would just observe, from my years of interviewing many different people, that careers which allow people to draw from information outside of themselves seem to yield substantial opportunity to create.

By contrast, careers that draw from only one's own authenticity might ultimately be more threadbare as time wears on. Take artists, for instance. I can observe—and again, this is not empirical—that the revelations of self-discovery would be incredible in the earlier parts of life. This would lead to books, songs, a sound, and a style that could peak early in life. Future creations might well be prolific but not necessarily fundamentally different from the creations that came before because they mimic the authenticity that drove the artistic creation in the first place. Think of how many musicians and writers you've cherished and about whom you have said: This reminds me so much of his or her or their earlier works.

In any case, Simonton concluded that there is plenty of evidence people can continue to create well into the latest hours of their lives.

"After all, late bloomers reach creative peaks at ages when early bloomers are past their prime," he wrote, "so the good news is that it is possible to stay creative throughout one's life span."

This is partly why creativity can so ripen with age. But I think there is an even more potent reason that explains the potential for creativity later in life: People begin to understand themselves and their passions better. They understand how things work.

Labor economists at Ohio State University analyzed hundreds of physics discoveries that led to Nobel Prizes, along with the ages of the scientists. A hundred years ago, a third accomplished their discoveries before the age of thirty and another third before forty. But that phenomenon has shifted sharply as people live longer, have more time to learn, and the fields grow more complex.

"The image of the brilliant young scientist who makes critical breakthroughs in science is increasingly outdated," Bruce Weinberg, an economist at Ohio State, wrote in an article published by *LiveScience*, a science-centric news site. "Today, the average age at which physicists do their Nobel Prize–winning work is forty-eight. Very little breakthrough work is done by physicists under thirty."

For others, the key discovery isn't about substance but about themselves. Longer life spans have provided more opportunity for people to hear themselves.

To that end, witness the inspired work of creators I mention in this book. Their contributions span their lifetimes:

- JIM ALLISON, born 1948, won the Nobel Prize for Medicine when he was seventy for work he did creating cancer treatments, work that covered forty years and traced back to the late 1980s. He continues now to try to expand the applications to additional forms of cancer.
- STEVE KERR won six NBA Championships as a player (while he benefited from the creativity of a guy named Michael Jordan, who was in his twenties and thirties), and three as coach, when Kerr was decidedly creative in his forties.
- JUDD APATOW, born in 1967, had been doing stand-up comedy since he was a boy. He's been relentlessly creative throughout his whole life. He's still going, well into his fifties, and some of his best-regarded work has happened later in life.
- JENNIFER EBERHARDT, a MacArthur Genius Award winner and Stanford sociologist, identified ways to rethink race relations and help police see their unconscious bias. She grew up somewhat shy, and her intellectual curiosity meandered. Then her creativity began to crystallize around the work of unconscious bias and police—making her a world expert in the field. She did groundbreaking work with police forces. She

published the book *Biased: Uncovering the Hidden Prejudice That Shapes What We See, Think, and Do*. It came out in 2019. She was in her midfifties.

- **ROGER MCNAMEE** made a mint on Wall Street in his thirties. Years later, he invested in Facebook and many other major internet companies. He founded a popular band in 2007 called Moonalice, for which he sings and plays guitar—he and the band perform in dozens of gigs a year. He later identified deep flaws in Facebook that allowed it to be co-opted by political ne'er do wells, and he has testified multiple times before Congress. He just keeps creating. He was born in 1956. So he was sixty-three when he published *Zucked: Waking Up to the Facebook Catastrophe*.

- **MIKE LEE**, who co-created MyFitnessPal with his brother, made several hundred million dollars and people a lot less fat. He did that in his late thirties and forties. He's looking for a new idea.

- **MIKE MONSKY**, who created the Clean Remote—after he was frightened by the goop on the television remote control—found himself in the middle of the most creative and inspired period in his life during the pandemic after hotels and hospitals started asking him to build his creation for them. He was in his seventies.

- **GARRY TRUDEAU** was the first writer of a comic strip to win the Pulitzer Prize for editorial cartooning. Okay, neato, pretty cool, for sure. One Pulitzer Prize. How about this figure: 15,000. That's how many comic strips he'd created by the strip's fiftieth anniversary in 2018. In the meantime, though, Trudeau was constantly churning out new ideas and each time we chatted, or had a meal, he had an inspiration to share—for television or for the screen. How old is a creator? In this case, the answer is: Any age will do.

- **DARRIN BELL** was the first Black cartoonist to win the same prize. He's one of those guys who, like Trudeau, became one with his muse early in his life, making cartoons as soon as he could lift a drawing tool. He's since expanded his creations. While I was writing this book, Darrin—now in his late forties— was working on a television show based on his comic strip *Candorville* for the comedian Kevin Hart and writing a two-book illustrated autobiography for a major publisher, all while writing *Candorville* and regular editorial cartoons.
- **DAVID MILCH**, a Hollywood legend, born 1945, wrote *Hill Street Blues* in 1982, and *Deadwood* in 2004. Both were epic, genre-changing shows.
- **BRUCE SPRINGSTEEN**: To be clear, the truth is that I put in a dozen calls to Springsteen's "people," and didn't get so much as a "maybe." No wonder. He's creating relentlessly. He started not long after he heard Elvis Presley on television that epic Sunday night, and he'll be buried with sheet music. At the time of this writing, he'd just put out yet another album, and it was a rocker. He's in his seventies. Thank you, Bruce, and I'm around, Bruce, if you want to chat.
- **RHIANNON GIDDENS**: Born in 1977, in her midforties as I write, she has expressed one after the next of the multitudes inside of her. In fact, truly, one of the challenges Giddens posed to me as I interviewed and wrote was that she kept putting out new ideas during the construction of this book. Mini-concerts, online performances, group musical projects. I finally told her: "Rhiannon, when you read this book, it's going to feel dated given everything you keep coming up with. I can't keep up with you."

Then there's Jake Schroeder, the perfect final profile for this book because he exemplifies the power to hear one's voice late in life but also the ability to jettison other peoples' ideas of creativity in favor of his own. He'd been a rock star. He decided he was more inspired by helping to heal relations between police and poor and minority young people.

His story also shows how much progress was taking place before the troubles of 2020. Every little creation helps.

Two Short War Stories

ONE MUSE

In June 1944, Normandy, France, the first amphibious transport boats were cutting through the surf to Omaha Beach. It was time for Frank DeVita to do the job from hell. As the boats reached shore, he had to lower the protective metal ramp in the front. This let the soldiers crouched behind it rush forward.

That meant the men would be walking directly into unimpeded German machine gun fire that spat thousands of rounds a minute from pillboxes dug into the beach. DeVita knew that when he did his job, his friends and fellow soldiers would be instantly killed.

The coxswain yelled: "DeVita, lower the ramp!"

DeVita pretended not to hear.

"Goddamn it, DeVita, lower the ramp!"

DeVita lowered the ramp.

The Germans decimated the troops, including one soldier who happened to be standing directly in front of DeVita.

DeVita lowered the ramp in about a dozen such landings that day.

In December of 1944, the Nazis launched their last counteroffensive of the war. It led to the Battle of the Bulge, with furious fighting in France and Belgium. Like a dying beast, the Germans lashed out with the full of their cruelty, their soldiers and stormtroopers laying villages to waste in a murderous spree. Bradley Thomas, an infantryman, was sent to fight the Nazi scourge along with the other Americans. This was a break from the usual rules. Thomas is Black. He helped beat back Hitler's malignant creation. He felt so proud.

Then the war ended and Thomas rode back in the bottom of the ship, with the other Black soldiers. And when he got home, he was not allowed to vote because of the color of his skin.

So he folded up his uniform and put it in a box and swore he'd never look at it again.

What unifies these men is their sacrifice, the agony and moral ambiguity of war, and one more thing: Their stories became an inspiration for a wildly creative program aimed at healing divisions between police officers and poor, minority youth in urban America.

They inspired a history buff and empath named Jacob Schroeder. He got a wild hair of an idea to have these men and other World War II vets tell their stories to police officers and to youth in hopes of having the two groups learn the history, feel the power of common purpose shared by these soldiers, and, more than that, so that the cops and kids would get so lost in the moment that they'd shed conceptions of each other and get to know one another as individuals.

"It's hard to generalize about people once you get to know them and like them," Schroeder told me.

He was nearly fifty years old at the time. It might seem late in life for the muse to strike. And he'd already been a great creator—at least in the eyes of others.

Schroeder was a rock star and lead singer of a band called Opie Gone Bad. It was one of Colorado's most popular bands ever, having headlined the legendary venue Red Rocks nine times.

In a video of their show from July 10, 2001, Schroeder stood in front of thousands of screaming fans, very much looking like a rock star, shaved head, big frame that commands the stage, and the voice. Holy cow, the voice. Pitch perfect, with the ability to create a huge range of sounds, gravel, light melodic, spoken word, and he let it go, laid out his soul there on a gorgeous Colorado night with the crowd dancing and singing, raising their beer cups in joy to Opie Gone Bad, the band Jake led. So he didn't just look like a rock star. He *was* a rock star. He married a Denver Broncos cheerleader.

Schroeder was not happy.

Music did not totally inspire him. Yes, he liked singing, and the gigs were heady, the tens of thousands of people standing out there, dancing to his beat. Before each show, though, so much uncertainty. "I'd tell myself before I went out there: Nobody is going to be there, nobody is going to dance," he said. "I would always talk myself down before gigs so I wouldn't be disappointed if it wasn't great."

Schroeder wasn't putting so fine a point on it then, but he was performing then, in the sense that his experience was more about the audience reaction to his performance than about his internal motivation and love of the experience. Besides, he rarely wrote the songs, and so his role felt, as he looked back, a bit mechanical. It eventually caught up.

Long story short, he had a daughter with the cheerleader, got divorced, partied a lot, womanized, felt crappy about himself and dark about who he was, and then got tired of a life that might seem enviable but wasn't true to him.

Schroeder and I were friends growing up and we'd exchanged notes every few years. In the summer of 2019, we connected and something about him sounded different.

"I cannot wait to tell you what I'm up to," he told me as we sat down at a Mexican food restaurant. He started telling me about his new thing; his eyes lit up.

After Schroeder retired from rock, he settled into a suburban life. Married a woman he'd met playing coed hockey. Started a family with her. Took a job as the executive director of the Police Athletic League in Denver. The group sought to promote youth sports and positive relations between youth and cops. It spoke to Schroeder in a basic, quiet, emphatic way.

His music career was reduced to one song, the national anthem. He sung it at sporting events, particularly at the opening of the games of the Colorado Avalanche, the state's professional hockey team. He was a fixture there. One night, after 9/11, Schroeder got to know a group of soldiers who were escorting World War II vets back to Normandy. They asked if he wanted to go on a trip.

"It was something I'd always dreamed of—helping out and getting to be around World War II vets, and being such a history nerd."

His first trip was in 2012. During his second, in 2013, he found himself in a Toyota packed with young American soldiers who'd served in Afghanistan and come to see Normandy, along with a Normandy vet who had walked with his company into a German ambush, losing nearly everyone.

Walker opened up to these soldiers as if they were siblings. "The young soldiers were like holy shit. This is like you go through some gate and go back in time.

"That's when it hit me."

He went home and he crafted a plan to raise money to bring police officers and youth from Denver to meet the veterans on the D-day battlefields. He was connecting very disparate dots: Normandy and aging vets, police officers, minority youth. But his certainty about the idea eclipsed any song he'd ever written or tried to write.

He recalled thinking: "I'm going to do whatever I can to bring as many kids and cops as I can."

In 2016, they took three kids, four vets, and four cops.

In 2017, two more trips, including one with kids from Columbine, the school where the infamous school shooting took place in 1999. One of the kids was Alejandro Rizo. He was thirteen.

Alejandro, called Alex by his friends, lives in the poorest part of Denver and had written an essay at his school about why he'd like to go to Normandy, had been selected, walked the beaches, looked at densely filled cemeteries. "You don't really experience it until you see all the white crosses," Alex told me.

He was particularly moved by his experience at the small church in the village of Sainte-Mère-Église in Northwestern France and the nearly centuries-old blood still staining the pews. Not all the bloodshed was from the mortally wounded. That's because of the work of two American medics, a pair of nineteen-year-old young men stationed in this eight-hundred-year-old church to help Allied soldiers but who then agreed to take on all the wounded, including Germans who had counterattacked. The medics were credited with saving eighty-one lives.

"They saved a little girl from this town," Schroeder told me, as he stood outside the village square in early October of 2019. Rain started to fall. Jake seemed overcome by what had happened here, marveling at the notion of the compassion amidst "all this battle stuff, all this death and destruction."

Alex had the same experience.

"Seeing that in the church, it was like a complete stranger was willing to sacrifice his life for the better of my life in an unconscious way, if that makes sense."

At night, at the residence where the group stayed, Alex said he spent time talking to the Denver cop, a homicide detective. "I saw him not just as a man in uniform, but I saw the dad, the husband, the son," Alex said. He said they became friends. "You can have so much in common with someone you sometimes think poorly about."

It's not that Alex intrinsically disliked police. His grandfather had been an officer in Mexico before being killed, and Alex had learned from his parents a respect for law enforcement. On the other hand, when Alex was twelve, a friend of his who had stolen a car was killed by multiple shots from a cop's gun, with the police officer claiming he was trying to stop the young lady thief from hurting anyone while behind the wheel.

The day before I interviewed Alex, a white cop in Texas had shot a woman in her own house; she was playing video games with her nephew, and she was studying to attend medical school. Two weeks earlier, a white cop had been convicted of murder for killing her neighbor, an African American, who was in his own apartment.

I interviewed cops involved in the program too. But that was during the 2020 unrest, and they feared having their names used because the situation had become so politicized. They told me about getting to know these kids, spending hours with them, chatting about this or that.

He sees young men and women and cops transformed, "experiencing this together and something so much bigger than themselves."

Sometimes, Schroeder says, the grandeur and spectacle and solemnity of Normandy just seem to overwhelm what's going on back home—in a good way.

"I remember this kid coming up to me, and I said: 'You know that guy you were talking to? He's a cop.'"

It goes both ways.

"These aren't racist cops. These aren't bad guys," he said. "But that doesn't deny the systemic issues, especially with African Americans." He said the trip became an opportunity to discuss the issues through the lens of discrimination at the time. "There are a lot of brave African Americans who acquitted themselves just as amazingly as white soldiers and then took the bottom of the ship back home and weren't allowed to vote when they got there. We highlight that."

The lessons of Normandy aren't clear-cut, the morality tricky—death and destruction, discrimination. This reality is exactly what allows Schroeder to extract lessons and dent prejudices.

"You don't have to solve all the problems. I think about a rudder on a cruise ship and how hard it is to turn, and so there's this little tiny rudder that starts the rudder for big turns," he said. "What we are is a little rudder—even if we touch a few kids a year or a couple of hundred kids a year."

That's one takeaway from this story. Helping a few kids and cops a year means more to Schroeder than the thousands of screaming fans. Creativity doesn't need to be a Big C to be a powerful one. Maybe Schroeder is helping provide shoulders that allow a perch for a great creator.

A second takeaway from this story has to do with the lessons of creativity and age. Time served in this lifetime should not be a deterrent to creativity. It can lend the wisdom and experience that allow a muse to blossom. In Schroeder's case, the experience of rock stardom paled by comparison to the inspiration he felt from his Northern European Campaign.

There's a third takeaway, much grander. It puts the creative cycle into some perspective, providing a context for the great challenges of the year 2020.

I told you that Alexander Fleming discovered penicillin. That happened in 1928. It came from mold. In other words, a human being, through keen observation, found a lifesaving application in an organic creation. After that, the would-be medicine got tested in mice. Then it was used to treat an English policeman in 1941. The constable's recovery was "remarkable," as accounts have it. But there wasn't enough of the drug, and the man relapsed and died.

In the lead-up to the invasion of Normandy, twenty-one companies cooperated to make 2.3 million doses of penicillin, according to the National War Museum. The antibiotic became known as the war's "miracle drug," the museum notes.

What a creation! What innovative and powerful production! And it was inspired by the chaos of the war.

The D-day invasion succeeded in no small part thanks to the innovations of an Englishman named Alan Turing. He spearheaded efforts to break the German "Enigma" code that the Nazis thought allowed them to secretly communicate their troop and submarine movements and strategic plans. Turing helped develop the most basic principle for modern computing. His team of cryptographers at Bletchley Park in England used a special machine called "Colossus."

By now, across the pond, work had begun, using related mathematical principles to build the first computer, the Electronic Numerical Integrator and Computer. It used 18,000 vacuum tubes to make big-number calculations, with an initial aim of making ballistics calculations for the US army. On February 14, 1946, the *New York Times* published an article about the previously secret project: "One of the war's top secrets, an amazing machine that applies electronic speeds for the first time to mathematical tasks hitherto too difficult and cumbersome for solution, was announced here tonight by the War Department."

The war had just ended, thanks in no small part to one of the creations of the atomic bomb, an ingenious, devastating killing weapon dropped twice on Japan.

These are among the mere handful of creations that came from World War II, itself the product of a kind of virus of fascism, ravaging the whole of the world. Roughly seventy-five million people died in the conflict.

Disruption, creation, disruption, creation, nature's call-and-response.

In the year 2020, nearly one hundred years later, the world felt crystallized with challenge as it had never been before. In some ways, that was true—there was a novel coronavirus, and a new, widespread type of social unrest in the United States. In other ways, these threats paled by comparison to prior challenges (World War II, and World War I, and the 1918 flu pandemic, and a Cold War that led the world to the brink of nuclear obliteration, and racism, sexism, homophobia) so much more extreme and that had given way to extraordinary creativity in law and policy and enlightened industry.

The creative turns often met with resistance, and sometimes it took a common enemy, like the Nazis, to allow change that led to progress and that made the risk of change worth it.

Schroeder put that dynamic in very personal terms when he described his idea of inspiration to me.

"It's when I lose the shame of feeling like I may not be good enough to do something like this," he said.

That freedom and overpowering inspiration hit Jake in his forties. Circumstances, emotional state, and expertise all combine in different people to allow for the creative spirit to take hold at different times.

Does it matter?

Vocabulary

FOUR C'S

It may not seem like creativity science would lend itself to moments of crises. Not like, say, virology, where a new virus emerges and, absent quick intervention, people will die. So it might seem dramatic to say that creativity scholars James C. Kaufman and Ronald Beghetto, over appetizers in San Diego in 2009, identified what they saw as an urgent and serious problem in creativity research.

But they found the matter so pressing that a few days later James flew to Eugene, Oregon, where Ronald was on the faculty at the University of Oregon, and they sat up until two in the morning kicking around ideas looking for a solution.

The problem had to do with the C's. The Big C and the Little C. This binary construct had been bedrock ideas for decades. The Big C, of course, referred to the geniuses whose transcendent ideas changed our lives, or the foundation of a field, or art or molecular biology, rock and roll or computer engineering. The Little C referred to the rest of us.

But what about George de Mestral?

He changed the world, but James kept wondering how he'd be labeled—as a Big C, or a Little C—if he hadn't changed the world. You may not know De Mestral's name. But you may currently be in close contact with his innovation: Velcro. One of the stickiest innovations of all time.

The origin story of Velcro traces to one day in the late 1940s while De Mestral was walking in Switzerland with his dog. The innovator noticed that burrs from the surroundings had become attached to the dog's fur and to his own pants. How did these burrs attach?

At that moment, the observation was a nugget, nothing more.

"He could've shelved it and never thought about it again," James told me. "That wouldn't have taken away from that moment."

Kaufman and Beghetto started to wonder if a distinction was to be drawn between a discovery that is seen through to the end and one that is a mere observation. This was a variation on the philosophical question: If a tree falls in the forest and no one is around to hear it, does it make a sound?? If a brilliantly creative observation was made but was not ever acted upon, did it count as a Big C? Did it count as anything?

Or take the example of someone like Vivian Maier. She also vexed Kaufman and Beghetto, as they thought through the idea of the prevailing notion that there was a Big C and there was a Little C.

Vivian was a nanny in Chicago. As a hobby, she strolled the city with a Rolleiflex camera. She later traveled the world, taking photographs, often not having the negatives made into pictures, and she went unpublished and was seemingly uninterested in being published. After her death, a real-estate broker in 2007 found the collection of some 150,000 snapshots and realized their brilliance—searing portraits in black and white, capturing street culture, faces struck in moments of conflicted emotion, groups on stoops, children in summer dancing in a hydrant's geyser.

Much acclaim followed, of both the critical and viral nature (her collection became an internet sensation). That was nothing she had sought, though. She hadn't even bothered to get her pictures developed.

A brief *New Yorker* profile in 2014 told of a documentary about the photographer and captured a bit of the conundrum. "Maier's story is titillating precisely because of how it deviates from the familiar narratives about artistic aspiration. They (filmmakers and fans) can't understand why she never put aside her profession for her passion. People who never saw her without a Rolleiflex around her neck express bewilderment that they were in the company of a great talent," the profile reads.

What would these photographs have been called if they'd never been discovered? Was there a category for that? Was that a Little C turned Big C? Did that mean the creation had to be appreciated by others for it to have Big C value?

Kaufman and Beghetto, the scholars who met in San Diego and then went deep into the night brainstorming in Eugene, could find dozens of loopholes to the two C's, big and little. Was a solid essay of an eighth-grade English student the same Little C as the essay of a professional writer who, inspired though she might be, wasn't changing the world?

It all felt personal to Kaufman. He hadn't wanted to be a scholar. Instead, he said, "All my life I wanted to be a creative writer." As a kid, he wrote story upon story, did sports reporting for his high school newspaper, went to college to get a degree in creative writing. Then he applied to graduate school programs to get a masters in fine arts, and one of the universities he applied to sent him a standard letter urging him to think hard about applying. The note essentially said: Before you apply, you should know that our MFA program graduated twenty students in a single year and there are about thirty jobs for MFAs in the entire country each year.

It was around this time, Kaufman says, that he realized he was "good, but not great."

He wound up going to Yale University to study psychology, and, ultimately, creativity. He continued to write too, including creating a musical called *Discovering Magenta* about "a mental health worker trying to help a catatonic patient." It was produced at a small theater in New York.

This wasn't Big C, of course. Was it Little C? Like the Valentine's Day poem you write your spouse? And what is that anyway? What should the name be for a new recipe that you think up at home and that the family or dinner party raves about but never goes further than that?

Kaufman and Beghetto came up with an answer that, for my money, is extremely helpful in understanding the field of creativity and our own behavior.

Introducing the Four C's.

The Mini C

The Little C

The Pro C

The Big C

The Mini C.

Their definition: novel and personally meaningful interpretation of experiences, actions, and events.

This category of creativity is much more about personal satisfaction than anything else. That doesn't mean it's not valuable. If De Mestral had never mentioned his observation about the burrs sticking to a dog's fur or his pants, it might have been pleasing to him, a powerful observation based on curiosity, maybe novel, but mini in its essence.

We have Mini C's all the time. So do our children. Random observations: the empty Kleenex box is a hat!; the fifth-grade essay—the dog and the cat lived together in peace; and the Lego tower looks more like an upside-down pie.

Kaufman's own example of Mini C is coming up with a twist on a dinner recipe that feels exciting to the creator even though it may or may not be well received by the family. "I put cinnamon in mashed potatoes. No one would go within ten feet of it," he said. "But every so often I make something my boys and wife will eat, and I step over that threshold."

It's not a huge threshold, but it is one. The step up to Little C.

The Little C is a Mini C that makes a ripple, enjoys recognition, however modest.

In the Kaufman household, the boys and wife say: "James, this chili you made is actually pretty good. Will you make it again?"

Little C!

Or this is the essay your fifth grader writes that stands apart enough to get emailed to the family, or it might be the third grader's painting hung on the refrigerator.

"If the Mini C is something many people experience multiple times a day, the Little C is something nearly all of us can do."

That doesn't make it a throwaway. It counts. It really does. In your own life, this might be the song that you write on your guitar that your spouse asks you to play when guests come over because it really inspired. It could be the workshop you build in the backyard, or the treehouse you make with your kids that causes a neighbor to say: "It really does look like a pirate ship!" It could be the work you do in a field not your own.

It could be the work of a well-known creator in a field in which he is not a professional.

During the COVID-19 shutdown, I got a note from a friend of mine, Linwood Barclay, a top-selling thriller writer. As the world slowed to a halt, he'd stopped writing and marketing his books—having recently turned a draft in to his editor—and stopped going to festivals to promote. He'd heavily invested his time in building a model railway system. It grew to be an obsession, taking over an eighteen-by-eighteen-foot room, train cars traversing a cityscape, the base of a mountain range, through tunnels and over bridges, finding rest in a train yard.

"I've always been a model-train nerd, since I was a little kid," Linwood said in a video he posted on Facebook. I asked him about it in a note and he said: "I figure I spend my days imagining a world in my head, and so it's nice to unwind building one with my hands."

It would be accurate to call what Linwood did a "hobby," but that doesn't diminish a creation that merits recognition of an inspiration acted upon.

I am putting a fine point on the Little C because it is a place of authentic and deliberate creativity. And yet it shouldn't be confused with the next step up, a big one, the Pro C.

That's what Linwood does with his books.

Meet the Pro C. It's a big deal.

In my humble view, this is the most important new category, and the most complicated. The Pro C is reserved for creations by, you guessed it, professionals, the pros, and these creations often are recognized as very good, or even great. This makes for a really big span, so much so that this brief section is where some really well-known exceptional creators might feel somewhat insulted. That's because Pro C lumps together such a wide spectrum.

"The beginning of Pro C," Kaufman says, "is the publication or acceptance of an article, where the level of the work goes from having a small local impact to, in some way, having an impact on the domain, even if *that* impact is small."

The Four C's paper that Kaufman and Beghetto wrote, is a Pro C of a slightly more elevated variety. So too for some of Kaufman's books, like the *Cambridge Handbook of Creativity*, now in its second edition, and *Creativity 101*, a more conversational but still largely scholarly book—"the stuff I'd tell you about creativity in a dinner conversation," Kaufman said.

Like the fact that all four of these C's—mini to big—have "dials or notches, or like a dimmer switch."

None more so than Pro C. Because here's the thing: it includes professional scholars like Dr. Kaufman, but also professional writers like James Patterson and James Ellroy, or world-class performers from Billie Eilish to Shakira, comedian Trevor Noah, Iron Chefs, *Squawk Box*er Jim Cramer.

And then many, many people who may have made very little name for themselves or a name only within their domain. Almost on a daily basis in my day job as a *New York Times* reporter, I interview politicians, scholars, authors, and others who have developed pedigrees and expertise and who demonstrate creativity but are not at all thought of in the same echelons.

Dr. Charles Dinarello, a National Institutes of Health researcher who in the 1970s discovered the molecule that causes fever, is in the same category as the singer James Taylor, and also some middling writer like me, along with countless Silicon Valley engineers and innovators.

And while it might seem really unfair to them to have their creations lumped in with those of us who haven't sold ours for half a billion dollars, the key facet of the Pro C is not money, or fame, and not even talent. Creators must have enough practice and training in the field. They don't break the mold, but their fingerprints massage its shape.

Pro C's make a significant difference and belong to a large category populated by talented, creative thinkers who are good at what they do. Millions of people live in this rarefied air. Not like with the Big C.

Tiny. Rarefied. Air. And it's even more elusive than it might first appear to be because there is one aspect of the Big C that no creator can control: time.

The Big C label here is reserved for truly enduring creators. In fact, their contributions can in many ways be measured only over decades or even centuries. There's a fun mental game in this, which is to spend a moment to take a stab at which contemporary people might qualify.

"The way Ron and I conceptualized it, Big C is for the ages," Kaufman said.

Abraham Lincoln, Jonas Salk, Harriet Tubman, Steve Jobs, Paul McCartney and the Beatles, Bob Dylan, George Washington Carver, Winston Churchill, Gandhi, and Martin Luther King, Jr.

When I talked to Kaufman about this, I ventured one person who seemed a likely candidate: James Allison, the Nobel Prize winner whose story I wrote about a few pages ago—and who you may not have heard of until then.

But, Kaufman cautioned me against comparing a scientist to a musician or an athlete to an actor. The Big C must be, he said, domain-specific. "If you're talking about something like medicine and someone like Jonas Salk, it's a pretty unfair comparison to almost anything and anyone else."

This, he said, is where "creativity and fame aren't the same thing."

He told me about Norman Borlaug. Y'know, right? C'mon, really? You don't know your agronomists? Or your Nobel Peace Prize winners?

He was both.

He won for discovering new strains of wheat to vastly increase crop production. The biography for his Nobel Prize, which he won in 1970, notes that: "To his scientific goal he soon added that of the practical humanitarian: arranging to put the new cereal strains into extensive production in order to feed the hungry people of the world—and thus providing, as he says, 'a temporary success in man's war against hunger and deprivation.'"

Norman Borlaug, tireless creator, man of the field, a Big C you've never heard of.

Borlaug also hints at another defining characteristic of Big C creators—their methods and ideas get copied, borrowed, become part of the foundation of their field.

"Haven't you heard the joke about the Velvet Underground?" Kaufman asked me, referring to the sixties rock band led by Lou Reed. "They sold four hundred albums and all four hundred went to people who would go on to start a rock band."

"What about," I asked Kaufman, "someone like Bruce Springsteen?"

Immense influence in his time (now), extremely well regarded by his peers, prolific creator who developed a sound and ethos of his own. Could it be that he would be only a Pro C?

"In four hundred years, will everybody know his music? No. But will people who are into music in the twenty-first century say: 'You gotta listen to these three or four people,' and will he be one of them? Absolutely, yes."

Hey Boss, you're in.

To Kaufman, the overriding characteristic of a Big C, the one determining factor that makes someone a no-brainer candidate, is whether their creative contributions are enduring and they represent a way of thinking that is very divergent from the way their field, or domain, had been progressing. They, in effect, reestablish a field, and the way they do so becomes a new foundation.

So the plain reality is that only history can really dictate the impact of a creation—which of the four C camps it belongs in.

The only thing people can control. That's what this has all been about anyways. You.

BOOK IV

SALVATION

The Secret Ingredient

Brains, eyes, and ears, an average IQ, an imagination, at least basic understanding of some field or another, access to the internet, the ability to be curious and open. These are traits that I've tried to illuminate through science and story as crucial to the pursuit of creativity.

Most people have most of these traits, if not all of them.

And everybody—*everybody*—has the secret ingredient: themselves. Their individuality.

The secret ingredient to creativity is: you.

This is one of the biggest takeaways I learned in reporting this book. In the end, creativity is born of the connection of ideas and snippets of ideas that emerge from the darkness of a person's mind. The pieces that emerge, and the way they get processed, are as individual as an individual's genetic makeup, or fingerprint. Much among us is identical. We are close but we are not clones.

That helps explain the origins of creativity, but not the reasons for it. Earlier in the book, I mentioned that I'd been asked a question by a highly accomplished Hollywood director: "What is the purpose of creativity?"

The director was Mark Romanek, whose work I've described. I told him about what I'd learned about creativity and its connection to evolutionary biology. Creativity is essential to us because it allows us to survive. This answer seemed unsatisfying to him. "By that definition," he asked me, "isn't everything about survival?"

Well, yes, I concede. Our underlying programming dictates we pass on our genes. Creativity helps us do that.

Is there anything else to creativity?

As I considered the answer in the days that followed, I found myself thinking about a piece of research from one of the leading scholars in the field of creativity science. I've described work earlier by Jack Goncalo, one of those thinkers who is not afraid to ask "smart-dumb questions," and wise enough to come up with good ones. He discovered through one of these questions a partial answer to Romanek's question: Being creative makes people happier.

In 2015, he and others published an article titled "The Liberating Consequences of Creative Work: How a Creative Outlet Lifts the Physical Burden of Secrecy."

The research shows that when people create, it allows them to experience relief. The creators feel as if they've shared themselves with the world. This is true, the compelling research shows, even if the creator doesn't share their most intimate secrets.

Let's say, for example, a person cheated on a partner or spouse, or merely has thought about doing so. This is a real secret, or an authentic feeling of shame. But it might not be an idea to share widely.

The secret weighs heavily. It can lead to preoccupation, unhappiness, obsessive thoughts. It can also create a burden not unlike a physical weight. Research shows, for example, that a person carrying a troubling secret may view a hill to be walked as steeper than a person not bearing the weight of the secret.

Goncalo and his colleagues characterized the fear created by that secret as coming from the idea that the person holding the secret considers the thought to be "amoral." The secret is "out of the box" of what is allowed, allowable, and even thinkable. This characterization makes a ton of sense. Otherwise, why not just start sharing it around?

In fact, the underlying idea of shame connects directly back to the fourth-grade slump and the idea that, as we mature and assimilate into the world, we internalize all kinds of rules. When we feel we've violated those rules, we can feel shame.

Goncalo and his co-researchers did a series of three related experiments to find out how the act of creation impacts the weight of carrying a secret. In brief summary, the researchers asked study subjects to think about a secret of their own—some would think of a small secret and others a big secret. The participants were told to write down something about the nature of the secret, without revealing it, and then were given a communication that asked some to come up with creative solutions and others to come up with practical solutions to the same problem. (The word within the parentheses varied depending on which group the participant was in.)

"A restaurant near campus has recently gone bankrupt, and there is now an empty space where the restaurant used to be. Please generate as many (creative/practical) ideas for new businesses that might go into that space as you can in ten minutes."

Then the researchers asked participants to engage in a physical task that had been previously shown to measure "physical burden"— the participants were asked to throw a bean bag at a target. In other studies, the burden of a secret caused participants to overestimate the distance—it looked farther than it actually was—thus causing them to overshoot the throw. Lo and behold, the participants who had been asked to keep a big secret and to do the creative thinking did not overshoot the bean bag by nearly as much as those who came up with more practical solutions.

"The results of three studies showed that the opportunity to be creative feels liberating—feelings that can, in turn, lift the physical burden of secrecy," the researchers wrote. "The results of study three also showed that the unburdening effect of creative work was strongest when the task permitted wide-ranging exploration across different types of ideas, rather than a specific focus in one domain."

To put that another way, creativity let people express themselves out of the box—to the point that it was a physical relief—when they felt they couldn't express an idea that made them think they might be seen as "outside the box."

Imagine! The more creatively people think, the less burden they feel. This argues for all kinds of far-reaching thinking, unconstrained by barrier, connecting dots across plains and fields, disciplines and media. Everyone, after all, has secrets. Being authentic doesn't mean spilling them, and they may be fuel nonetheless, even unspilled.

This research helps answer the question I'd been searching for myself and that Romanek asked about. Why create? This is not about saving the world. It might be in no small part about saving yourself.

Over and again when I heard from creators—from the business-people, investors, musicians, visual artists, writers—they described joy of losing themselves in a creation, of authentic self-expression and of independence. It makes a strong case that creativity and happiness are close relations. In fairness, happiness might be a component of survival—the happier you are, the better able to survive—but it can feel like salvation too.

Additional research supports other reasons why this might be.

Some of the insight comes from James Kaufman, the same Kaufman who helped come up with the Four C's. In a 2018 paper titled "Finding Meaning with Creativity in the Past, Present, and Future," Kaufman explored decades worth of research into how creative supports lead to meaning. He began with a premise: "Everyday creative people are less stressed, happier, more successful and more satisfied with their jobs."

His overview then shows that this is because creativity gives people a deep sense of meaning. There are various reasons why. One draws from the study of people who have survived "atrocities, ranging from Hiroshima to prisoner-of-war camps." The research in this field finds that people in these situations tend to crave "symbolic immortality." A key way to achieve this, the researchers find, is through creative contributions that leave a legacy, or are perceived by the creator as leaving a legacy. Kaufman argues that the creation of ideas is a parallel to the passing along of genetic material through having children.

Fairly, a reader might see this as a form of survival—the preservation of self even beyond the grave.

Kaufman points to other ways creativity leads to a sense of meaning. One has to do with how it helps people make sense of the past. A book, song, a diary, any representation of a reflection of past events can help bring "coherence," Kaufman notes. To this, I say: Amen. Show me a writer whose first novel isn't partly autobiographical in theme or philosophy and I will, as my grandfather would say, eat my straw hat.

Broadly, Kaufman writes: "Such creativity activities can be a vehicle of self-expression, a way to understand one's past, or a method to heal earlier traumas or upsetting events."

He also argues that creativity can create meaning around "present" events (rather than past ones). One reason is because it leads to a kind of intimacy. For instance, he said, when a creative project is shared and appreciated, "it can be the ultimate connection."

When the connection happens it is inherently collaborative because it involves sharing of perspectives—"the creative equivalent of walking a mile in someone else's shoes."

Also, simply, creativity is "a distraction." Kaufman cites research that shows that people who are drawing pictures wind up in a better mood than those merely copying shapes. Interestingly, research shows that people who use such art as a distraction see their mood improve more than when they use the art to vent a source of negativity. So here's a good reason to create: beats feeling rotten.

"Creativity and art," Kaufman writes, "can serve as much-needed distractions during difficult times."

Finally, Kaufman looks at how the creative process creates meaning as someone looks ahead in life, to the future. Again, he finds that creations, through helping others or being part of big projects or as vehicles for self-expression, lets people feel they are leaving a legacy. They feel remembered, passed on, and connected.

As I consider all these ideas, they seem to convene around the idea of happiness. I also have to concede that happiness, in the end, is part of survival. Your chances of making it through are better if you're not depressed. So in a nod to Mark Romanek, the fine music-video director who asked the purpose of creativity, I'll admit that yes, much of it is about survival. But if creativity is a means for being happy, and thereby enhancing survival chances, that sure beats eating your vegetables.

One flaw in this line of thinking would be if creativity actually makes some people uncomfortable. I did argue earlier in the book, for example, that creativity means taking risk. Risk is scary. Authenticity is scary.

So the question ultimately becomes whether there's a way to take risk, traipse into the unknown, and not go over the cliff. To be creative, need a person throw it all away? Must a person be a starving artist, entrepreneur, a dancer, musician, writer flirting with skid row?

Turns out that's not so at all. I learned this years ago when I got some clichéd advice—you're your day job—that is (to use another cliché) now more true than ever.

Don't Quit Your Day Job

Here's a personal tale about why creators should keep their day job.

In 2004, I wrote the beginning of a fictional story. In it, a man in his thirties sits reading in a crowded café when he sees a woman's slender hand put a note on his table. By the time he looks up to see who it is, she's disappeared into the crowd. He picks up the note and follows her. When he gets to the doorway of the café to follow her out, he opens the note.

It reads: Get out of the café. NOW!

The café explodes.

As he sits in the rubble outside the café, having survived, he finds him thinking of his ex-girlfriend. She had died five years earlier, and he's been thinking of her ever since. But that's not why he's thinking of her at this moment. It's because he recognizes her handwriting on the note.

After I wrote this opening—although in slightly longer form—I felt inspired in a way I'd never felt before. I was consumed with writing the story to figure out what had happened—and whether the girlfriend was still alive.

To that point, I'd never written a book nor ever wanted to write a book. I knew colleagues in the newspaper business who had written them and the whole idea seemed nuts. Who could ever write that many words, or want to try?

I started writing a mystery-thriller, and couldn't stop. I didn't really even know how long a book was. At night, I'd pick up books and count the number of words on a line, multiply it times the number of lines on the page, and then multiply that by the number of pages. I figured a book was around 100,000 words. I thought I'd try to make my story about that long.

Enraptured by the muse, I wrote the first draft in six months. Writing those pages felt natural, easy, sometimes thrilling, like discovery and invention.

The book came off well enough that I was able to get a book agent, Laurie Liss, who remains my agent to this day. She and I talked about the book, and she helped me come up with a gigantic twist at the book's end that, in turn, allowed it to be sold to one of the most elite editors in all of publishing. He had just started a small influential publishing imprint named The Twelve, which was novel in that it published only one book a month (hence: Twelve) and all of the authors had significant notoriety—except one. I was the outlier, along with people like John McCain, and Christopher Hitchens, and Christopher Buckley.

I used to call the list The Eleven and a Half to reflect my lack of notoriety.

But who am I kidding? It was so heady. The book was eventually called *Hooked*. I didn't get crazy money for it, not anywhere near the kind of money you hear people bandy about, but it was almost a year's salary. And the publisher got several big-name authors to write blurbs for the jacket. They said the most wonderful things, and this was long before I understood that's partly how blurbs work.

I wrote a letter to one of those authors thanking him for his kind remarks. He wrote me back with kind words, and then pointed ones: Do not quit your day job.

I don't think he was telling me that the book was inferior, though he might have been. What he was telling me is what I'm telling you now: Being creative for a living is very, very hard. It requires immense luck. Even people who make Pro C contributions don't often make lots of money from them.

Hooked came out with decent fanfare and reviews. Then it did what most books do: sold okay, and then more or less disappeared. Do you realize how long a book that doesn't become a runaway best-seller stays on the shelves of bookstores? A month or two. Then along comes the next batch of well-blurbed books pushed by terrific editors and inspired writers.

And that was the old days. Now the competition is so fierce for reader attention that the likelihood of going big-time is modest.

But.

That is not at all a reason not to create. In fact, quite to the contrary. It is an argument for giving yourself freedom to try. And my own experience, which is very common, also is an argument for how people's skill sets and their hobbies do merge over time. In fact, one reason to keep a day job—besides the obvious need to eat—is that it can actually lead to the development of abilities that may lend themselves to the skills and structures upon which creativity can be built.

Many of the great creations in the history of the world (see: small-pox vaccine) came as a kind of sidelight to a skill set.

I've written ten books since *Hooked*, including a children's book. I still have a day job, and, in it, I play by rules. But the books I write, and the songs, also inform my journalistic work by nurturing creativity in the storytelling I try to do.

My point: Creativity is not an either/or lifestyle.

Late in the reporting of this book, I had a conversation with Rhiannon Giddens that added a wrinkle to this point and that helped me to understand how lucky I was to have discovered her and featured her in these pages.

We'd spent nearly a year chatting and I'd gotten to know the story of a blessed talent and her journey. It's a very American story too, for good and ill. Giddens's slave roots connected her to a perspective, legacy, to dark skin that made her a target of racism, still. On the flip side, she soared in a society that is freer than most, rose from circumstances that were hardly royal, and made a life for herself. She'd confided to me the innermost emotions of her emergence as a creator, how she'd evolved to let herself create in her own voice and in her own way. She'd confided too that there were parts of her that she could not yet draw from creatively, aspects of her childhood that felt too scary to explore.

There still felt a piece missing for me. She had been on a track for great stardom and she had not taken it. She could have quit her day job, so to speak. Well, I suppose she had quit her day job in that she was doing what she loved. She was so highly regarded in her circles and among a huge range of musicians from Elvis Costello to Yo-Yo Ma. In August of 2020, she'd been selected as the new artistic director for Silkroad Ensemble, a global music collective that Ma, the peerless cellist, had founded in 1988 as a way to foster creative collaboration amid the chaos of a frenetic, globalizing world. Giddens, in short, was major-league big-time.

But she'd made a choice somewhere along the line not to go all in on the life of a creator of great fame or to make her life as commercial as it might have been.

I'm not sure I even realized how important this missing piece was to the story of creativity until she and I spoke near the end of 2020. I'd contacted her that morning to ask about the period in her life when she began to hear her own voice. It had come, as I've written earlier, when she was an up-and-coming voice in music with a band called The Carolina Chocolate Drops. She was increasingly unhappy, touring and making music that, while popular, didn't feel truly authentic to her.

This was true even after the release of her 2015 solo album called *Tomorrow Is My Turn*, her regular appearance on the hit TV show

Nashville and various star-studded sidelights, her virtuoso performance at the CMA Awards in a duet with Eric Church. When I watch the video of that performance, I am blown away by the power of her voice, and the apparent inspiration. Now that I know Giddens, I can almost pick up the tension in her face. She's wearing makeup, looks almost doll-like in her perfection. "I was the thinnest I'd ever been," she said. "I gave it the old college try." She was in the game, playing it well. Not liking it. "I realized: I'm not cut out for this shit."

"I hate the photo shoots. I like wearing whatever the hell I want to wear," she told me that morning we spoke in 2020. I'd picked up that much by that point, although I don't think I'd appreciated just how much that connected to the larger picture of her emergence as an authentic creator. It wasn't really about makeup and photo shoots and much more about what those external demands said about the creative choices she was making. Those demands are part of creating music and telling stories aimed at appealing to popular culture. Increasingly, she wanted to tell the stories of her ancestors.

"I kept wanting to talk about slavery and play the banjo."

In 2017, she put out her acclaimed album *Freedom Highway* that included the song "Julie" that she'd long held inside her, and included other such narratives, like "At the Purchaser's Option." It also included several cover songs, including a potent version of "Birmingham Sunday," written by folksinger Richard Fariña.

She loved that stuff but she didn't feel compelled to be locked into it either. She wanted to learn new instruments and she had this idea for an opera. It is titled *Omar*, and it is about a Muslim-African named Omar Ibn Said, who was kidnapped by slave traders and taken to South Carolina in 1807.

During our conversation that morning, she told me about how a major aria from it had poured out to her as she sat in front of a fireplace at the house of a friend on the west coast of Ireland—"the words just tumbled out and the tune tumbled out of my fingers."

The work has been commissioned by a major arts festival for performance at Carolina Performing Arts in Chapel Hill. A story in the *New York Times* announcing the opera called Giddens "the musical polymath." (Yes, I had to look it up: person of wide-ranging knowledge or learning.)

That morning, in our call, she also told me about the work she's doing with Elvis Costello.

What Giddens has done is to truly free herself to create what inspires her, at any given time. She told me there is no difference between her life and her creative life. "It's just me. It's my thoughts. When it's ready to come out and hit at the right time, the door is open."

She doesn't spend much time assessing whether what she creates is good, perfect, and certainly whether it's good enough for someone else.

"My creativity is what it is. My abilities are what they are—constantly developing."

As the conversation wound down, I realized I'd been handed quite a gift in Giddens. She is an authentic creator and that's not because she resisted the trappings of fame and a greater fortune. It's because she made herself available to her voice and she followed it without discrimination, recrimination, second-guessing, or fear. She meanders from project to project and one creative burst to the next. Sometimes, that means just doing a lot of baking. Her twitter feed has filled up with various baked items she's crafted.

"I am," she told me, "the happiest I've ever been."

I began this chapter by noting that it makes sense to think of creativity as a hobby, and to keep a day job. The wrinkle that Giddens adds to this piece is, simply, this: once the creative portal opens, it will find a way, whether or not time gets spent on the day job. Creativity is a state of mind. If you allow it, it will find a way.

Right around this time I had a conversation with a near-total stranger who sees an explosively powerful way to tap that state of mind.

This is the brief story of Todd.

Todd

In early November of 2020, as the year came to a close, I found myself reporting a story for the *New York Times* about a creation that had sprung from the pandemic: recovering substance abusers had begun holding their therapy sessions online. They had to. It wasn't safe to meet in person.

This was a pretty cool development because it meant salvation for people who rely on these meetings to survive. One of the people I spoke to was named Todd Holland.

Over the course of thirty minutes, he became an object lesson in creativity. This was only in small part because he explained to me how much the pandemic had helped fuel a creative way of doing meetings. What hit me much harder is that Holland, in his own way, helped inspire an idea that is as powerful as any research that I'd done over two years in explaining how to think about courage and creativity.

My interaction with him showed me once again that the ideas that fuel creativity can come from unexpected places.

Holland started using drugs when he was eight. "Anything you had," was how he described for me the limits of what he would ingest to get high. He grew up and lives in Utah, in the northern part of the state.

He finally got clean around 2012 thanks to Narcotics Anonymous. Using the 12-step program, he freed himself from the terrible outside menace of opiates and methamphetamines and cocaine and alcohol. He'd learned to surrender, he told me, which is a common refrain. I've not totally understood the idea and asked Holland to explain.

Holland said that he had learned to accept that he was an okay person but also that he was not any more okay a person than any other person. He surrendered to his basic humanity.

These were his exact words: I AM WORTHY, BUT I AM NO MORE WORTHY.

The words hit me hard. They were words I'd been looking for over the many months since I began understanding the creative process. Many people believe they are worthy of trying to create, and as worthy as anyone else. But they are not more worthy, which is just as important to the creativity equation as feeling worthy. That's because people who feel "more" worthy are, by definition, feeling entitled. They imagine themselves superior to other people. That almost certainly means that they are unable to see and hear information from people they deem themselves superior to. They have limited greatly the spices they can draw from in the spice rack of creativity.

Furthermore, a person who feels superior likely will see the notion of trying to create as putting them at risk of failing, and becoming like one of those "inferior" people.

I am worthy, but I am no more worthy.

When I heard these words from Holland, I understood that these were the words I could attach to my own emotional collapse in my twenties. I had surrendered to the fact that I was merely human, no more, and no less. It was only thereafter, when I'd emerged from darkness, that I could hear myself, my voice, and trust that it was okay.

BOOK V

CREATIVITY IN THE TIME OF CHAOS

Two Steps Forward

ONE AND SEVEN-EIGHTHS STEPS BACK

Occasionally, I've heard someone longing for simpler times say: "I miss a world where we got our news from Walter Cronkite."

Cronkite anchored the *CBS Evening News* and regularly was voted "most trusted man in America."

His voice became synonymous with some of the most extraordinary innovations and news events of the century (see: moon landing).

This one source provided so much clean, clear, unambiguous information.

He was nearing the sunset of his career when a group of techies met in Silicon Valley and built the technological and philosophical underpinnings of the internet. There are many pieces to this story, told much better in other settings, that include military and financial inspiration, but one of their core principles was that information would be decentralized by the internet. This was done partly to help keep the sources of information safe from an attack. More hubs of connection meant less chance that a nuclear missile, say, could take down the whole system.

That inspiration came from fear.

Another came from the opposite side of the coin: hope.

Early techies thought that decentralized information would be more democratic. More people would have a voice, and a person needn't work for the *New York Times* or have a book contract or be Walter Cronkite to have a say in the world.

And it wasn't like the world under Walter Cronkite was all that perfect. Sure, there was a streamlined source of information. But Walter Cronkite's world was a bit like the world of the Cold War in which relative peace came because there were two superpowers—the USSR and the United States—and their overwhelming power and the threat of nuclear war kept everything in check.

Beneath the surface of a Cold War world and a Cronkite one, things were a mess. In the United States, such basic order denied African Americans their full rights and gay men and women had no place in society, along with dozens of other simple truths put to the side in the name of a simpler order. Internationally, the simple hegemony of order hearkening to the words from the Bible that began this book: Much of the world remained in pitch black, wanting and desperate for light and creativity, innovation and change.

This is not to say that the world hadn't come a long, long, long way from darkness. It's only to say that each new ray of light was accompanied by the risk of unintended consequence. Antibiotics gave way to drug-resistant infection, cars to an epidemic of road deaths and the riskiest activity most of us will engage in during a lifetime: driving. Guns defended many and murdered an equal number. The world's dominant economic systems led to more wealth and comfort than there ever had been, and immense gaps between rich and poor.

So it would be with the internet. On the plus side, it came with more power to express ideas from more people.

More?

Understatement of the century.

One study found that 90 percent of the information ever created in the world happened from 2016 to 2018. And that figure is growing by the year. Each minute during 2020 there were millions of tweets, Facebook posts, Instagram photos, TikTok videos. This wasn't mere folly. Some of those social media posts came from presidents and prime ministers.

Communication came hand in hand with innovation and economy, as people began moving across international borders, sharing ideas that seemed so heretical to many others, and building products that changed the world but that, in the process, challenged the world.

In this period, the very idea of "truth" fell into question. How far the world had come from "the most trusted man in America," to "fake news!"

Noxious, certifiably crazy ideas spread and people believed them. One idea took root, planted supposedly by an anonymous tipster called Q, that elite Republicans and Democrats in the United States secretly belonged to a satanic ring of pedophiles. Not even I, in my worst moments as a thriller writer, would propose a notion so absurd. But many people believed.

It is certainly possible to bemoan the extent to which some people sought to manipulate information, weaponize and create skepticism over the most basic scientific or rational fact.

Step back for a moment, though, and realize just how likely the year of 2020 was when seen through the lens of creativity.

Few, if any, powerful creations have ever come with unintended consequences virtually equal to their power for good. Think about the Bible and the other enduring works of scripture, used both to preach morality and as an excuse for tribal bloodbaths. Fire brought us out of darkness and destroys villages, forests, and now even the climate that we rely on to survive.

And then we create in response—laws, customs, technologies, businesses. We learn, and develop Mini C's that lead to Small C's, Pro C's, and then someone, on the shoulder of giants, creates an idea so potent, powerful, responsive—so inspired—that light shines again where darkness had regained a foothold.

This is the math of creativity: two steps forward, one and seven-eighths steps back.

That may seem arbitrary—to add seven-eighths, when I could have added nine-tenths or nine-hundred-ninety-nine-one-thousandths.

I'm not good at math. You get the point. We burst ahead with innovation and then discover unintended consequences.

During 2020, a creation of nature called COVID-19 ripped through society because it was able to take advantage of prior creations, like urban living and domestication of animals and open markets and borders; and it ravaged us. And we responded by taking advantage of some of the same levels of international cooperation that created a fecund place for virus by developing vaccines at breakneck speed.

The tightly knit nature of the global economy, bringing lower prices and great efficiencies and spreading labor costs, made of all nations dominoes that could fall one after the next. And the massive multi-trillion-dollar international investing markets that worked when combined with fast-twitch electronic trading systems brought competing impacts to the masses of humanity: For the first time, individuals could trade stocks from their desks with ease; but the true power and wealth was amassed by the wealthiest, who had immense ability to profit from the system. These tools democratized us and divided us all at once.

Mobile devices allowed great communication, from every nook and cranny, along with so much entertainment, and delivered us all that news. And these devices entranced us and delivered narcotic-like bursts of information, addictive signals through the eyeballs that wondrous creators of apps and games and news sought to propagate.

In this period, a term was also coined and gained prominence in various news articles. It was called "decision fatigue." So much information, so many products in the food aisle, and so many cultures around us; so many directions the world could go because of the plethora of ideas and creations, and therefore an equal number of choices. Choices are alone challenging. They are harder when they mean change. It is an essential part of creativity and innovation.

Creativity forces us to come to terms with change. On a regular basis. Change is like vomit and toxins, the creativity scholarship teaches us. Change is death—of an idea, a way of behaving, the passing from darkness into low light, and into pure light itself.

Only as we look back through the lens of history can we know if a creation would serve us well, and to what extent.

Does this mean we are helpless in the face of creativity?

The answer is no.

With creativity, there are a handful of truisms:

Creativity is inevitable, because it is in us. This much I have shown you.

Creativity has unintended consequences, and this requires of us an awareness of the power of change to disrupt and overwhelm, in ways that are good or bad. This is precisely why we have public policies that help to set boundaries. There's a reason that nobody can walk into a five-and-dime store and buy a nuclear bomb.

The New Jerusalem

The story in this book began in Jerusalem the week of Thanksgiving 2019. It ended on an aging cracked green leather couch, in San Francisco, precisely one year later. Creativity was at war with itself.

The deadly creation that had emerged in Wuhan, China, as I walked the Old City was now everyplace. Worldwide, 1.5 million dead. In the United States, 275,000. Government officials here warned that the number could nearly double in the coming months.

People had shut themselves inside. Businesses closed. Millions of people lost jobs. Food banks scrambled to feed growing ranks of the hungry. Isolation and loneliness had a new calling card in nursing homes, where 100,000 died in the United States, most unable to say goodbye to loved ones in person.

Then humans created their way back into the game.

The very day before Thanksgiving, one year to the day after I walked the Old City, the Centers for Disease Control and Prevention announced that darkness might soon give way to light.

"Within the next month, messenger RNA vaccinations—also called mRNA vaccines—are likely to be some of the first Covid-19 vaccines authorized for use," the CDC's website read.

The way these vaccines work boggles the mind. They entail creating synthesized strands of genetic material, called mRNA, that essentially help instruct the immune system to attack the novel coronavirus. The scientific details are for a different book. But the way these vaccines came about belongs here because it is a quintessential story of creativity. It started with the spark of a stubborn creator.

———

Her name is Katalin Karikó. She's a Hungarian-born researcher who, in the 1990s, became obsessed with the idea that mRNA holds the key to great advances in medicine. She believed that bits of genetic material could be synthesized to give instructions to the body and override, complement, or replace instructions that were happening inside the body already but not in sufficient ways to tackle a disease.

This was not merely a creation, but, in its own way, the creation of life itself—a synthesized, souped-up version of our own defenses.

She found little support for her work. That's because the technology didn't seem to work.

"Every night I was working: grant, grant, grant," Karikó said in the profile, which appeared in *Stat*, a scientific journalism site. "And it came back always no, no, no."

The profile reads:

> By 1995, after six years on the faculty at the University of Pennsylvania, Karikó got demoted. She had been on the path to full professorship, but with no money coming in to support her work on mRNA, her bosses saw no point in pressing on.
>
> She was back to the lower rungs of the scientific academy.
>
> "Usually, at that point, people just say goodbye and leave because it's so horrible," Karikó said.

Long story short, she and a collaborator named Drew Weissman persevered and figured out the way to allow mRNA therapies to work: The concoctions had to be tweaked so they didn't cause the body's immune system to attack the synthesized genetic strands. She came up with a solution.

That discovery, described in a series of scientific papers starting in

2005, largely flew under the radar, the *Stat* profile reads. But: *it was the starter pistol for the vaccine sprint to come.*

And even though the studies by Karikó and Weissman went unnoticed by some, they caught the attention of two key scientists—one in the United States, another abroad—who would later help found Moderna and Pfizer's future partner, BioNTech.

These were the very companies that had prompted the CDC, on the day before Thanksgiving, to write that new vaccines were coming. The work of two creators working in darkness a quarter of a century earlier had become the basis for vaccines that could save millions of lives. And the mRNA technology that these companies had harnessed in the crucible of the year 2020 also offered promise to help solve other diseases.

This was no modest creation. This was life itself, a synthesized complement to our own genetics. The human species would not be outcreated.

I took in this news from my phone, sitting on the old green leather couch we'd inherited from my in-laws. The household was quiet, the kids not awake yet, my wife catching up on sleep too. I turned on the television and clicked on the gift that awaited me. It was from Taylor Swift.

Early on in COVID-19, Swift started writing a new album. It wasn't like her previous work. It wasn't filled with pop songs. It was deeply personal, reflective, cerebral. She didn't tell her record label. She just wrote. It felt right. She was right. The album, called *Folklore*, was no less than a brilliant creation.

Thanksgiving morning, Disney+ debuted a video performance of the album shot in a house in upstate New York where Swift sometimes lives. The video was shot with two musicians who co-produced the songs with Swift—at a distance, during quarantine. Now they were in person for the first time. They sat on the porch of the house and spoke briefly about the origin for their work and how they collaborated without seeing each other.

"In the dismantling of all of the systems of life that we've known, during pandemic, you're left with two options: either cling to it and try to make it work or say, well, I guess I'm going to chart a new path," said Jack Antonoff, one of her collaborators. "You kind of get a frontier mentality.

"It's a thrilling use of quarantine to say: Everything's a blur, so I'm just going to rewrite it."

Swift said she finally went to her label when the work was finished and confessed she'd written this very-different kind of album. She was nervous to tell them.

"But my label was like: Whatever you want to make, we're down."

"You ready to play this?" one of her collaborators asked.

"Yeah, I think it's really important we play it. It will take that for me to realize it's a real album. Seems like a big mirage."

"It does," her collaborator responded. "I've never worked on an album like this, and I don't know if I ever will again. I don't know if this is how albums are meant to be made. It just works right now."

"There's something about the complete and total uncertainty about life that causes endless anxiety," Swift said. "But there's another part that causes sort of a release of the pressures that you used to feel because, if we're going to have to recalibrate everything, we should start with what we love the most first. That was what we were unconsciously doing with this."

She added: "It turned out that everybody needed a good cry, as well as us."

On Thanksgiving Day of 2019, I ate turkey on a kibbutz in northern Israel, and a day later bumped into the Kangaroo Man. I felt determined to understand creativity and to see its manifestations in every part of life: artistic, scientific, sociological.

When the pandemic hit, I started to wonder: Has creativity been put on pause? Are we locked inside, alone, maybe able to hear our creative voices but unable to act on them? "I felt listless and hopeless," Swift said in her account of the making of *Folklore*. "For the first three days."

A year later, I realized that creativity, far from being contained, exploded. And, by then, I'd come to understand why. It is in us. Each of us. History may be the only judge of whether any of our various creations make a mark deep enough to become the stuff of legend. But history is not the *best* judge. That's because the creations that inspire us on a daily basis are the seed corn of the creations that keep our species alive and progressing.

And we need not be gathered in creative enclaves, the way great creators of religion played off one another in Jerusalem. The home office is the new Jerusalem. Cafés and small gatherings, tapped into technology, connecting across borders, feeling inspired, hearing a voice and creating harmony with the voices of others—that is the new world of creation. It is even more ubiquitous than the virus.

On this Thanksgiving, I am truly grateful for what our species has created, and what we are destined to yet create. Imagine that.

Inspired

To truly appreciate the power of inspiration is to witness it. To see it unfold, in real time. To watch it come alive.

This is not only possible, but I've witnessed it with my own eyes, as have many others. Many times. I'd like to describe one of them to you. It took place on August 24, 2018, before the pandemic shook the world. The inspiration belonged to Yo-Yo Ma, one of the world's most renowned creators. He played a brief, twelve-minute concert on the internet. He started the Prélude from J.S. Bach's Cello Suite No. 1 in G Major. It was the first piece Ma learned at the age of four, and he's played it many times in his sixty-odd years.

As he played, his fingers and bow synched with unmatched ability. They traveled an unseen, delicate web of connections among notes, tapping, touching, sliding. Yet watching Ma's playing isn't really where the action is.

Where the inspiration unfolds is on Ma's face. In the two minutes he plays, Ma's face goes on a long journey. It travels a rugged terrain of emotion, thought, instinct. No stirring seems to go unexpressed by his chin, eyebrows, lips, forehead, by a twitch, at one point even the edges of an utterance. It looks like you're seeing a topographical map of his soul. It's a soul that looks, from his face, like it is at once old as a timeless mountain and childlike as a preschooler.

First his eyes closed, his face in a dream state, then there was a slight frown turned wry smile, a flare to the nostrils, then a little more air in the cheeks, chin up, lip curled down, then his mouth opened and it seemed there could be words as if he might speak in tongues, instead his chin dropped so that pressure built terribly on the lower lip and squeezed the bottom of the face, and finally, as the piece resolved, Ma experienced an awakening, eyes open, a return to the world.

Ma had, as the kids say, let it all hang out. The mechanical training had long since happened. But the interpretation, the way he played, and so the way we felt as listeners, were a product of his inspiration—in that moment. To that end, Ma explained a moment later what makes each version of this piece different from each prior version. "I've lived with all of this music all of my life. Embedded in the way I play is actually in many ways everything I've experienced," Ma said.

He said that the whole of his being, in that moment, let through. He used an interesting term for the ability to read his being in that moment: "forensic musicology." He had shown us his muse. It was beautiful.

Two years later, I interviewed the brilliant cellist and thinker for this book. It took place over Zoom in February 2021, the end of a long winter, literally and figuratively. The first vaccines had been spreading since just after Thanksgiving. Ma reveled in the collective creativity that had led us to this point. Quickly, we began to discuss the state of the world and I witnessed in Ma a trait that surfaced repeatedly in conversations with great creators: unyielding curiosity. He seemed very happy to forgo the traditional interview and traipse into this subject and that.

"Let's focus on you," I said.

Okay, Ma said. But that's not really what happened. What followed was a high-level master class on creativity. He not only described from his perspective where creativity comes from, how it works, what it might achieve but he exhibited the very qualities that creators exhibit and lead to creation. Listening to him, I could hear the essence of creation.

First, there was his innate curiosity and openness. Creators don't seem to preach as much as to listen, interact with the world, gather, synthesize. They give themselves permission to ask the "smart-dumb questions." They don't rush to judgment by choosing to mimic what they've learned. They test, probe, ask with some fearlessness about where the answer may lead.

Going back to his college days, Ma explained he had been fascinated by anthropology, social biology, and evolutionary biology. These fields, he said, help us understand why we are creative. New ideas spring from us, naturally and persistently. Many of these ideas are small, and then, BANG, something extraordinary happens.

"How do things evolve—do they evolve at a steady state? No," he said, "you kind of move along and then every once in a while there's a sharp jump."

"Agriculture, the wheel, metals," he said. These are examples of the broad nature of creativity—well beyond what Ma called the "accepted categories" of creators, like musicians or painters. "Adam Smith was a creator, so were the people who came up with the East India Company, Karl Marx was a creator, and Freud and Einstein."

When I think of the breadth of creativity in our world, I sometimes think about how Ma couldn't play the cello if a creative woodworker hadn't first built the instrument. The lesson is that creativity takes as many forms as does the singular nature of our individual genetics. The secret ingredient in creativity is you.

At the same time, the nature of the creations that rise in each of us can very much depend on the circumstances around. How much access do would-be creators have to tools, other information, cooperation, ability to share what they have learned? Throughout history, collections of people—fueled by competition, cooperation, collective inspiration, and external threat—have led to various concentrations of creative output. Ma believes we are amid one of those moments of intense creativity—a "Golden Era of Creativity," he said.

I wholly agree. Digital technology gives the creative tools to the masses, to all of us. This is a time of immense creative potential—for the individual and our species.

It also is a double-edged sword. Creations, even the most brilliant, have unintended consequences. See: nuclear weapons. You might fairly say that no great creation goes unpunished. So what happens in an era like this depends partly on luck but also partly on how much energy we put into using our tools and creations for good.

For instance, Ma pointed to the power of massive computing, to artificial intelligence, and to what he called "the algorithm," and how it has often been used to create tools to snare our attention. Not always in ways that serve as individuals or as a society.

"We could actually use those for knowledge building, creating curiosity and creating access and creating collaboration," he said. Not only could we, he said, "We are in the midst of it."

Ma, for his part, hopes that these circumstances will lead to the creation of a new way of thinking, a philosophy or worldview that would bring together great ideas that have floated about, put a new spin on them, offer a way of widespread peace and prosperity, health and happiness. "The millennials may be poised to write the underpinnings of a philosophy that could carry the species forward," he said.

The arc of the human story bends with creativity. The fate of our species ebbs and flows with our creations.

But, in my humble view, the most important point I can convey in these pages is that creativity isn't at its core about outcome, or influence. It's not about the end game or even about process. Those come second. First, foremost, creativity comes from personal inspiration. It starts with an impulse, a gut feeling, idea, a spark. Creativity is not elusive, highbrow, the province of the lucky or the few. Ma has made great creations. But what he has felt is what we all can feel. Inspiration.

"This is what happens to me every time before I do something," he said, describing his experience. "I'm sitting there, kind of bereft, depressed, not knowing which way is up but then I start to collect information about something, almost subconsciously. I collect and I collect until I feel enough solidity that I can look over the edge."

To what?

"Something that was scary before—personal edge, or societal edge. Maybe subject to criticism, maybe laughed out of town for saying something," he said.

Even the greats confront a reality of the creative process: creativity is terrifying. The science shows us this. Creativity scares us. It means change and confronting the conventional. Creativity can involve discomfort, for the creator and for the people who then try to digest this new idea and take it into their lives and way of living.

Creators thrive when they give themselves permission to peer over this edge. To consider the new. The science shows that the courage to create can be stoked by parents and teachers who give children permission to go to the edge, not just to stay safely within the confines of the conventional.

"And then," Ma said, "I take a leap."

I asked Ma whether he could help but take the leap.

"You can't help yourself," he said. "You are obsessed." He added: "It's like falling in love."

You can see this on Ma's face when he plays. He leaps, right there, in front of the world, undaunted by our presence, fearlessly creating a new version of a masterpiece. He comes to this edge, and he leaps and he knows he will land. Will it be his best piece? Will it change the world? That's not what drives him in that moment. It is the release of his inner creator.

What sets a creator like Ma apart is that he had faith in it—he *has* faith in it. Ma trusts that the inspiration is there for a reason—that it is in him and that it is its own treasure, as mysterious and essential as love. All the lessons of these pages can be summed up by the look on his face, and the permission and faith that he manifests.

Be inspired. It is natural. It is a thrilling path forward. For the individual. For our collection.

"We need to be the authors of our own narrative as we proceed," Ma said.

We are the creators. Each of us. Together. Into light.

Acknowledgments

This book owes its existence to the time and energy given by the people I've written about. They are immensely busy creators who indulged multiple interviews, questions about intimate process and emotion, repeated fact-check and clarification. The book itself is an acknowledgment and thanks to all those included.

A pointed thank-you to Rhiannon Giddens. Your patient, frank, soul-searching participation provided an anchor for my understanding and ability to describe the creative journey and process.

I owe immense thanks to a group of usual suspects: Laurie Liss, outstanding agent, sounding board, and business and creative partner for near two decades; Peter Hubbard, world-class editor, friend; Vicki Yates, minister of early reads and copyedits; Liate Stehlik, soulful publishing executive; a full cast of tenacious and creative types at William Morrow and HarperCollins who do covers, copyedits, publicity, sell the book into stores brick and virtual. Without you, no book.

Thanks to Noel, Josh, Bob, for the sounds dogs hear.

To my parents. This curious creator came from someplace. You!

Finally, thank you to my wife, Meredith, and to Milo and Mirabel—the point of the exercise.

Index